Philip Rieff / Fellow Teachers

Philip Rieff /
Fellow Teachers

New York, Evanston, San Francisco, London
HARPER & ROW, PUBLISHERS

1817

901.9
R553 f

Portions of this book appeared in *Salmagundi*.

FIRST EDITION

Designed by Sidney Feinberg

Library of Congress Cataloging in Publication Data

Rieff, Philip, 1922-
    Fellow teachers.
    Includes bibliographical references.
    1. Civilization—Philosophy.   2. Education—
Philosophy.   3. Man.   4. United States—Civilization.
I. Title.
CB19.R47   1973   901.9   72-12103
ISBN 0-06-013554-9

In memory of J. P. Nettl

fellow teacher/dear friend

33015

Prefatory Note

Fellow Teachers is addressed, first, to Robert Boyers and to Robert Orrill, both members of the faculty of Skidmore College. I have maintained the fiction of its address to them because the starting point of this theoretical book remains, indeed, a personal exchange between myself and those two readers of my earlier published work.

In March, 1971, I went to Skidmore College to give a public interview, responses to previously submitted questions from both faculty and students. Most of the questions clustered around the theoretical chapters at the beginning and end of *The Triumph of the Therapeutic;* those chapters had grown out of the concluding chapter, titled "The Emergence of Psychological Man," in *The Mind of the Moralist.* The intention was that an edited transcript of the public interview should be published in a special number, on "Psychological Man," in the journal *Salmagundi.*

When I came to edit the transcript, my doubts about public interviews led me to begin this book, explaining how I felt about such occasions as part of the larger effort to meet expressed interest in the direction of my work. It was agreed that an early version of the book would appear in *Salmagundi* (No. 20, Summer-Fall 1972) and some later version, my summa of work done between *The Triumph of the Therapeutic* and now, in what follows.

P. R.
University of Pennsylvania
Winter, 1973

Philip Rieff / Fellow Teachers

Fellow Teachers

Is it possible that my invitation to come to Skidmore on 26th March, 1971, to be publicly interviewed, was based upon a happy misunderstanding? Did you imagine that I am a herald of the therapeutic? I am neither for nor against my ideal type. Nor am I Freudian or anti-Freudian, Marxist or anti-Marxist, Weberian or anti-Weberian. I am a scholar-teacher of sociological theory; as such, I try to help myself and my students to see not only what the theorist has seen, but through him to see what is at stake in his vision. Anyone who knows how to make his way toward the light will find himself in shadows. For example: there are long shadows, of Jew-hatred, cast by Marx on the Jewish Question. Even so, some of my Jewish students resolutely prefer the shadows; they come away from their lessons confirmed in their self-hatred. For more general reasons I shall try to explain later, I cannot resolve that self-hatred. My job, as I understand it, is to convey the highly specialized objectivity that derives, not from some impersonal methodological gimmick, but from attempting to get inside the theoretical work of my predecessors, and of their objects of understanding. Once inside orders of creation not necessarily obvious to their authors, exploring the interior space opened up and shaped by the work and its objects, my students and I sometimes find ourselves earning further entry into that space, a little way deeper into it than the author may have imagined—always

1

within the discipline and for exercise in the classroom, which is a rather small part of life. The real test of a good college class is what its teacher learns from it. Students, alas, too often come away with the impression that they have learned something when, in fact, they have been entertained or excited or directed. Preaching is not teaching, except in a church.

As teachers in the humane studies, our sacred world must remain the book. No, not the book: the page. We teachers are the people of the page—and not only of a page of words but of numbers and of notes. To get inside a page of Haydn, of Freud, of Weber, of James: only so can our students be possessed by an idea of what it means to study. Music, philosophy, the literature of human conduct in cases or fictions, mathematics, I suppose, all disciplines of theory, are visions of the highest formalities; the visionary disciplines are what we should require of our undergraduates; then, at least, they may acquire a becoming modesty about becoming 'problem-solvers,' dictating reality. Such disciplines[1] would teach us, as teachers, that it would be better to spend three days imprisoned by a sentence than any length of time handing over ready-made ideas. To that which we ourselves relearn,

---

1. I do not know what biological discipline ought to accompany the aesthetic and sociological in strengthening the minds and hearts of our students; my intuition would be microbiology, with its deeply concealed bacterial cultures and procedures for revealing them. One procedure here for revealing what I think is at stake in the text, its inner dialectic, is through the use of footnotes. As students are to my classroom, readers are to this book; they come to it, and it to them, as strangers. In the classroom, as sometime strangers work through the text, I deliver to them at such pedagogically strategic moments as may occur, a 'footnote,' some aside that has prepared its own way during our workings-through. In this book, as in my classroom, the footnotes are my asides, in which a concept may be pointed separate from the text and sometimes superior to it, I hope. One height of the scholar's art would be reached, according to my reckoning, if a book could be read, at least equally, for its footnotes. In any case, I am unable to think without footnotes, superior or inferior. One reviewer of *The Mind of the Moralist* paid me the honor of noting that he had "run across a footnote that was more significant than the page of text."

as we teach, no digest can do intellectual justice. Moreover, the new mass-media predigest everything and can reproduce everything as intellectual nullities, finished products; that I consider dead knowledge, suitable for the training of technicians but not for the education of intellects strong enough to feel their ways through works of art and science. Why should we imitate our enemies, the mass mediums of dead knowledge? Perhaps we can help more than a few students resist the ever-present temptation to slap tourist labels, such as 'Repression,' so readily on mysteries as if they were light travel baggage. I refer here not merely to abusers of the word. What good are statistical formulae, which students can learn in a fortnight, if they do not learn as well the forms of statistical argument? What good are huge record libraries, if what our students hear are familiar quotations? Better to concentrate repeatedly on, say, the fifth, in Haydn's Op. 76. There are formalities enough in the Largo of that D Major to direct me through interior spaces I can enter in no other way. In my private discipline,[2] during this writing, not for the first time, Haydn has been the accompanist serving my workday, then the entirely attended soloist of my evening—evenings, I listen as his most obedient servant. When I manage to concentrate, Haydn rewards by moving me a little farther inside those walls of sound, shaping purities, nothing like the world mess and myself in it. However secure we are made by the sanctuary of those walls, we theorists cannot hope to be deeply immersed enough, each day, for safety in and through the initiations of our masters; try to imagine, though, a student or teacher who has never been over his head in the work of his superiors. Impossible. I believe in total immersion for adults, regular re-baptism. 'Repeat that, repeat,' called Hopkins to the singing birds. Only so, by creating repetitions, does mortal mind survive. (If his god-terms were immortal, as Hopkins believed, then it is because his belief, that 'Christ minds,' is a superb mindfulness.) If our education were then truly con-

---

2. As for the discipline of pictures, hierarchies of color, ennobling formalities: I have not yet found a way of bringing my students in sociology, apparently self-selected for their interest in the significances of social forms, into the discipline of looking intently at colors, lines, volumes—arranged in space.

tinued, we might be able to make known the music of our minds.

We people of the page, intent gazers at what there is to see, invisible to the naked eye, because of how we know, know also that the world, mindless, regularly refuses to become a text analogue. Living between those two worlds, respecting both, our vocation is to make interpretations that will not collapse one into the other. An interminable making of interpretations is the duty of the teacher; in this duty of mindfulness, never fully to be discharged, he is freer than most other citizens. That unique condition can only exist if academics do not try to destroy it by a frequent taking of sides, as auxiliaries in the ever-changing struggle for power. The university has been only grudgingly exempted from full and immediate participation in those many-sided struggles. If we teachers understood those struggles, we would stay out of them; battle lines are not to be trusted. Fighting attitudes do not mix well with analytic. Criticism is not superior to advocacy. Neither describes that close, personal and positionless understanding which constitutes the true objectivity of the scholar-teacher. Our task is to understand all sides, to analyze all reasons—including reasons of state. Trust only that the sides will change faster than we can or should change our minds. Our duty is to hang back, always a little behind the times.[3]

Our objectivity, always from within our culture, has nothing whatever to do with the cant of 'value-neutrality'; we cannot derive our insights from that ideological slogan of the positivist movement. Rather, one of our tasks is to analyze all insights as they derive from movements, including those that derive from the Marxist. We must try to make our stands outside all movements. If we try fastidiously enough, then even our failures will be instruc-

---

3. Studied hangings-back require a disciplined historical memory, more acutely of rejected than of accepted times. For example, Israeli teaching intellectuals had better remember who was Israel's most reliable backer in 1947. There are endless examples of how changeable political sides are. Now is always the wrong time in which academics can make up their minds, without the tension of historical memory, which, rightly exercised, is likely to leave us always refusing to announce the ardors of the moment. We cannot be advertising men for any movement. Herald nothing.

4

tive. The worst thing about us teaching intellectuals is our arrogant assumption, now fashionable, that we have to oppose anything we wish to understand. As a method, this gegenüberstehen is no more intelligent than empathy. And even empathy, the tribute of internal mimicry paid by one self to another, implies its own aggression; opposition grows, and may achieve a sympathetic end, through bouts of mimicry. What a strange perfection of everything human that an object of desire can be pleasurably obtained through opposing it. Think of Benedick and Beatrice. Moreover, once they have succeeded toward their desire by opposing each other, Benedick is a shrewd enough critic of their future to suggest they have a dance before they are married. For tolerable relations, a certain dancing distance should be kept—the imagination of an armslength preserved to avoid the disaster of too close an embrace of opposition. But this advice may be good only for customers who would keep cool; certainly my advice implies no method. If a theory is superior, then facts will rise to imitate it. (See, e.g., *New York Times,* March 7, 1973, p. 46. "Each party claimed victory. 'It's a perfect marriage,' said John W. Mazzola, managing director of Lincoln Center.")

There is no Method for achieving the proper distances of feeling intellect; there is an institution within which we can keep trying. Only in our schools can our students hope to achieve a humane and perceptive inner distance from the social struggles in which they may be—need be—otherwise engaged. School can be drawn too close to society. To make distances may help save this society from its cruel infatuations with one damnable simplification after another. The most complex analyses grow brutally simple as they become public objects. The negative condition of all objectivity is that it escape, for a time, the success that will transform it into publicity—dead knowledge—making it over, thereafter, into one of the techniques of power and modern commerce. There is nothing culturally more subversive than the modern commerce of quick turnover in ideas. Our second pedagogic responsibility is to keep our ideas to ourselves—and to those others who may be taught how to concentrate their interest—for as long a time as the disciplined ego will allow. The last thing we have to do, if then, is to deliver a message, even to our little world.

5

As a teacher, positionless, I had no business allowing myself to be interviewed; that medium is fit only for messages. Interviews yield too obviously to the marketing of positions. Messages and positions are the death of teaching. As scholars and teachers, we have a duty to fight against our own positions. If the university is still to be the temple of the intellect, mind entire, then its high priests can only worship the intellect, which does not worship itself. The enforcement of intellect, upon ourselves and reluctant students—that is our one force; it is to that force that we have a duty, uniquely unchangeable. Because the university must be the temple of the intellect, uniquely unchangeable in that respect, it is a sacred institution, the last in our culture. If the university is not the temple of the intellect, then it is not a university. In the temple, as its servants know, there are no students' rights, except the right to be well-taught. A university is neither a political democracy nor an oligarchy; it is an intellectual aristocracy.

In my service, as a sociological theorist, I do what I can, in practice, to defend the university against becoming a training center for technicians, equipped with quantified slogans; I am equally opposed to the teaching of my subject as a high moralizing entertainment, with the professor recast as guru, dispensing final solutions to over-eager young activists who have discovered that they are guilty of merely thinking about the world when what it so obviously needs are the changes by which innocence will be achieved, at last. In their own way facile as the undertakers (i.e., problem-solvers) they profess to despise, the gurus are profaners of our sacred precinct. How can we outwit these profaners if we ourselves aim at positioning our students, by being popular and direct in our teachings?

Yet here I am obliged to say something that will respond directly, unmediated by a gauntlet of pages in books, and despite the lack of study together, to your special interest in my published work. In the contemporary theatre of ideas, we shall not escape the theatricality of our situation. Our exchange cannot be disciplined, objective, personal—a complex of indirections, set by close attention to the work of our predecessors. We who meet at meetings have no continuing intellectual relation to each other or to the past; without this continuity, there can be no successive generations of knowers privileged to see how easily interest in an idea may twist it beyond re-cognition. Except as re-cognizers, we professors of the present may become minor actor-managers in more or less provincial roadshows; students and townsfolk never know how right they are when they tell us, after such shows as we gave on 26th March 1971, how much they 'enjoyed' it; I cringe at the thought of my performance, and at their evident pleasure in it.

How seriously these audiences take their pursuits of pleasures is evident in the commercial success of an astonishing number of 'value'[4]-change actor-managers, who parallel in a minor, less profitable way, the managerial entrepreneurs of the research grant industry. In relation to their audiences (most corrupt of all when transferred to a classroom), the quick 'value'-change artists on the college circuit are not much different from the managers of Big Science, who direct the operations of an ever-expanding horde of dependent technicians. Managers of the knowledge industry produce whatever facts are needed, while, in the new division of labor, the actor-managers of our culture crisis produce 'value'-criticism—and, nowadays, what is worse, rude personifications of those criticisms. More and more, orchestrating youth protest, the 'value'-managers feel they must act out their criticisms. To do good is to put on a show of evil; thus the 'value'-managers surpass their critical apostle-genius forebears. If Nietzsche ever acted out, then at least he did truth—which is repression successfully, though never finally, achieved—the honor of going mad. Acting out the eccentricities of prophets does not make a prophet. Even that great priestly theorist of social reform, Ezekiel, was not who he was because he baked his bread upon dung, or opened up his mouth to eat a scroll, with a message of guilt upon it. By their play-acting at the prophetic role, making a holocaust of the priestly, actor-managers of total criticism have reduced our complex binding traditions of

---

4. Whenever I hear the word 'value,' I reach for my wallet; the word should be left to the barkers of schlock on the mass media, giving good 'value' for your money. 'Value' is a word which should only be used for purposes of marketing spoilt goods.

7

prophecy, which are incitantly conservative, to primitive rudenesses. Now primitive rudeness is honored with a sociological rubric: 'counterculture.'

No primitive was rude. Our college-trained primitives have been charmed by the idea that rudeness of manner, speech and thought is criticism personified. They express not criticism but hostility to culture in any form. Their chorused obscenities and temper tantrums are the debased liturgical form taken, nowadays, by the high nineteenth-century religion of criticism, about which they have not the slightest knowledge. Only projects—inputs and outputs, quickly made—really interest them. These projects have come to be called, in modern times, 'personality' and 'personal' experience. The cult of personality, with all experiences to be summoned forthwith, pharmacologically induced, if need be, has destroyed the mannerliness inseparable from culture. Good manners are protective, against the thrust of those short-term, even instant, projects that are the bureaucratic version of the quest for experience.

Experience is a swindle; the experienced know that much. Try to conjure, as if it were actually happening, the latest swindle in the academy: 'Experience' for course credit; that is how I imagine the academic bureaucrat could make a total travesty of our inherited socratic idea of the examined life. As a program or in principle, Experience is profitable only for licensed projectors, Merecrafts,[5] who now have advanced degrees chiefly in the subject of how to get more profit out of their projects. The feeling intellect is a long-term project, which would be blessed by less capital funding for Research and far less publicity. Meanwhile, the apparent enemies of the gurus, the bagmen of a commercial technological culture, are learning how to ape everything, including Revolution, for which there is a market. Attracted to the university by the new money and status in it since 1946, the bagmen and the gurus between them are destroying our sacred institution. Both sides are

---

5. Here I conflate the characterological language of seventeenth-century capitalist enterprise and twentieth-century welfare-bureaucracy. 'Merecraft, the Projector' is a Jonsonian morality, in *The Devil is an Ass: A Comedy*, acted in the year 1616, by His Majesty's Servants.

equally ready to make over the temple of the intellect into whatever it cannot be: research and development center, political camp, college of therapists.

Teachers cannot be therapists; nor can they be 'Projectors.' In a society, god-terms cannot be parody godheads; nor can they be bought and sold or offered as cures, modern relics miraculously efficacious on being mouthed. Because those in therapy take their pleasures too seriously, they can only take their god-terms too lightly. The order to which we teachers belong is authoritative and commands its members to prepare for long mindful devotions to the understanding of god-terms and their social organization. The academy does not exist as a place from which to depart; it is not therapeutic. Our colleges cannot be made over into orders for order-hoppers; the rapid turnover of our students mocks the tenacious concentration necessary for study. We scholar-teachers are the university. Yet, in our hurry to get somewhere, to some conclusion that will not hold, we are helping make over the university into a therapeutic institution. Nothing more desecrating has ever been introduced into the temple of the intellect than the present dominant alliance: between a) political theatre, by demagogues of Eros, and b) data-management, by bureaucratic undertakers of the knowledge industry. Do not despair. Even together, the gurus and the undertakers have not quite resolved that transference, in disciplined and specialized intensities, of a privileged knowledge which can only be in the personal gift of modest masters to patient students.

Returning to the question of our public interview: if (I say, only, *if*) our personal knowledge is a teaching privilege, not readily or publicly available in its constant re-cognitions, then how can we teachers transfer it, by public interview, among almost total strangers who have come, more often than not, to be carried away to some new conclusion? Privileged knowledge—the most objective, closest, personal re-cognitions—can only be conveyed by the art of concealment. We teachers are called to represent the god-terms, in all their marvelous indirections, inhibiting what otherwise might be too easily done. Even Christ, as he revealed, precisely in order to reveal, concealed—lest he be too easily identified, in his love, as a being identifiable with everything. Jesus struggled against his

9

acosmic love, to conserve his saving No. One of his reasons for coming was to change not one jot or tittle. Concealment is the most necessary pedagogic art, without which there are no revelations. If I have written anything worth rereading, then it is necessary and right that you should misunderstand me. I write as I teach, with extreme caution; indeed, I am a rewriter.[6] If you read in order to conclude, for or against, then read at your peril. There is nothing conclusive here.

What terrific dangers there are in revelations that are not, equally, concealments. Some revelations end badly, as fighting attitudes, and specially so for those not gifted with the revelation itself, the student follower. The most terrific danger, however, is in the teacher who personally asserts a break through established interpretations. Even Jesus, who appears possessed by this danger in its supreme form, understood that, for us mere disciples, misunderstanding may be the highest form of prudence. Grown imprudent, understanding, which can be as self-aggrandizing as love, develops an equally acosmic tendency. Both love and understanding, too hard pressed, can confuse themselves with the world and its history. The heart may have its reasons, but they cannot be made into a political science without becoming sinister.

There are other reasons, involving less danger than obligations hinted earlier, why a concealing transfer of privileged knowledge is the unchangeable work of teachers: being mere interpreters of interpreters, not ourselves prophets, we are authorized only by the greatness that has preceded us, from which we make knowledge our own. You will now understand why my students are rarely allowed to read, under my indirections, living authors. Plato, Haydn, Beethoven, Freud, Weber: all our greatest teachers are always dead. Yet God enlivens their minds in us. Except for us, their scores become too settled; they need constant performance in order to be realized. Our task is to perform them, in order to see what lives. When, prepared slowly enough, a student can make his own sudden plunge through the words, into the interior space

---

6. I am a reteacher. The one student who takes my course over and over again is myself. That course is never the same; when it becomes the same, I hope that I shall know enough to stop teaching.

shaped by those words, then he inherits his share in the living authority of our great predecessors. So, and only so, students, like their teachers, may acquire personal authority; so, together, we come into possession of, and are possessed by, our inheritance— and may even improve upon it. That improving possession—slow, never certain, not always practical or with a happiness output— constitutes the activity peculiar to life in a university. As a work of art shapes its audience, so a book shapes its readers. In both cases, audience and reader are so active that they find themselves reshaping the work. So they become the true objects of the work, its contemporaries.

As modest interpreters of interpreters, the highest for which we can hope is to become the truest object of our predecessors: to become such an object implies no superiority—rather, a sur- passing modesty, an act of interpretation impossible except through the discipline of our predecessors. Again, I refer here not only to the interpretation of the literature of human conduct. Our constant performance may be mathematical, or musical, or biological. Without considering the slim chance that one or another of us may actually advance a little beyond our great teachers, or do some- thing incommensurably great, we are required to submit to the discipline of entering their minds. That discipline, the critical per- formance rightly transferred, is highly personal; it is also risky; however well disciplined, we risk failure. I see no way of repro- ducing a true interiority exactly, from one time to another. Exact reproduction constitutes the destruction of the interpretative per- formance; it must be impersonal. A masterful interpretation exactly reproduced becomes what Broch once called, referring to a master- piece reproduced millions of times, a "genuine fake." A true interpreter never can repeat himself exactly so long as he is learn- ing something from one of his masters. The mind that is alive in him is too alive for reproduction, which is the contrary of interpre- tation. Note, here, the obvious danger to personal, i.e., hermeneutic, knowledge in the machined reproductive spread of it, which has so displaced teaching activity that we teachers ourselves have lost feeling for the difference.

For machined performances, research managers and technique operators are superior to interpreters and teachers. Splicing tapes to make a performance can never be an interpretative performance. The more research is managed, the less its managers have to teach; on the other hand, technique operators grow less efficient as they are immersed in their subject. Do not blame these facts; blame the research managers who have all but completed their takeover of the university and, at the behest of State and Corporation, train students as if the best thing they can become is a technique operator. Not that all students resist their fate. The captains of the knowledge industry are safe men. Moreover, they have the money; it follows that the timid and the careerists will flock to them. Except to intellect itself, there is no risk involved in the new academic productivity.

We scholars are gamblers against the odds; so must our best students become. Gambling takes a certain intense calm. Anyone who is possessed by the objectivity of close and personal understandings must run the risk of that possession: the risk is in destroying one's own position. Before this risk, some flee. Others violently disagree with the sheer continuity of the teaching effort, all the more violently when they discover that agreements and disagreements, in the temple of the intellect, should not matter less. Some insist that their teachers function as gurus, supplying mini-social orders and, at the same time, the intellectualized emotional dexterities with which to hop from one mini-order to another. As teachers, we must be at war with the cultic 'life style,' with the endless order-hopping of the questing young, often formatively encouraged by their still questing parents, for whom the quest is an escape from the untaught authority of their own pasts. Authority untaught is the condition in which a culture commits suicide. For the suicide we witness, the responsible generation is the elder, not younger. 'Youth' has been taught that to be willing victims of untaught authority constitutes some new freedom, surpassing any experienced before. For this freedom, the default of authority, student youth is taught only how to sacrifice the life of the mind; there are so many ways—one of the most ardently sought is being a professor. What a good deal: the professor, in principle mindless. No wonder the teaching profession is so crowded. Any fink can think—but to act! Witness the new elite: of professing actors.

12

To be a scholar-teacher, neither guru nor entrepreneur, is to continue the life of study; at best, a scholar-teacher is a virtuoso student. There are alternatives: to play the virtuoso of prophetic views, plugged into Criticism; to be the friendly manager of your local data-bank, plugged into Method; both are easy roles nowadays. But the rhythms of teaching and learning are slow and unpredictable; the progress we teachers achieve is hard to couple with the advance of any social movement. Henry James offers one splendid example of complex, unprogressive teaching, unaddicted precisely to ideas. In Eliot's description of James's genius, we may take a hint of the perfect teacher: "most tellingly in his mastery over, his baffling escape from ideas; a mastery and an escape which are perhaps the last test of a superior intelligence. He had a mind so fine that no idea could violate it. . . ."[7] Here is the trouble with us, and with the masses we educate: our minds are too easily violated by ideas. We paste ideas on our foreheads, in order to follow them. It is not simply that a little learning is a dangerous thing, or that virtue cannot be taught. The case is more desperate. In the age of universal higher education, we excite minds that are never given time enough, or the inner strength, to learn how to avoid immediate violation by ideas; Weber, using Simmel's phrase, refers to the 'romanticism of the intellectually interesting.' There

---

7. Both James and Eliot were writers of supreme intellect. By 'idea,' Eliot meant ideology, I think: those ideas that excited minds acquire when they are released from patient thought—for example, the 'idea' that American culture is 'repressive.' No artist was ever more thoughtful than James. No novelist thought through his fictions more carefully. In his famous excoriation of a Trollope novel, James wrote: "Our great objection to 'The Belton Estate' is that we seem to be reading a work written for children, a work prepared for minds unable to think, a work below the apprehension of the average man or woman. 'The Belton Estate' is a *stupid* book . . . essentially, organically stupid. It is without a single idea. It is utterly incompetent to the *primary function of a book of whatever nature, to suggest thought*." (My italics) Perfectly said. Much of what passes for 'Liberation' writing and chat, nowadays, is below the apprehension of the average man or woman, intended for the expanding market of educated fools, the Sniffpecks of our anti-culture. (See, further on Sniffpeckery, p. 44 below.)

are students who are defenseless before any idea, or phrase, that excites their interest; they apply what they cannot understand. By this thinly intellectualized acting out, the young betray their own trained impatience with both ideas and life, as if each were a recalcitrant parent, unwilling to yield to their demands. How shall we cope with a universally critical style? Popular criticism— what we hear from the reprobators of our inherited culture—is so unprepared, so unprivileged, so swiftly acquired that it possesses no intelligence disciplined enough to master and escape the violence done by its own popularity. Against authority, paranoid styles flourish; chaotic characters spin out symptoms as if they were systematic ideas. Demonstrations of hostility, pathologies acted out, are supposed to activate the destruction of truth.

Students should be least subject to transformation into that sociological contradiction in terms, a critical mass. The activist conflation of hostile feelings and critical idea-mongering is in part a result of the banausic non-teaching to which students are subjected, the learning of formulae—all sloganizings, expressionist or scientist. It remains our pedagogic duty to oppose the orgiasts of criticism and their counterparts, the entrepreneurs of programmed Reason; research gimmicks are the entrepreneurial parallels of the latest Experience bag. Methodized reason, like orgiastic experience, consumes culture. Memory-data banks and retrieval systems are what Culture[8] is not. Our data banks and exciting ideas have no authority; they cannot compel us to indebted thought, as can a presiding intellectual presence, a Plato or a Freud. To preside is not to rule; here is the hairline that makes all the difference in the world between culture and politics.

You asked, early during our performance, within what *tradition* I taught. That is easy to say: my tradition is the one that would draw hermeneutic circles if it could. In my teaching tradition, I am one link in a long chain of interpreters. That chain has been broken in many places. It may be beyond repair. As in the Freudian thera-

---

8. A term to cover the death of our great traditions first made, for consumption by high-minded professional audiences, by Arnold the younger.

peutic model, the tactics of interpretation grow more treacherous as interpretation itself is trapped within final and resolutive rather than tentative and reproductive modes. Our pedagogic task remains to repair the old and forge new links, not to continue breaking old ones already so broken that our students have scarcely done more than heard rumors of their existence. Without links to intellectual authority, our students cannot know what they are criticizing, nor respect the complexity of all true criticism. (I shudder at the simple-mindedness of my Fanonist students, who do not respect Fanon enough to read him closely; indeed, few students know how to read a book and fewer come out of families still blessed with oral traditions, upon which abilities to read build up.) How do you teach totally unprepared students? The American universities are now producing tens of thousands of failed intellectuals and artists of life; this mass production may lead to the destruction of culture in any received sense. That received sense, without which the university destroys itself, must be active—never passive—a 'traditioning' in continuities of interpretation across successive teaching generations. (I shall return to 'traditioning' and its deadly counterfeit, 'tradition,' our lip services to the authority of the past, on p. 185 and again in footnote 125, pp. 194-195.) The one true announcement we teachers can make to our students is that all prophets of the new are false, precisely because the age of prophecy is past; its authority lives only in our interpretations of it.

To teach is to conserve the related benefits and penalties of our inherited existence, beyond earlier transferred observations of what is not to be done; and to sharpen our observations of what exceptions there may be to rules that constitute no game, no scenario, no psychodrama, no Third Kingdom, no movement of natural or historical forces. To act out, in the classroom, our one and only role, is to teach in defense of the privileged knowledge that must be constantly reconstructed from acute constructions already made—and for us to remake. How dare we dismiss the authority of the past as if we understood it? From that past we gain our regulating weight, to hold against the lightness of our acts. We should try to teach our students as if they were to become weight-lifters and, by this practice, themselves weightier men. The academic tradition in which I act is open to talent, exegetical, not least to discipline our ignorant passion for originality. Most of my classroom time, I am stuck loyally within the text. Yet I am willing to venture beyond it, in a certain way, when the context of our lives demands that I do so; that way has an ancient name—apophasis. Denial, the discipline of double-crossing your own position, is an ancient tactic of exegetical teaching. That tactic may help prevent us from transferring to our students positions they will then be less prepared to treat with a distancing intelligence.

The transference of theory, our hermeneutic art rightly worked, resists its own ambition. In all effortful theory there is the danger of asserting itself as practice; such assertions show a failure to respect the limits theory itself teaches. The triumphs of our art are confined to our art; too readily transferred to life, those triumphs have always mocked the teacher's vision. Were there ever more obvious mockeries of Platonism than in Plato's practice? To be Marxist in Russia under Lenin, Trotsky and Stalin? The psychoanalytic professionals of Freud? Let me know if you can think of any mockeries more obvious. Christendom and modern scientific technology supply abundantly horrific examples. Our presiding presences are better after we respectfully digest them, at the sacramental feast of learning. How nice it is to know that Marx pretended, at least once in his life, that he was not a Marxist; that Jesus declined tenured appointment as King of the universe; that tragedy returns as farce. We teachers are duty-bound to insist upon all the junior power-seekers under our instruction running the gauntlet of our fastidiously prepared hindsights. However hard they try, power-seekers end in one of two ways: as winners or as losers. We aim neither to win nor to lose; we try to see a society in its orders and disorders, not least so that our own parts in it can be known by us the more truly. Never will the whole appear from its parts. To aim toward the whole is the glory and danger of every theory, and implies our first responsibility: to cultivate a modest sense of the different spheres of life.

For the safety of our own souls, to prevent the mental disease of praxis, we teachers of various theories have to imagine truths still to be stable old men, never fickle young women ever itchy to bed down with the latest winners in a perpetual intellectual-political style show. To imagine such truths, however, is not to make words like 'necessary' or 'need' dress up, imperative in either their interdictory or transgressive modes. This means our temples of the intellect can never be put into the service of any politics and that we abjure prophecy. Nor are we problem-solvers; real social problems are not solvable by any method that can be taught in the classroom—or taught on any rational model.

For us, in our priestly roles, everything there is is there to be interpreted; outside the temple, we are not priests. We have no objectivity. The closeness of our personal understandings is removed by life itself. Who among us can live as he teaches? It is a monstrous possibility; or a godlike one. Because it is not for us to organize any methodical conduct of life, outside the temple, those to whom we make our interpretations cannot be a large or unprepared or remote public. It is our duty, as teachers, not to be public men; as public men, we cannot teach. Teaching cannot be public or occasional. Moreover, societies are not vast academies. They are vast public networks by which secret lives are linked one to another, and yet at a distance remote enough for each life to remain as it is, inviolate, secret from all others. Publicity, calling itself democratic or scientific, more and more exposes the secret life, as if under some mandate to ruin the only life worth living, which is one not too well known, or necessarily too well liked, by others.

Yet through these crowded streets, we teachers are asked, even commanded, to be guides. How shall we be guides and yet not in power? The classical answer was to become the uneasy advisor of those in power. Every political world exists in its own right only when it can justify itself. 'Inner justifications,' authority in the right, can be so only because there is that which is wrong, and those who are wrong-doers. If to be 'justified' once meant, as it did, to be freed from the penalty of sin, through grace and not through merit, by the highest authority, then our human justice must involve the tragic relation of right authority as the penalty of wrong-doing. Authority is as of right action, reserved for acts of wrong. Only thus is the exercise of power ever remotely near the condition of being just. Therefore no justice can be said to exist without reverence. This is the principle of order without which there can be no law, as Protagoras rightly teaches. The

17

one way to destroy authority, in its right, is to establish as a principle of order that there can be no wrong. Thus would perfect anarchy supersede imperfect order, in all its tragic consequence and critical vulnerability.

Our higher schools have the burden of teaching the art of critical interpretation; but they cannot, at the same time, serve as bases for thrusts of power against established authority. A true disestablishment of authority can only be of itself, from within. The arts of criticism can remain true only when they are unarmed. Otherwise, all god-terms die in their very utterance and men are free to become demons. As the Marxist case demonstrates, even the highest criticism, armed, will defend its own establishment soon enough and prevent mind from entering those interior spaces opened and shaped by our continuous interpretative sciences, in institutions reserved to that end. Our schools must be powerless institutions of the political orders in which they exist; otherwise, they cannot be schools. Falsely positioned in any struggle for power, the school reserves its autonomy as an institution of authority so long as its task remains to draw circles of interpretation around all those capable of doing more than adjusting to power as it is. The relation between political power and pedagogic authority can never be simple and direct without becoming brutal, inartistic.

Even as he practices the art of critical concealments, not fit for all to learn, a practitioner in the academic order, more theoretical than practical, needs to resign himself to the treachery his interpretative activity must create within the political order. In return for the indirectness of these treacheries, those who administer the political order must allow them; so long as they are not directly political, they are inseparable from academic freedom. Academic freedom is the historic compromise between sophisticated academy and philistine state. To inhibit its treachery, every successful interpretation is bound to develop its own defensive cadre; without defensive cadres, interpretations run wild and impose themselves too immediately upon life. True criticism is never armed. Marxism lost in truth what it gained in power when it gained power over the Russians. I shall refer again later to the dirty trick embedded in the Marxist party theory of change, from truth to power, in which

18

all members of the Soviet public are to change their minds in order to accommodate the latest turn of the wheel of power.

No public should be too quickly ready for Change. Such readiness indicates a breakdown of culture. Interpretative efforts gain their inner strength from continuities of their preparation, outside the world of fashionable ideas; the life of study is inherently cautious and cannot be rightly politicized. Only as links in a chain of interpreters, keeping a cautious distance from the political order, as from a vicious animal, more than apologists, more than critics, can we teachers achieve our ineluctably privileged and dangerous knowledge, favored neither by officialdom nor revolutionaries (defined as an officialdom not yet taken office). My argument against taking sides is one of principle not prudence. Machiavelli made the prudential argument, which is for taking sides. In politics, as a matter of prudence, Machiavelli's argument was correct. Genuine neutrality never pays off in the struggle for power: the friendlier side will not be grateful; an enemy does not grow less hostile in victory.

A genuine neutrality will not lead us to moral indifference, no more than genuine politic partiality will lead us to moral superiority. On the contrary, to be inwardly and institutionally distant from every political order, however just the critical truths of that order once may have been, is not to ride loose to all symbolics, outside every constraining hermeneutic circle. We teachers are not free to hop from one circle to another. That critical style, more than any other, has blunted our inherited acute constructional senses, substituting a crude animus against culture in any form. Such an animus is likely to serve the immediate needs of those struggling for power without authority. At our best, we can only interpret an authority which is not reducible to power. Such authority can help to inhibit all sides in the struggle for power. Indeed, a neutrality in service to no side would be inhibiting. The greatest teachers are deep inhibitors of the latest conclusions—and of final solutions, of power and its justifications.

On various sides, presently in the endless struggle for power, are two apparently opposing cadres: 1) rationalizers of technological reason; 2) orgiasts of revolutionary sensuality; these cadres converge in the cult of violence. By 'cult of violence' I mean that

19

openness to possibility in which nothing remains true; in this original of cults, all oppositions are welcomed as if life could be an endless experience of political, technological or interpretative breakthroughs, against orders recognized only for purposes of disestablishment. Both cadres are hostile to culture in any form and transmit this hostility under apparently opposed means: as rationalizing science or scientific irrationalizing. Politically, this double condition of modern life expresses itself in the resolution of authority as the triumph of the powerful and of what follows from their power—the freedom to pursue pleasures. That freedom exists only at the very top and bottom of polities, which is why top and bottom, potentates and plebes, find themselves allies against all autonomous or independent centers of both power and authority. The regressiveness of the sensualists is as dangerous as the progressiveness of the technologists: both implicitly assume that the authority of truth inhibits the endlessness of power. I suppose that assumption to be correct. No strategist of power can maintain the authority of truth. As a consummate strategist of power, Lenin tried to break the inhibiting character of authority when he remarked, following Engels, that nothing is more authoritative than a revolution. Indeed, nothing has been more authoritarian than The Revolution in power.

To oppose the double movement of modernity—technological-political and sensual-political hostilities to culture in any form—is not, however, to become a pietist of culture; such pietists continue to represent the failure of the high culture[9] just before our own, when the pursuit of pleasure needed a Kreutzer sonata to blame for the mendacious games our re-educated classes have learned to play in order to raise their consciousness of possibility. Tolstoy correctly grasped the tension between a work of art and the pursuit of pleasure. A work of art is a moralizing form; moved as we are by it, no work of art can be neutral in the eternal war of culture. Art is the most subtle form of social direction. Either a work of art deepens the thrust of culture into character, creating ever greater loyalties to the godheads most fully alive in (and only in) their deepest order; or, as in its present extremity, art sub-

9. On *high* culture, see below, p. 67 *et pass.*

verts that order, goes down to murder its own godheads, and, often, to mock its own use of god-terms. It is interior space that is first reshaped, preliminary to the reshaping of social order.

In the academy, Plato first taught us to understand the mutually endangering relation between art and social order. But even before Plato, and more certainly than he, the interdictory cadres of ancient Israel, now all but excluded from our academic canon, taught this lesson. The unique quality of our lives refers not to an alternative space but to so many spaces opened up that even the least cultivated are aware of the vast emptiness inside: all our symbolics are manufactured for instant use; none are constraining; all oppose constraint, which is itself the main conceptual term of opposition to the opening up of new interior space, within which humans get a different sense of themselves and others. Because mental events are compound inhibitions and releases from inhibition, cultural revolutions are massive changes of mind. Sociologically, the metaquestion is never 'to be or not to be'; rather, our metaquestion is 'to act or not to act.' The predicate of sociological analyses of the moral should be that 'Man,' the most capacious of ideal types, is capable of everything. That predicate, the possibility of action without limit, must lead sociological analyses to insights that are defensive, against the very predicate of its special understanding.

The 'Everything New' syndrome, an unconstraining spaciousness, however the space may be divisible and rearrangeable for multiple uses, is ready-made for eternally youthful order-hoppers. In this architectonic for infinite interior Change is one predicative cultural condition from which we have, coming to us, our future unremarkable absence of soul: an endlessly developing Self, mocking, by its consumption of them, all constraints. Against this coming pliancy, the professional architects of Culture have proved helpless to maintain the constraints integral to its business of soul-making; indeed, even our mere architects, in their designs for habitual buildings, put on their mask of impiety and make interior spaces for infinite changeabilities. They have misplaced, somewhere on their drawing boards, the inherited knowledge of their craft, which was of space made stable and trustworthy.

The pietists, behind their masks of age, are equally untrustworthy. Cultural piety cannot make itself functional as the equivalent of a godhead and so conserve human beings in their particular distances from one another, in spaced orders; too often, we pietists of culture have become professional curators, guides for masses of tourists intent only on hurrying through our museums so to declare they have been there and had it. Cultural pietists are no better than any other among all the putative guides who disclaim authority as they conduct tours among artifacts that are not authoritative but only 'valuable.' Practically everyone, nowadays, has been to the Uffizi and to other even holier places. When traveling backward, we are all tourists and believe in nothing we can see and in nowhere we have been.

If a past has no authority, then it is dead, however expensive its artifacts. There can be no culture without living authority, right and proper demands superior to competing immediacies, not reducible to nor identical with power, which is the successful assertion of one's own immediacy over another's. Modern rulers have no authority. Our governments cannot be ordained remedies for sins we no longer can commit. Because the civil order, too, retains no presiding presence, it has become inherently unstable. The old interdictory motifs into which the remissions were once woven, the fabric of authority, no longer hold. The abuse of power cannot be justified as punishment. That most obvious break, in the connection between power and authority, is one way to state the subject matter of sociology in its triple probes—of culture, society and state.

Weber identified authority, as distinct from power, with service to ends, and ends with faith. But his faiths—"rational, humanitarian, social, ethical, cultural, worldly, or religious"—are a functionalized psychology of motive. Faith, as an 'end' to be served, is not a concept that carries the slightest particularizing resistance of truth against immediacy in it. Weber's ends, the *causes* there to be served, are means of acting; they cannot escape service to power. That knowledge of inescapability describes the Protestant pathos from which Weber suffered. The pathos is equally clear in Sohm's understanding of the Church as a legal institution emerging (inevitably, as Harnack thought) out of its first charismatic

22

organization.[10] At the despairing edge of the Protestant pathos, to say, "some kind of faith must always exist," as Weber said, is to implicate *therapy*, the great conceptual term beyond Weber's historical vision, for the justification of all immediacies.

Beyond some kind of faith, therapy describes the social procedure of release from the authority of the past. It takes at least two to commit a therapy. Beyond the dyad is a triad and so on. A variety of faiths suits the complexity of human relations; yet it may be the purpose of one variety, in its truth, to reduce the complexity of our relations. That reduction is what 'world rejection' means. Not Weber, not any theorist of my acquaintance, knows how to escape the modern functionalization of faith into therapy. No therapy can be world-rejecting. A 'world-rejecting' therapy parodies world rejection in order to defeat it. Here is one example of how our culture revolutionaries mock the very form of culture and not only its particular historical content. The modern revolution is against culture—and not just our own. Buddhist culture is not less interdictory than ours once was. True, a faith may be, as Zen Buddhism is, iconoclastic and anti-ritualistic. Yet Zen remains interdictory everywhere, even when it is remade for export and consumed in a radically different culture, as in its chic Californian varieties. At the heart of Zen is an intuitive looking into things that constitutes a satire propaedeutic to the reception of stronger discipline. The Noble Path does not permit certain callings. What callings are we now sure to prohibit? What do we know to be absolutely suspect? What knowledge do we have of evil?

It was in response to the reality of evil, irreducible to its 'causes,' that *faith* became one word for the most privileged knowledge: of the ways in which humans justify their behavior. Faith is the horrified suspicion of justification. Because this suspicion is horrifying, no justification worth calling to mind has ever satisfied its user; look at old Calvin's ravaged face, or read Luther's

10. See, further on this subject, my Introduction to Adolf Harnack, *Outlines of the History of Dogma* (Boston, 1957), pp. xv-xxxviii.

table talk. Yet to act without justification is more terrible. Few have been able to tolerate their acts unjustified. Mind begs to be violated by ideas. To be a professional student of violating ideas is to know what bizarre justifications there have been, and with what bêtise the human animal flocks after them.

Every genuine community has been credal; men love to conceal their acts, specially the most violent, which challenge justification, in an order of justifications. Perversely, it is thought that the most violent actions seal justification as if the latter serves on behalf of the former. Ideas are falsely sanctified in blood. The tension inherent in every community between the life of the mind and its disordering violations makes it imperative that teachers, if they must be guides, exercise a passion for good manners, grace, wit, decorum—whatever will keep the life of the mind and its enacted violations a little distant from one another, away from the taste of blood. Without taste and tact, theorists, who can see for themselves only when they see through theorists preceding them, grow ugly and hateful in each other's company. Gurus sanctify; teachers educate. If we must have him as a unifying figure, then let Eros wear heavy, concealing dress and eat modest rations of his followers. Let Eros be an old man.

With enough taste and tact, we professional interpreters will know enough not to produce new justifications where some old and tried ones already found wanting enough to be tolerated, will do. The hardest job for intellectuals is to prevent themselves from over-intellectualizing, not least on their own behalf, which is tantamount to demagogy. Too often we teachers become arrivistes; to be intellectually fashionable is to produce ever more justifying violations of mind, most often nowadays in the name of criticism or progress. Scientists produce new facts; orgiasts produce new experiences. We teachers should produce nothing new, no breakthroughs, until we produce, first in ourselves, those protections of older wisdom which may help stave off arrogant stupidities parading as originality, modernization, revolution—and, of course, 'values.' Respect for what is long known is not charismatic. We have no business making over our students into followers, least of all by offering them breakthroughs as if they were gifted with genius or prophecy. Privileged knowledge is rarely revolutionary.

24

On the contrary, our privilege is to know in detail how slow deep down things are to change, and equally to know what superficiality and blasé attitude is encouraged by mystiques of change.

In his superb Terry Lectures, *Islam Observed*, Clifford Geertz refers to faith as a "steadfast attachment to some transtemporal conception of reality." With Geertz, I find all efforts at defining faith futile. The first phrase of his packed reference specially invites unpacking, I think. However else it works, faith attaches to itself, in interdicts *and* their remissive modalities, actions that are not so "steadfast" as they may appear. That "steadfast attachment" to which Geertz refers hides ambivalence as the primary psychological modality inside culture. Where there is faith, transgressions are always possible. Without the moralizing authority of the interdicts and their remissions, no faith attaches itself to us. I know of no faith without interdictory implication—which is to say without submission to authority and to its presiding presences. This is true even of 'atheist' faiths such as Buddhism. Faith implies both 'alienation' and 'organization.' It was not easy for a Jew to learn the Law and he could not learn it, rightly, alone: Torah is taught and the learning of it interminable. Buddhism cannot be abstracted from its teaching orders. Faith is no less social a procedure than its opposite, therapy. Inquiry, as *Socrates/Plato* teaches, is equally a social procedure. By the notation *Socrates/Plato*, I intend to indicate a metamorphosis. Our received Socrates is changed, platonic, as Plato becomes socratic. There is a substantial change of both Socrates and Plato, a reciprocity. The metamorphic relation between x and y takes the form x/y.

The classic example in modern literature that stipulates the form x/y is Kierkegaard's *Either/Or,* subtitled "A Fragment of Life, Published by Victor Eremita." These accidentally discovered scribblings by two unknown 'authors' are labeled by the 'publisher': "A's Papers" or "B's." As revealing fragments of anonymous lives, *Either/Or* was first published in Copenhagen in 1843. With these fragments—dazzling shifts between what is personal and what theoretical, toward their unity—Kierkegaard played out the critical change of his intellect and passion into something that included both and yet was entirely different from either or both. This fundamental yet inclusive change in his life, Kierkegaard's anointed work, he found himself compelled to work through in his writings; he published these workings-through under either various pseudonyms or his own name. Pseudonymous, *Either/Or* established Kierkegaard's fame as an author.

To give an author—and, in particular, an author who is a genius—the benefit of every doubt is a mark of our respect for his achievement; so respectful are we that we rightly tend to include his person in his achievement—e.g., the divine Mozart. I am not embarrassed to refer, in the respect I hold him in his work, to the divine Kierkegaard. This respect raises its own questions. A genius lives in his work. In the case of Kierkegaard, how can authorship be excluded from the authority that he found recognizing his life in his work? Like questions may be asked of the socratic Plato and may help us see a reason why Socrates authored nothing; he merely taught. Oral tradition is one thing; tradition and its individual talents, published, quite another. 'Tradition' now exists to be broken through by the individual talent. This subversive activity gives its meaning to 'creativity' and 'originality.' It is a breakthrough that can be swiftly appreciated by its public; the appreciation of what has been broken through takes longer. Where oral traditions operated, there precisely the reverse was the case: it was the continuity of presentation that could be swiftly appreciated.

What authority is it that commands obedience through acts of authorship—even sacrificial acts in that manner? The occasion of Kierkegaard's literary success, the sacrifice built into the success of *Either/Or,* is known to have been his broken engagement to Regina; that occasion includes the nearest Kierkegaard may be said to have come to a chosen profession. Say, rather, that Kierkegaard was chosen, somehow, and did not choose as we ordinary doctors, lawyers and merchants do. Even so, Kierkegaard became an author rather than husband and family man—as if his choice involved the most significant order of decision.

Compare Kierkegaard's decision with that of another famous author and translator, Luther. Author and translator, Luther chose also to be a parson, teacher, husband, family man, sometime friend of princes. The inclusiveness of Luther's metamorphosis from monk is greater than that of Kierkegaard. In both cases, Luther's and Kierkegaard's, their metamorphic inclusion of much personal stuff,

26

highly personal efforts to signal fresh obediences to a distant yet final figure in authority, excluded the one thing that Kierkegaard protested (more often than did Luther in his *Table Talk*) would be unambiguously superior to any and all published workings-through of his obedience: a piety of silences. Those published workings-through of obedience may be said to constitute Kierkegaard's great failing; in achieving his own right distance in relation to final authority, he wrote for publication, later and decisively under his own name.

How ambiguous is the metamorphosis in print of the classic relation in which we may be condemned: *authority/obedience*. Publish that metamorphosis and it appears specially liable to its reversal, *obedience/authority*. In that reversal, the highest criticism becomes an act of faith in an authority always to come and our religions cannot be distinguished in yet another way from our politics. Judgment is implicitly condemnatory; under the reversal *obedience/authority*, a way is opened to the judgment of authority itself by those who obey it. The theoretical problem of reversals operates far beyond the moral field, indeed, wherever there are questions of order, however formal. For example, in aesthetics the problematic character of reversals is stipulated in the interaction of color, when one color appears as two, looking like the reversed grounds; in that interaction, the reversal itself again appears inclusive.

Kierkegaard's metamorphic writings will not separate for us from his acts of faith; neither will our social organizations separate from authority itself, however imagined by those analyzing the dynamics of their differences. In the case of Kierkegaard: I suspect that he was more a genius of criticism than he was what his genius tried to evoke—a fine specimen member in the cult of Jesus, who lived recognizably the one ideal existence. In Jesus, Kierkegaard saw genius and apostle one and the same. Under the authority of Christ, the one ideal existence to which each can relate his real life, Kierkegaard became, of all things, an author. Not even Tolstoy took his later, religious authorship to be so inclusive. Free of such messy obediences as come with Tolstoy's or any other colony of the faithful, Kierkegaard's organizational struggles were acted out critically, himself gloriously alone and perfectly obedient inside his authorship. By contrast, Luther's criticism of authority ended, to his pleasure and conscious surprise, in messy new obediences. Yet, for all his experience of its messiness, Luther celebrated his act of reversal, *obedience/authority,* and made it a credal statement. Luther's justification by his faith only helped reduce authority to whatever obedience we feel inclined to authorize.

Kierkegaard's critical career ended in no organization founded or refounded, but with his published *Attack Upon Christendom,* as if a common faith could ever really belong to virtuoso authors, loners like himself, charismatic organizations of one in which the follower is endlessly critical of his leader. The beautifully critical paradoxes of Kierkegaard's concluding unauthorized *Attack* come nearest their end in a passage titled: "That the crime of Christendom is comparable to that of wishing to obtain stealthily an inheritance to which one is not entitled." What nerve Kierkegaard had to write of stealth and the tactics of gaining an inheritance without being in legitimate descent. To conflate his protest with faith, and then to call that conflation "My task"; further, to deny that he can call himself a Christian: all this preaches their higher illegitimacy to lowly legitimates.

Kierkegaard's teaching on authority is in an apophatic tradition familiar to virtuoso believers, especially among the ultra orthodox. His denials are so refined that none except candidate virtuosi can be included in the real, and least visible, organization. Critical protest, as against the reversal *obedience/authority* or *organization/charismatic,* is no faith for ordinary descendants; encourage those sorts to think themselves extraordinary by denying their ordinary parents and you risk making the family romance into a kind of theology, with yourself playing the favored son. Criticism successful, even popular, the higher illegitimacy, taught to those who have not worked themselves up to it through their inherited condition, may be carried so far that the primal order, of descent, is threatened. Virtuosi of the highest criticism are bound to have their vulgarizers, poor readers who subject everything in the order of descent to suspicions of illegitimacy. Then, in apparently simple faith, the lower legitimates may refuse to marry, or marry and have no children, or have children without marriage, and so forth. Even Kierkegaard's real and visible organization of one could not have survived long, I think, if Kierkegaard had lived to lead it.

And after Kierkegaard: what shall we say of virtuosi of faith as criticism? In its sociological metamorphosis, this virtuosity amounts, at its beautiful best, to faith in criticism. Our present position as the truly beautiful people, feeling intellects, intellectuals: faith in criticism. To us intellectuals, the faithful in criticism, Kierkegaard's reply, as I interpret it, seems at one with that to the Organization men: *Neither/Nor*. Neither faith in criticism as the higher legitimacy, nor faith in being uncritical—'faith' as what every decent, hard-working janitor needs if he is to stay sober and a good family man.

What faith can survive the culture Kierkegaard's *personal/ theoretical* obedience implies, at least for those who are not geniuses at one with their creations? Take, for an example, his analogy of faith at work to an ordinary man who drinks heady stuff without considering his reward in the matter. If you have this simple drinking habit, as a matter of course, then, in your "honest intemperance," you are faithful. To pursue the analogy where I think it leads: that "of course," with no reward following the act, may produce a few ecstatics; it is likely to produce many more alcoholics. The culture of honest intemperate faith can only destroy itself; the alternative is a more cultivated faith.

Not only culture, but faith, too, in particular for those of us who share the modern faith in criticism, depends upon what Kierkegaard dispraised as "refined intemperance." Faith may be an acquired taste, for which you need a clear head and trained palate, some experience in the matter and manner of taking in the stuff. Taste seems least likely to be acquired by "honest intemperance," by knocking back any stuff as a matter of course. Just how either taste or faith is acquired is a mystery to me. I do have personal knowledge that the act of drinking needs refinement if it is to end in some tipsy humane condition, without brutality or retching.

I know, too, that it should be considered in bad taste to talk about faith or name its objects of oppositional desire; yet it must be the case that pieties of silence are surrounded by talk—which then may yield, in its way, to silence. With "refined intemperance,"

faith cultivated, there are certain institutional entanglements, rewards and penalties referring to the manner as well as matter of it. "Refined intemperance" means disciplined drinking, among others who chatter on, giving reasons for the superiority or incomparability of this wine or that. Refinement comes through the collective talk about the wine that hedges in the individual drinking. You need to do both: drink and talk, which implies the silence of listening. Faith is not simply the drinking; it includes the more or less subtly competitive talk that hedges in the drinking. No wonder drink is so often a part of ritual. You have to learn to drink your way refinedly into faith. If not, you are likely to end either in abstinence or a roaring drunk and not even a writer on the subject; neither condition is desirable.

The trick is to drink and not get drunk. Faith is not so mysterious that we do not know it belongs to those who have learned how to live in the interdictory mood: hedgings in of that which we would do mindlessly, capriciously, indiscriminately, cruelly, impatiently. The faithless are like the mindless: impatient. (Have a look at our infant-bashers, in any courtroom: they are the dregs of humanity—impatient, mindless.) The faithful know that they should leave caprice, indiscriminateness, cruelty, impatience, to the mindful God; at least, in faith and with as little criticism as we can manage of that which was, is and ever shall be, we must try to act according to this supreme, most privileged knowledge of our limits. Once in faith we may understand how ungodlike we must be; then we may live either ethically or beautifully—and in both ways.

The opposite of being godlike is to be highly cultivated, a superior man, intricate in his restrained freedoms—and constantly at work toward their reenactment. Simplicity is a complex cultural achievement. I consider it a grave error, something dangerously Romantic and self-dramatizing in our (mainly) Christian tradition, to oppose faith and culture. That Romanticism had led to further false—even catastrophic—oppositions: as, for examples, between energy and morality, between achievement and decency. One famous author who was of my acquaintance sacrificed a wife for the writing of each of his major books; less major relations were sacrificed to minor works. How political the literary can be.

Just so far as his specially ambiguous authorship was inseparable from his faith, Kierkegaard became the last and greatest Protestant virtuoso of faith tensed against culture. He was not a surprised new organization man, like that original, Luther; more original, Kierkegaard was a virtuoso of faith in the shape of a professional writer on the subject, critical of the institutional life, which is always political, a constant shifting of sides.

In what way are we critics, too often mere entertainers of audiences, better than our enemies, the officials, organization managers? Is it that we are on the side of what has hedged us in? Then we must cease, whenever we can learn how, to have faith in criticism. That faith is merely our politics—author's politics against organizer's.

None, neither Kierkegaard nor any who have come before or after, have known how to keep their faith clean of politics in the largest sense—the manner of influencing decisions, if not the final manner purified, in downright violent struggles for power—to do unto others what you would not have them do unto you. Did even *Saul/Paul* know how to reorganize right relations in faith, the hedgings in of action that occur between authority and obedience? The dazzling analyses in Paul's letters of the right relation, and its immediacy in the cultic organization, the Body of Christ, have supplied the various great reformers of the cult equally with either their greatest deceits of escape from the closeness of authority and its social organization or with deceits of a greater closeness. Quakers are no less self-dramatizing, in their modest meetings, than Roman Catholics in their grand cultic gestures.

I cannot begin to count the metamorphoses of that ur-text of modern intellectuals: Luther's famous "Here I stand." I hope he never said it; if he had to say such a thing, knowing full well how he was shifting about, even as he said it, then I hope that Dr. Luther thanked every member of his Committee on Stands, in the first footnote qualifying his stand. How many deceits of resistance have followed since Luther's, to that same self-serving affect? Faith in criticism continues to shake the world without end. What makes Kierkegaard the last and greatest of the Protestant virtuosi, a genius never to be surpassed in his manner, was the way in which he protected himself against saying anything like 'Here I stand.' That kind of public utterance is far too ambiguous for Kierkegaard's spiritual taste and intellectual supremacy; he was too smart to set some fashion.

The latest way, still, round the double deceit of escaping authority through its close rival, obedience, is to accept seriously, as social science and functional religion, the reversal *obedience/authority*. Social and functional, the cross can return to Man as a cultural plus. What is good for Society is good for God. In Paris, a generation before Kierkegaard's Protestant agonizings about it, the reversal *obedience/authority* was enshrined without agonizings in a positive science of society that included among its prime functions that of 'religion.' By Saint-Simon and Comte, and by their followers, faith was changed fundamentally into the final and most inclusive science, Sociology, with its endless projects of change, acutely personal and yet organized for our health, education and most general welfare. *Obedience/authority* accepted, as truth earlier concealed in its primitive metamorphosis *authority/obedience,* there was no reason on earth why the Saint-Simonians, for example, should not experiment cultically in a 'God is a Woman' project; just so they did. Authority becomes obedience engaged in an interminable making of impersonifications; the real object of each impersonification is the impersonator. We are each becoming God. So our lives become intolerable, anything less than our desires fulfilled a humiliation; this God ends by killing or being killed.

In order to avoid becoming God, it is not enough for each of us to criticize the prime reversal. Reversing the reversal in authorship in no way restores the distant and right relation between authority and obedience. In our capacities to make reversals, we go beyond the usual thoughtless idolatries of self. We create our own lights, as if every day were the first in the original seven, and our lights the highest adornment. The light by which we live must be like other adornments, purposed to protect us against the danger of idolizing ourselves under the authority of our own feeling intellects, the most subtle darkness.

No author has ever written more critically than Kierkegaard of his own decisive thing as it appeared in public, his immensely thoughtful authorship. As a genius of Christian criticism, Kierkegaard had to suffer a fact of life he accepted: that he could not be an apostle; rather, he was a famous critic, rightly critical of his fame even as he wrote in defense of the apostolic possibility. He knew how to joke about the inclusiveness of his literary ambition: to leave behind the inner history of his decisive move.

Critical joking is less dangerous than humorless criticism. Compare Kierkegaard's joking with the deadly seriousness of the founding (and competing) father and son of Sociology as a discipline, Saint-Simon or Comte. They had dangerous minds; both were entirely humorless. That divine quality missing, Man without laughter, first at himself, theory then organizes itself the more readily into movement. Even in Marx, I cannot find a trace of laughter that is not bitter or savage—excepting always utopia, the permanent possibility that he really did make the primal joke about the movement, if he said 'I am not a Marxist.' There are plenty of jokes in Freud, but even I, often as I restudy Freud's mind and character, cannot say he jokes. Worse: think of what Comte made of his own version of Regina—a cult; less, a cult functional for the emotional development of mental workers acting in the historical stage of Positive Science. As the cult proved dysfunctional, it is not surprising that Comte grew more interested in himself as an object of worship. Between a Comte and a Kierkegaard, in the organization of ideas, there can be no contest. My colleagues may not respect their founding father, but we are fulfilling Comte's prophecy of a scientifically reorganized society: research workers investigating and symbolizing everything—culture, love, factories, the works—without laughter at their antic and endless abstracted ways, which can only be put together in the symbol of symbols, the grant of grants, Money.

Against the cynical seriousness of a Saint-Simon, with his New Christianity, or of a Comte, with his inclusive new Science, the faithful laughter of a Kierkegaard, with nothing in its object that people can follow, may serve as a warning against all those who would take his laughter and make it pay off, a routine. Spare us our performances. That co-existent founder of nothing, Nietzsche, serves us incommensurably well as a cautionary example, against making a school of critical theory out of our performances. That way the author plays his politics and may even cherish fantasies that it is he, and his sort, who ought ideally to be in power as well as in clover.

Where is the way out of our deceits of escape, beyond our authored projects of inclusive change? I ask you, as fellow authors. Whatever you publish is bound to your name, even if you resort to the tactic of concealing it; that is the fly in every apostolic anointment, nowadays—and perhaps also in *Saul/Paul's* time. After all, some scholars argue, cogently to my mind, that *Saul/ Paul* is the real founder of both Christianity and Christendom. Since *Saul/Paul's* time, that fly has landed on many a nose; and where it lands there it sits, implacable.

By way of exemplifying a metamorphosis, then, *Either/Or* is not only a text but, according to Kierkegaard's own authorship as a series of life-acts, also a text analogue. It was in this way, by virtue of trying to test himself as a text analogue in his texts, that Kierkegaard made himself the last and greatest virtuoso of faith in the Protestant tradition. By his life-acts he tried to deny that tradition its modal act, which discriminates sharply between text and text analogue, holy Scripture and its organization; 'charismatic organization' becomes a dubious category and the 'iron cage' an inevitability. The author Kierkegaard could not but sustain the sharpness of this Protestant pathos in his vision of faith as the one resistance landed, implacable against culture. I see in the Protestant pathos, ur-text opposing text analogue, the mood behind our established psycho-sociological discrimination "between a religious attitude toward experience and the sorts of social apparatus which have . . . customarily been associated with supporting such an attitude."[11] This Protestant distinction has led to a pathos now called the sociology of religion, a discipline for the religiously interested. Interdictory motifs are far from steadfast except possibly as they are embalmed in books of religious interest. Faith is no steady state; it is compounded of what is not to be done and yet done. Dostoyevsky understood the compound better than any sociologist. (That is one reason why sociologists of religion ought to read Dostoyevsky more and their colleagues less.) Great churches alter as faith changes character. Now, for example, we see the teaching church unteaching itself, under its own compulsive remissions. The church invests its ministry with powers to agitate for endless therapies.

---

11. Clifford Geertz, *Islam Observed* (New Haven, 1968), p. 2.

New charisms reveal old demons. There is no understanding the releasers of aggression in our age without grasping the unsteadiness of our received faiths.

Our established sociological analysis of faiths allows that the historical course of a religion "rests in turn upon the institutions which render these images and metaphors available to those who thus employ them."[12] Perhaps we can speak, equally well, of those who are institutionally employed by a particular historical variety of the interdictory form and its logic of remission. For example. The release of aggression against whites by young slum blacks, under the agitation of their militant street doctors, constitutes a straight reversal of the transgressive hatred by which not only did whites murder blacks, but blacks turned their aggression against themselves, thus doubly accenting the remissive motifs in American society. Culturologically, the most significant form of crime in America, nowadays, has its sources in this release and redirection of transgressive behavior. 'Religion,' in the Protestant imagination always turned institutional, is, nevertheless, too abstractly conceived; 'steadfast faith' is too high flown, a bird of fantasy, when it does not exist in street crime and its suppression. Through a vast apologetic of transgressive behavior, which is peculiarly 'religious' in its resonances, the line that divides culture from barbarism in this century is not the color line: that line is between the teaching of our inherited interdicts, so deep that men are not free enough to become neurotic, and the preaching of endless remissions so that men are free to become what they are not. That freedom is deadly. It is also so superficial that all action, under its jurisdiction, must become blasé.

The greatest theorist of therapy was neither superficial nor blasé about aggression. Freud indulged no mystique of change. On the contrary, he grasped—and, indeed, he approved, in the very different spheres of culture and therapy—"the slowness with which profound changes in the mind bring themselves about." One of the mysteries of Western spiritual history is how, specially in America, Freudian ideas were misused to violate the slowness with which profound changes take place in the mind. Freud accepted the constraints of privileged knowledge. His analytic couch

---

12. *Ibid.*, p. 3.

was not the world. The therapeutic relation was not a social order. Despite some lapses, as in the case of Dora, what is moral remained to Freud self-evident, as he declared for himself, but not for his patients or readers. The last thing in the world this interpreter of interpretations would become is an impresario of his own endless expressional quest. His first masterpiece, *The Interpretation of Dreams,* is masterly not least in its method: dreams revealed and yet himself concealed. You will seek Freud in vain if you do not see how he managed his reticences in the very act of making his interpretative breakthrough. That breakthrough was not to some autonomous inner being. Autonomy is given from the outside, in our reception of those interdicts and their remissions that settle down as we become ourselves and, so, cannot become an other. In its becoming, self is no performance; the performing self is a not-self, and takes on the instabilities that are the modern condition. I dare to use that hackneyed phrase because, I think, the quivering public instabilities of too many personality doctors and their patients are traceable to the instability of their culture. Psychiatry leads back to sociology.

One task of our third force in defense of culture, neither technological nor sensualist, but a cadre of teaching interpreters, is to keep close watch on what is being done by the impresarios, under their entitlements of Science and Art. We are subjected to endless breakthroughs, by hosts of mini-charismatics, intruding on our private selves, demanding that we abolish them. Against these breakthroughs, and their celebrants, revolutionary and regressive, we might try to imagine a science and art of limits;[13] our primal feeling, if only we could reconstruct it, must be for what we have long known is not to be done.

---

13. A neglected American theorist, my favorite teacher among the old wasps, Horace Bushnell, tried to instruct the chief cultural disciplinarians of the day, his fellow theologians, on the limits of their science. Read, at least, what he has to say on the art of interpreting theological dreams.

Observe that, when God is revealed, He will not, if He is truly and efficiently revealed, be cleared of obscurity and mystery. He will not be

Our cause cannot be hopeless, except as it grows mindless, and gives up the art of interpreting what cannot be cleared of mystery and obscurity. As a teacher, I cherish our slim chance. An old American alliance, between technological radicalism and cultural conservatism, appears broken. Battle lines are being redrawn. The technological radicals will merge with the cultural radicals. 'Counter-culture' is a purchasable gimmick. As the sides merge, strategic opportunities wait to be exploited.

I am aware that those who already know what is not to be done seem weaker than ever before, specially in the universities. We can scarcely make ourselves heard to ourselves; there has been an insolence of tumults even among our book-insulated silences. If we could justify the noises we ourselves make, specially about

---

a bald, philosophic unity, perfectly comprehended and measured by us. We shall not have His boundaries, He will not be simple to us as a man is. When we have reduced Him to that, and call it our reason or philosophy, we have only gotten up a somewhat larger man than ourselves, and set this larger man in the place of the Absolute Being. And if we perfectly understand Him, if we have no questions about Him, the colder, and in real truth the more unknown He is—the Infinite revealed away, not revealed. No; if He is revealed at all, it will be through infinite repugnances and contrarieties; through forms, colors, motions, words, persons, or personalities; all presenting themselves to our sense and feeling, to pour in something of the divine into our nature. And a vast circle of mystery will be the background of all other representations, on which they will play and glitter in living threads of motion, as lightning on a cloud; and what they themselves do not reveal of God, the mystery will—a Being infinite, undiscovered, undiscoverable, therefore true. But if we could see the last boundaries of God, and hold Him clear of a question within the molds of logic and cognition, then He is not God any longer, we have lost the conception of God. [Horace Bushnell, "Incidents of the Revealing Process," *God in Christ* (New York, 1877), pp. 144-145.]

Bushnell then goes on to say what all the faithful believe, although, for reasons hidden in Bushnell's argument, not steadfastly:

There is in God, taken as the Absolute Being, a capacity of self-expression, so to speak, which is peculiar—a generative power of form, a creative imagination, in which, or by aid of which, he can produce Himself outwardly, or represent Himself in the finite. In this respect,

public affairs, then our weakness would not be so alarming as it may sound, for we can only work to confirm and disconfirm authority, not to originate it. Old authority cannot begin to make its next right and proper claim upon our capacity for obedience through teaching in the classroom. Teaching begins long before a student reaches the classroom. Until there are vast numbers of true parents, we cannot expect vast numbers of true teachers—or true students. How can we teachers expect to achieve disciplines of the feeling intellect so late in the student day, and in a cultureless society— one that divorces us from the interdicts?

Moreover, we teachers now easily accept, so long as our jobs and affluence are not threatened, that same cultureless society into which our students have been born. Affluence is becoming only for restrained people. We Americans have never learned to reject enough new things; absence of restraint is the key to our affluence and to our populist inclinations. Very American, we teachers have no cause for complaint about our students. We are up on the latest and have become ex-somethings—ex-Marxists, ex-Jews, ex-bourgeois, ex-straights, ex-kin. How can we complain that the chain of interpretation has been broken? All new links must appear as forgeries if only the self is authentic. Our acceptances of experience are thought to be most satisfying when they are without precedent.

God is wholly unlike to us. Our imagination is passive, stored with forms, colors and types of words from without, borrowed from the world we live in. But all such forms, God has in Himself, and this is the Logos, the Word, elsewhere called the Form of God. Now, this Word, this Form of God, in which He sees Himself, is with God, as John says, from the beginning. It is God mirrored before His own understanding, and to be mirrored, as in fragments of the mirror, before us. Conceive Him now as creating the worlds, or creating worlds, if you please, from eternity. In so doing, He only represents, expresses, or outwardly produces Himself. He bodies out His own thought. What we call the creation, is, in another view, a revelation only of God, His first revelation. [*Ibid.*, pp. 145-146.]

How is it that, a century after Bushnell, we honestly think we can conceive all but what Bushnell still called, filially, 'Him'? Are we so muddle-headed that we can believe a concealment is only what we do not yet know? Does Herbert Spencer have the last word?

We have no stable old ruling ideas and, therefore, can have no stable old presiding class.

We cannot simply dismiss the argument that the struggle for power, revealed for all to see, makes our kind of work at best irrelevant. It has been argued that our transferable interpretations are now so contradictory that they can never again prepare for soul-making and ethics, but only generate neuroses. New scientific interpreters, marching out behind their quotation marks, as if they were shibboleths, aim to acquire an inner freedom to act—any role; this freedom renews the most ancient dexterity, the liveliness with which a human can step aside, as if no particular act represented the responsible I in the middle of his head. Putting all the god-terms and their necessary enemies, the transgressions—'defilement,' 'impurity,' 'lust,' 'untruth,' whatever breaks through—between quotation marks, the new interpreters, improving upon both science and democracy, have made ambiguous and entirely problematic all orders in which we might conceivably live. Our feasts of commitment grow more and more swiftly movable; eternally young and unsettled, we teachers ourselves engage in the most acrobatic hopping from one order to another. Yeats was mistaken: all centers hold equally well. Therefore, there is no center. To be radically contemporaneous, to be sprung loose from every particular symbolic, is to achieve a conclusive, unanswerable failure of historical memory. This is the uniquely modern achievement. Barbarians have never before existed. At the end of this tremendous cultural development, we moderns shall arrive at barbarism. Barbarians are people without historical memory. Barbarism is the real meaning of radical contemporaneity. Released from all authoritative pasts, we progress towards barbarism, not away from it.

Barbarism means more than radical contemporaneity; it means playing at being 'Man,' or 'Human'; barbarism means the universality of those re-educated or brutalized out of membership in the binding particularities of their culture and, being able to entertain all, inhibited by no new god-terms. One perfectly reasonable reviewer of a recent non-book of oracles backed me accurately into my historical corner, along with others:

> Philip Rieff . . . comes over with a touching nostalgia for
> the educated man who once could place himself in a usable

tradition. Now, the barbarians are taking over—the barbarians being classically defined as people without a history, and dwelling most naturally in America, a country dominated by 'an ingenuous will to transform, without regard to what is being destroyed and what is being constructed.' The source of the trouble is the revolutionary activity of the bourgeoisie, for the bourgeoisie is both greedy and rational, reckoning that neither God nor nature nor human nature set any limits to what it might do with the world. Against this Gadarene Rush, intellectuals are powerless; Rieff mentions in an aside that history is only stopped by 'prophecy', but that dark saying is left unilluminated.

Indeed, even under some pressure from their interviewers, the contributors who are asked for prophecy invariably back away. Werner Heisenberg talks some calm good sense about the silliness of the demand for 'new values' and about the idea that science can or ought to provide them. He is plainly right.[14]

---

14. See review by Alan Ryan, "Conference Smog," of G. R. Urban (ed.), *Can We Survive Our Future?* (London, 1972), in *New Statesman,* February 11, 1972, p. 182. Note, however, that I am not quite so ardent a bourgeois-basher as the reviewer makes me out. Bashing the bourgeois is the Marxist version of baiting the Jews. Do not blame the bourgeoisie. They are talented expressionists of the law that to those who have, more will be given; the law is applied, at times with a vengeance, by have-nots. To be realistic about the propertied is not to grow sentimental about the less propertied. There is no special virtue in either of these conditions.

The Bourgeois-Jewish Question will not wash out of the Marxist symbolic. If you do not believe that bourgeois-bashing is the Marxist link, backwards and forwards, to Jew-baiting, then read Marx on goods.[a] There are other equally infamous passages in the Marxist synthesis of bourgeois-bashing and Jew-hating.[b] Bourgeois-bashing and Jew-hatred aside, the distribution and redistribution of wealth remains the stuff of the struggle for power. But wealth, as the Jews should

---

[a]See below, p. 83 *et pass.*
[b]See, also, below, p. 78, footnote 47.

Another reviewer of those same sayings hints further our strategic opportunity:

> Herr Werner Heisenberg, the eminent German physicist, points out that utility is no longer a sufficient justification for new inventions or new applications of technology. Some broader, more socially responsible criteria are required. The point is reinforced separately and elegantly by the American sociologist, Mr Philip Rieff, from a perspective closer to politics, when he points out that technology carries no interior controls.[15]

Here is the negative point at which we teachers in the humane studies might realize our vocations. A science of limits, an interdictory order, cannot come from the scientists, so long as their sciences are limitless. From the scientist in their present minds we can hope for nothing except more of the same, science mocked by armies of intellectualizing bureaucrats who have learned the trick of calling themselves Scientists. What has science to do with bureaucracy? As well reduce interdicts to rules. But who will educate the new scientist to his limits? The humanistic scientists, like the anti-scientific humanists, are in desperate condition. One culture cannot be created by holding sensitivity sessions for scientists; the reading of novels and poetry as part of a new humanism suitable to the age of science, makes no more sense than all the interdisciplinary remedies that would make the literary take a course in basic science—whatever is basic to Science at a particular historical moment.

To see the beginnings of a science of limits, the scientists them-

---

know best, is not identical with power or even its predicate. It is as ridiculous to imagine a ruling class that is merely wealthy as it is to imagine a ruling class that remains poor. Property is an infinitely extendable entity. Stalin made the greatest of political fortunes; no one had more servants. It is not clear that Stalin enjoyed owning Russia. Alas, the rich are not happy; they have such responsibilities and they must live in fear of having less.

15. See "Doomchat," review of *ibid.*, in *The Economist*, February 12, 1972, p. 54.

selves will have to recognize the outside limit: that men must remain under the authority of death, the interdict of interdicts. It follows that the second interdict, in the historical order of our culture, is, at once, against the re-creation of life in the laboratory and the taking of life in the abortion clinic. Under this double authority, a science of limits can then explore a life that is again made meaningful. Those explorations can move us toward the interdictory instruction in which we are immersed, both in genetics and in symbolics. This is to say that a science of limits will have to be reconstructed under the authority of a genetics and a symbolic that cannot escape the modality of the interdicts. If the egalitarian political elites allow—which seems unlikely, at this time, because those elites derive their power from the manipulation of mass movements—then the meaninglessness that has all but conquered our mass education can be displaced by meanings already established.

A 'humanistic science' must remain as meaningless as modern social criticism so long as it seeks to tamper with the interdictory nature of authority. The life of the mind cannot tolerate the deceit of its own infinite malleability; once accepted, as Science, or as Culture without the interdicts, this deceit of mind emerges as anti-mind and grows powerful in the form of hostility to culture in any form. As the leading scientific character in Broch's novel *The Unknown Quantity* remarks: "There's either a mistake here or a miracle."[16] Our notions of the freedom and omnipotence of scientific thought were to be the miracle that would save us from ourselves; the mistake is here.

There are never two cultures, and literary studies cannot unite them. All spheres of activity have their special interdictory-remissive contents implied in the relations of those activities to those of other spheres. The one way to achieve one culture is in the way it has been received before, my fellow teachers: by a return to the authority of the established and ever-failing interdicts, complete with their repressions. We can only return to what we

---

16. Hermann Broch, *The Unknown Quantity*, trans. Willa and Edwin Muir (New York, 1935), p. 5.

already know; that is the zero-sum of our sciences and the blank meaning of our literatures.

If we teachers wish to make any sort of new beginning at the one necessary old science, of limits, then we can begin only by recognizing that our barbaric enlightenments have deinhibited the agency of inhibition: super-ego. The super-ego has not declined; it has undergone a metamorphosis. That agency made too active in any cause, rather than constraining, incites; modern criminals and would-be revolutionaries are not creatures of 'impulse,' as in the nineteenth-century imagination,[17] but more and more often, I suspect, driven creatures of high principle, militants of this immediacy and that. Rapists grow didactic. Apostles of the body flaunt their principles. Who is not to have his say and express himself fully? It is a resolutive contradiction in terms for the super-ego to express itself chiefly in transgressive activity. Such activists of easy principle are one price we are paying for packaging authority entirely inside quotation marks; inside those quotes

---

17. The new black is the old 'dangerous classes,' colored and caste, with infinitely understanding white empathy for the transgressive heroics of Supernigger, who is no less a figment of the racist imagination, now showing its fearfully worshipful side. For his often lyrical therapeutic prose, poor Fanon has been made the Supernigger of the revolutionary intellectuals. Perhaps Fanonism has been a fate that Fanon's prose invites. One good thing: Laughing Boy is a dead racist image. When will Supernigger, the sexual athlete turned revolutionary, follow Laughing Boy? 'Black is Beautiful' is just another racist slogan. One look at the 'black' population of America is all that is needed to persuade even the most casual observer that whites have always considered blacks beautiful enough. I suggest the following slogan, if black Americans must have one: 'Black is Brilliant.' That slogan commands a certain price. 'Intellect' cannot remain a dirty word in the militant black vocabulary. Such a slogan requires a return to Du Bois's doctrine of the Talented Tenth. How tragic the racist circle remains. The negative transference of young blacks against whites is not superior to a positive transference. Fanon himself understood perfectly the pathological connection between the phallic myth of the black and murderous racism, on either side of the colored mirror-image.

our principles no longer bring home to us the tragic sense of danger inseparable from all their enactments. Pseudo-sensibility develops into the finest art. How pompous our cultural revolutionaries are about their 'morality,' in all its preachments of honesty, lightness and play. Our academic world is full of Sniffpecks, who are full of abject snobberies about their effortful liberations from the morality of self-concealment. These Sniffpecks issue more vile sayings than our latest novels; precepts for a liberated Humanity are handed out like leaflets on a gusty day. Such revolutionaries must end each as a patriot for himself, trying to pose as The People. Our Sniffpecks are mere talkers of terror; but there are those who act out what they say.

How have we circled back to those exhibitions of personality, indignant as a revolutionary act, that that most scientific revolutionary, Dr. Marx, so distrusted? I do not know. I do know Marx is rightly served, hoist on his own praxis. With the ethical functionalized out of existence, under the concept of ideology, Marx could get no scientific grip on the fact that any aggressive action (e.g., class exploitation) must be transgressive and not a movement of the historical forces of production. By our own time, post-Marxist in the light of *Lenin/Stalin,* we know that transgressiveness knows no political boundaries, neither Right nor Left. Making a revolution (in the Marxist sense) is obsolete—along with revolution in its original meaning, as a return—except return to the orgiastic as original action.

Against this "originality," every artifice of culture, if it works, recreates us as obedient persons. A truth of resistance is not to impulse, but to transgressive behavior. Those who interpret themselves as activists for the 'counterculture' perform transgressively in spheres scarcely different from those of their political enemies; the difference is one of content rather than form. Business is business. Sex is sex. Politics is politics. Enter these different spheres and we witness different transgressions. But who now preaches a faith that will subject these differences, and their spheres, to a uniform set of interdicts? At least since Durkheim, we sociologists have known that modern societies are too complex for a catholic form, including a catholic Science—that fantasy of Durkheim's positivist forebears in which he himself could no longer believe. For Durkheim, science was to stand watch on the dynamics of all faiths; he had little hope in the dynamics of science itself as a basis for some new embracing social organization, as his predecessors, Saint-Simon and Comte, had hoped. As a collective effervescence, science and technology fizzled out in the century of their triumphs, the twentieth.

It is out of a highly differentiated society, spheres of action separate, none subject to the same interdicts, and all to fewer, that the therapeutic has been born. This ideal type is free, in the first place, because he can live his life among authorities so long divided that none can assert themselves strongly even in their own sphere —quite the contrary of Durkheim's quasi-syndicalist hope. There is, however, something new about the therapeutic: a conclusive freedom, all interdicts evaginated, so highly surfaced that none can survive. Why should the therapeutic feel anything deeply when he can exhibit his sensibilities? The contemporary man of feeling is equipped with a hidden weapon, his pseudo-sensibility; he demands, he appeals, he does whatever needs to be done, under whatever slogan, to assert himself. A slogan is an unrooted saying. Slogans are the language of a radically contemporary people. The American language has become a grab-bag of slogans. This massive abnormality has become the norm.

Living on his surfaces, as he does, the therapeutic is an acutely sensitive man; it is only deep down that he has learned to be less vulnerable. I was struggling toward this point in a passage from *The Triumph of the Therapeutic* of which you reminded me in your interpretative paraphrase of it during our exchange:

> With Freud, the individual took a great and final step toward that mature and calm feeling which comes from having nothing to hide. To live on the surface prevents deep hurts.

It takes a certain genius to survive the deepest hurts. Freud favored asking less of people, most of whom are not moral geniuses or any other kind. Most of us cannot transform our hurts into anything that does not hurt (ourselves or others) more. A true culture imposes certain limits on itself; it does not ask ordinary men to make extraordinary renunciations. But in a true culture, a genius is not considered a criminal, nor is criminality honored as genius. Life is not confused with Art. Terribilità should remain an aesthetic, not a political, capacity; it rightly belonged to Beethoven and Michelangelo, in their work, not to the condottieri, or Hitler, in theirs. An extraordinarily rare talent does not emerge in transgressions; rather, in works of art, or science, that control their own spheres with full interdictory force, called 'form.' Within its culture, every art work constitutes a system of discrete limits, each a paradigm of how a culture works; none are sovereign beyond themselves. A universal culture is a contradiction in terms. We Jews of culture are obliged to resist the very idea.

Confusing spheres, modern aspirants to freedom from all authority have produced a parody terribilità in all spheres. Our re-educated classes, rich consumers of everything available, are scarcely competent to perform the most elementary decencies—yet they are urged to fulfill themselves, as if each were a Beethoven, perhaps a little deaf to his own music and in need of some third-ear hygiene. Freud called psychoanalysis a 're-education.' In our own time, post-Freudian, everything new is a re-education; mind fawns over mindlessness and tries to find fancy names for it. So the therapeutic teaching of transgressive behavior confuses art and life, rare genius and common faith, public life and private. Encounter-group teachings, for example, mainly by therapists of the revolutionary rich, follow the precedent set by the technological radicalism of those same rich in their earlier scramble: for more.

That the opposing sides of the American scene, deviants and straights, are both suspicious of authority, is mainly the fault of what passes for authority in our nation; the officers themselves are so often inferior persons that their offices cannot conceal the absence of any reference beyond themselves to a presiding presence. Modern revolt has no authority and is all the more dangerous because there is no authority against which to revolt; we are stripping politics to its barest form, struggle for power after power, violence. What Mill called 'savagery' and 'barbarism' scarcely applies so well to his notion of static societies as it does to our own dynamic one. We and our students shall have to be reminded that "discipline, that is, perfect co-operation, is an attribute of civilization," not of mass rationalization. Mill tells us that to be capable of discipline in great things, "a people must be gradually trained to it in small."[18] Such training cannot be politicized without inverting the meaning of discipline, from civilization to barbarism—from a not-doing of what is not to be done to a routine doing of precisely that.

Presences have never been encouraged to preside—now less than ever before. The therapeutic has no presence. It is impossible to revolt against him. All revolution worthy of the name has been against authority, giving rise to a new presiding presence, without which authority cannot exist; for example, Jews cannot exist without the Mosaic presence (as Freud understood, in making his attempt at a resolutive interpretation of the Jewish historical character). Suppose, however, there is no authority—only power and its theatrical affects? How can there be a crisis of authority? Among our reflexive sorts, there is much fashionable talk of crisis, of our times of trouble. I doubt the gravity of the crisis, not least for all the crisis talk; the time seems to me less gravely troubled than some others. What can 'trouble' mean if our society is growing cultureless, without presiding presences and a public order of meaning? Guilt is much overestimated as a working force in the new society, usable mainly as a tactic toward its continuing dissolution. During a year in Germany, I met precious few guilty people. My German friends were having an authentically good time. My American friends seem equally guiltless, although they throw up their hands regularly as if aghast at their sense of guilt. I think they are playing games. To feel guilt takes a certain submission to authority. There can be no transgressive sense without someone (and his theory) to transgress.

No guilt is true except as it subserves the interdicts. Guilt is false, 'neurotic,' as Freud taught us to call it, when it subverts the interdicts. Far from separating crime and morals, the radical psychologizers treat certain kinds of crime as (politically) virtu-

18. John Stuart Mill, "Civilization," *The Westminster Review*, Nos. V and XLVIII (April 1836), p. 3.

ous; in the name of 'humanization,' false guilt subverts the interdicts by proclaiming that everything human is permitted. The
radical psychologizers have greatly increased the incidence of
false guilt because culture cannot tolerate such direct openings of
possibility. Our politicized therapists are the sickest people among
us—and our most liberated. Their quest for health has generated
an acute dis-ease, 'Liberation,' the latest mockery of all god-terms,
including the pagan.

We professors of the present have in stock a large supply of
god-terms and can conjure orders galore, from the grab-bag of
things past, passing and to come. Precisely in the age of the
therapeutic, the dead gods cannot rise from their graves. None
are alive; any may be talked up, for an occasion, if the talkers
like to drop those kinds of names. Our god-terms mock their
ancestors, the gods, in one special respect: no god-term worth
using can be merely heuristic, a device for extending intellectual
reach. God-terms must have binding authority, compelling not
merely intellectual interest but also suspicion of that interest. Our
God can only reveal as he conceals himself; ask that, concealment
with every revelation, and you have understood why the major
questions must always continue as if unanswered.

Without concealments, revelations yield none of those com-
promises which make life tolerable. Imagine the length of the
casualty list when a universal publicity reveals everything to all,
at once, when nothing is handed down slowly, in generational
dances of time. Sociology awaits its theorists in the classic style.
Since the positivist takeover, in the first third of the nineteenth
century, my discipline has tried too hard to remain permanently
advanced, young enough to produce an endless barrage of
originalities. Such youthfulness and originality—trendiness, some
call it—are fatal to the life of the mind. Violent excursions
toward death and perverse behavior are occupations most fit for
the young, when they will not think through what their predecessors
have thought. To leave the great past unremembered is to be lost
in the howling present; then the best an intellectual can do is
shoot off his mouth.

When the god-terms lose their inhibiting dynamic, then they
become protean. ('Protean man' does not descend from the god

Proteus. He has no descent, and therefore no existence.) The barbarian who is emerging, stuffed with tactical advice culled from the ages, can hop from order to order, committing himself, as in modern marriage, to a serial monogamy that is massively polygamous. ('But I'm always true to you, darlin', in my fashion' —what is the name of that old hymn? I will not remember. Was it: 'A Mighty Fortress,' as Erikson believes?) To say this barbarian is universally faithless is only to say that no character becomes authoritative in him. Only cultureless societies can exist without presiding presences. No presence can preside when all are subject to abandonments quick as their adoptions. Our passionate truths are so provisional, they move so quickly with the electrified times, that none can prepare us to receive them deeply into ourselves, as character; they do not become compelling in their interdicts but endlessly attractive in their remissions. Where creeds were, there therapies will be. Our new way, re-education, is an unlearning. What, then, have we to teach?

It is as the typical creature of a cultureless society that I have imagined the therapeutic. I do not imagine him as a serious man. Seriousness is a state of possession by god-terms, even to the negation of justified violence in their defense. Serious attacks on authority must breed new authority. In the therapeutic, I imagined someone who takes nothing seriously. Of course, a therapeutic can resonate empty militancies that signal an acceptance of their emptiness. Opposing this experimental life, in which all god-terms can be taken lightly, rather as heuristic devices, there can be only a culture of militant, opposing truths—god-terms that are interdictory before they are remissive and thus to be taken seriously because humans will oppose the interdicts with all their wits. (To take a god-term seriously, however, is not to be without humor; on the contrary, as I have said, no justification worth calling to mind ever sets it at rest. What may be taken lightly is not the god-term, but oneself. Luther called this the joy of the faithful.) A culture of truth opposing self—what culture is, understood sociologically—abides experimental lives only in its own service; thus, for example, monasticism, which opposed the corporate self-glorification of the church, served culture. Except through insti-

49

tutional services, before they harden into further glorifications and false guilt, experiment belongs in the laboratory and to art, most rarely to publicized individuality. Our continuous publicity for experimental living predicates that totalitarian disorder of which fascist movements gave one premonitory flash. I shall return, below, to the important point that, as Mussolini grasped, fascism is not a creed but an opportunity.

Now I am in position to answer the question for which you prepared me before our interview (perhaps the result of our happy misunderstanding): whether the coming of the therapeutic is to be welcomed insofar as he is free from any need of a common faith. With this emergent type, you ask, will we be delivered from the nightmare history of the last half-century, and spared its mass brutalities? No; I suspect we will not be spared. Violence is the therapy of therapies, as Dr. Fanon, the political psychiatrist, suggests. There is less and less to inhibit this final therapy, least where the most progressively re-educated classes seem ready to go beyond their old hope of deliverance, from violence as the last desperate disciplinary means built into the interdicts, as punishment, to violence as a means toward a saving indiscipline, as self-expression. Geniuses of this saving indiscipline roam the college circuit, selling their guidance toward a cultureless society, without interdicts deeply installed.

Which cadre of putative guides to the new freedom will you follow: our rationalizing functionaries[19] or our functional irrationalizers?[20] Never mind: they will meet at the end of their roads. The functional irrationalizers are well on their way to becoming our next rationalizing functionaries. Both cadres will produce endless therapies. With the end of authority, no violence will be illegitimate. Rather, as they destroy the civilities basic to cultured society, the brutalities of direct action will be differently understood. Victims are being taught their complicity, their role, in brutal acts. Let every actor play his variable part, without indignation—except when indignation promotes the part. The new society already has the look, both in America and in the Soviet Union, of

---

19. E.g., engineers, social and material, of control.
20. E.g., therapists of release.

50

a hospital-theatre—in contrast to the old society, which had the look of a church. The successor to our failed credal organizations will not be another credal one, not even Marxist, which names the last major credal effort to reorganize western society; we shall be dominated by anti-creeds and think ourselves free.

Our own culture has taken form in credal organizations. Priesthoods and intelligentsias are but two of the forms credal organization, ancient and modern, may take. However, the defense of it, implicit in my theory of culture, does not make me an advocate of some earlier credal organization. In particular, I have not the slightest affection for the dead church civilization of the West. I am a Jew. No Jew in his right mind can long for some variant (including the Party)[21] of that civilization. Its one enduring quality is its transgressive energy against the Jew of culture; those transgressions have been built so deeply into the church-organized interdicts that they survive even now, after the main interdictory motifs of Christendom are dead. Christian transgressions are still so vital that the recent well-publicized statements of Christian remorse are likely to be a condition of further transgression, as the Jews continue to resist their assigned roles and, worse gall, refuse to disappear into the universalist future 'Man.' The gospels were not good news; the ungospeled present has its supremely pleasant feature, the death of the church—or, less pleasant, its conversion into naively therapeutic institutions, hawking a few antique graces to ornament our triumphant gracelessness. A contentless faith in 'faith' is but one of the rather noisy rhetorics of

---

21. But, see, on the concept 'political religions,' my remarks on functionalism, pp. 187-188. I doubt that the Party, which Gramsci saw as the Prince of this world, can be understood as a 'secular' (i.e., successor and functional) equivalent of the Church. Indeed, I doubt that penetrative thrust inheres in the concept 'secularization.' We can do better without 'secularization.' The concept obscures interdictory-remissive shifts of indirective content. Secularization specially encourages false homotonalities, an ease of transitions that may falsify true oppositions: as between pastors and professors, for example—as if becoming a Professor really does express in another form (perhaps up-dated, superior because up-dated) earlier religious aspirations.

51

commitment to movement—any movement—that characterize the superego turned against itself, against inhibition and for action. As in space science, so in the new reforming amorality, to be distinguished from the old Reformation morality, the count-down slogan is "All systems go."

I, for one, am not keen on being where the direct action is; there brutality and the horror of total politics, uninhibited by any presiding presence, will be. One necessary thing that we inactivists, we academic men, suspicious of all politics, have to teach our students is how not to invest in the nostrums of direct action now being hawked. It is our duty to protect and nurture, in our academies, a few enclaves within which to practice an inhibiting subtlety, to think in something like late Jamesean sentences.[22] If we are not allowed indirections, slowly ordered, if we must serve some program, one side or another, then the academy has no unique service; it is least fit of all institutions to take stands or rationalize them. The more directly political it becomes, the more certainly the university must commit itself to shifting posi-

---

22. Then, after James, we may graduate to Proust, who grasped Chardin, master of the ordinary and of still-life. Prepared by Chardin, Proust could grasp Vermeer, master of that little patch of yellow wall and, more profoundly, of the ordinary moment, quietly revealed. To receive Vermeer's revelation is to become quiet oneself. Looking at a Vermeer, Proust saw how inhibiting are the supreme subtleties and how hierarchical, orderly, beautifully precise and commanding those subtleties are. This praise is not for old Art. Modern art can be equally inhibiting. It is mere ignorance, parading as traditionalism, to praise the formalities of a Raphael, or the eighteenth-century painters, while dispraising the formalities of modern painting, which begin with Cézanne (to whom Roger Fry makes the best introduction, still, I think) and continue, through Braque, to our best contemporaries in painting. But exclude—from my canon, at least—those talented impresarios (e.g., Duchamp) of a constantly innovative art who, as innovators, lead what is tantamount to a campaign for the abolition of art. Duchamp's *ready-mades* intend that 1) everything is pleasurable; 2) because the pursuit of pleasure can be totally democratic, everything is art. This is cultural egalitarianism with a vengeance, first against art itself.

tions, in the endless war for advantage, and so destroy its intellectual integrity. To resist endless politicizing is made more difficult when politics and therapy merge in fancies of a student culture opposed to study. Yet, despite the erotic incitements on campus, some of our students remain ardent to be students.

The threat to study is double: not only from masses of students who do not study, but from faculty who will not teach. By their gurus and Research paymasters, the collegiate young are being re-educated before they have been educated. From our collegiate ranks, the therapeutic will appear a re-educated man, one who can conquer even his subtler inhibitions; his final know-how will be to irrationalize his rationality and play games, however intellectualized, with all god-terms in order to be ruled by none. In their moral modesty, therapeutics will be capable of anything; they will know that everything is possible because they will not be inhibited by any truth. Far more destructively than earlier interdict-burdened character types, the therapeutic will be the warring state writ small;[23] he may be even cannier, less sentimental, stronger in ego, shifting about his principles and his impulses like so many stage props.

Of one condition that could make him less capable of brutality, the therapeutic, conqueror of his feeling intellect, is likely to be incapable: *inwardness*, the quality of self-concealment. That has become, as Kierkegaard predicted, an aberrancy. The growth of this aberrancy is linked to the mistaken idea, held by both rationalists and sentimentalists, of an autonomous inner man. What is referred to as 'inner' and 'autonomous' expresses responses of obedience to interdictory-remissive predicates that are as complex before as after they are taken in as character.[24] Cultures are con-

---

23. On this small matter, see below, pp. 152-153, footnote 99.

24. E.g., Jewish moral demands have a complex *We-They* order that, when taken into character, are not entirely defensive, according to my judgment. *I-Thou* is too pure a symbol to cope with the interdictory-remissive dynamic of *We-They*, in the ordinary life of Jews. The *and* between Buber's primary word, *I-Thou*, signifies, for him, an "act of pure relation" which, in its 'purity,' comes too near that emptying-out of revelation and its credal order characteristic of nineteenth-

stituted by interdictory contents, and their remissions, in multiform cults. Few of those cults are recognized in their multiformity, now that all have been overwhelmed by the cult of personality. Within those cults we are free to choose among authority relations; authority generates, as culture, its indispensable interior flexibility.

A student once revealed to me the new cultic untruth, from within which there will be dispensed an unprecedented flexible exteriority: "We are all going to be—we all have to be—'up front,' " she said. I gleaned from her the idea of a human who exposes himself completely and reveals nothing. She was training to be a therapist—welfare work and all that—mainly with clients released from psychiatric hospitals. Almost all her clients were already 'up front,' she said. How glad I was for her; she had found her vocation—not as a director of conscience, but as a semi-official tactician of outwardness. My one-time student, who scarcely understood a word I said or wrote, could be easily imagined as a functionary, herself in permanent therapy, in the coming total welfare state.[25] What every state can best use are empty people,

---

century idealism before it led toward its counter, the anticredal order of our time. I suspect a language in which "Man receives, and he receives not a specific 'content' but a Presence, a Presence as power." That sounds to me like the late Protestant emptying-out of the interdicts, by a too general affirmation. Historically and sociologically, in this way, 'Meaning' is anything but assured. Quite the contrary of Buber's vision, mine is that nothing can any longer be meaningful when 'Man' receives a 'Presence' without "specific 'content.' " [Cf. Buber, *I And Thou*, trans. Ronald Gregor Smith (Edinburgh, 1937), pp. 109-110 *et pass.*]

25. Nietzsche wrote, in 1886, of my student and her social welfare teachers: "It is almost always a symptom of what is lacking in himself when a thinker senses in every 'causal connection' and 'psychological necessity' something of constraint, need, compulsion to obey, pressure, and unfreedom; it is suspicious to have such feelings—the person betrays himself." How have we Americans lost our suspicion of this type? How have we developed our tremendous apologetics for those who "do not wish to be answerable for anything, or blamed for anything, and owing to an inward self-contempt, seek to *lay the blame for themselves somewhere else*" [Nietzsche's italics]? How well Nietzsche

without the gift of self-concealment. Beyond the concealed life, opposing it as once our souls (and then our historical neuroses) opposed therapy, lies the kind of naked life in which everything is exposed and nothing revealed. How we moderns love to undress. So I imagine the political order of therapeutics, for whom all uniforms will fit perfectly and none are to be reverenced. My ideal type is no idolator, not even when standing in front of the mirror. Rather, there he will appear in his most revealing disguise, as a comic figure.

Let me escape my own imaginings, into John Barth's, which are virtually real. *The End of the Road* is the story of a naked man, entirely exposed—and yet, not quite so. Something remains concealed, even from himself: a still unyielding truth of resistance. Barth's virtual reality, Jacob Horner, finds himself in trouble when his residual inwardness gets in his way; his endless movement stopped, Jake is trapped in a compromise of his honesty from the moment he cannot accept (and even tries to resist) Rennie Morgan's decision to commit suicide rather than bear his (illegitimate) child. Jake should have passed the point in his cultural development when, as Kant said, self-murder need be considered 'heinous.' Jake is no judge; equally important, there is no god-term by which he need be judged. Unjudging and unjudged, a therapeutic can achieve his perfection.

Are Jakes so rare, even now, among our re-educated classes? What crime is now abominable? What needs expiation? Who is not to be subject, by personality doctors of our ever new societies, to rehabilitation? Under the enlightenments of therapy, teaching

---

understood the intellectualized varieties of this type, with their contempt for inwardness. "When they write books, [they] are in the habit today of taking the side of criminals; a sort of socialist pity is their most attractive disguise" [Nietzsche, *Beyond Good and Evil,* trans. Walter Kaufmann (New York, 1966), p. 29]. Here is prophecy, which most often takes the form of forewarning. The type Nietzsche imagined rare in 1886, is common today in our universities and bureaucracies.

orders of law, dependent as they must be upon orders of authoritative persons, appear as penal colonies; we re-educated ones cannot comprehend our own received punitive writ; it is a meaningless legacy, handed down by some presence no longer presiding. It is punishment that will become the crime. If our points of view, old writ, can change swiftly enough, then no interdict can settle downward. Everything that does not seriously disturb the power of the state will be permitted, even encouraged. In a cultureless society, the total welfare state will become all-powerful, and, moreover, make common cause with its criminal opposition. A society that does not have the tragic sense to punish must die at the hands of its decriminalized transgressors—at the top and bottom of the social structure. Compare this condition with the law ordered by Zeus, "that he who has no part in reverence and justice shall be put to death, for he is a plague of the state."[26] Where is our Dr. Zeus? Since Nietzsche, who has spoken well on his behalf? Only some of the least educated, in their private suspicions of the new public wisdom.

Barth's Jake does not yet exist in this new state, without reverence and justice. He exists between orders, where death is casual and not a judgment. Some residual reverence in Jake, unacknowledged, makes death an inexplicable foolishness and not a sentence. On hearing Rennie Morgan's announced intention to kill herself, Jake Horner's constantly shifting point of view freezes, as if in horror. He rushes about, trying to arrange an abortion. Better abortion than suicide. Why not suicide? (Indeed, why not murder, incest —who can say what is not therapeutic?[27]) Jake is trapped in his

---

26. Plato, *Protagoras*, 322d.

27. The movement to abolish law—i.e., to evaginate all interdictory contents, first by removing their superstructures—has many converts, not least in our schools of Law. I quote from a heartening, enlightened editorial, in a conservative newspaper, the Toronto *Globe and Mail* [February 3, 1972, p. 6], under the title "New Vitality at U. of T.": "[The newly appointed] Dean of the School of Law . . . is a brilliant legal thinker and innovator, and a teacher of formidable reputation. He is a member of the Law Reform Commission and a consultant to

residual inwardness, for reasons so deep that they are concealed even from the author. We mere readers will never know; the author cannot tell us and knows better than to try.

In contrast, there is Joe, Rennie Morgan's husband: he is a rationalist; he wants to know everything. Joe celebrates the drive for clarity. He is one of the Cartesian sort, who are deaf to what barking dogs have to say in the variety of their barks. Our junior Descartes, who distinguishes himself too definitively from the brute, wants to know what Jake and Rennie *meant*, by going to bed— together; his moral demand is only that they explain themselves, propositionwise. Relentlessly propositional, Joe is capable of horrors for which the term 'brutal' is grossly unfair to brutes, as all of us who live our intimate lives with dogs as well as humans know best. This reminds me of a little book (for Humeans and against Cartesians) titled *My Thoughts*, written down by my wife and myself at the command of our Dandie Dinmont terrier, Darcy, that unfailing, decent and comic representative of what a presiding presence must have been like. You are aware of what *dog* is, spelt backwards. The motto of Darcy's book is taken from the *Summa*

---

government. But he is also a figure of dissent and perhaps even a gadfly to the legal Establishment.

"He is probably best known for his work on Bail reform that culminated in the Government's accepting his thesis that an accused person's liberty should not be jeopardized because of poverty. But he is also on record as calling for a separation of laws and morality, a rejection of codified Victorian puritanism. Noting that the Criminal Code has been updated to some extent by fairly recent changes involving homosexuality, abortion and birth control, he wants similar thinking in such areas as obscenity, bigamy, incest, drugs and gambling.

"[The appointment is] encouraging and welcome."

Once again, I say: the propertied classes are not conservative; we need not continue to mistake invincible stupidity, and petty rancors, with the defense of culture. The propertied classes, their lawyers and editorial writers, are self-interested, which is not the same as conservative. Modern culture is constituted by its endless transitionality; the people at the top have learned to want it that way.

57

Theologica. I refer you to the *Summa*, Part I, Q. 13, Art. 5,[28] in which Thomas[29] records the objection that

> If the name *dog* be said equivocally of the barking dog, and of the dogfish, it must be said of some univocally—viz., of all barking dogs; otherwise we proceed to infinitude.

By such relentless intellectualizings, as the divine Thomas pillories, Joe would proceed to infinitude, where he cannot be. "No name belongs to God in the same sense that it belongs to creatures. . . . Therefore whatever is said of God and of creatures is predicated equivocally." Joe does not understand the difference between god-terms and godheads, and therefore must be false to both. As Thomas remarks, "in analogies the idea is not, as it is in univocals, one and the same, yet it is not totally diverse as in equivocals; but a term which is thus used in a multiple sense signifies various proportions to some one thing." Joe mistakes equivocals for univocals. He pretends to treat god-terms as if, understood, they would leave no room for human maneuver—as if in their revelations they had nothing to conceal. Under such compulsive misapprehensions, Joe must go on working on his parody *Summa*, suicide or no. Joe makes heavy going of all god-terms, and, misguided by his own seriousness, makes his life over into a seminar.

Jake, too, is proceeding to infinitude, but by another road. Because he takes all god-terms lightly, scarcely acknowledging their existence except in the classroom, Jake is at his worst when trying to do his best—when he commits himself to act interdictorily, in order to prevent Rennie's suicide, and yet without knowing that her danger is himself. We can name the death of God only from the death of those who are, in a sense, doglike creatures.

---

28. [The Dominican Fathers translation (2nd rev. ed.; London: Burns Oates, 1920), pp. 158-162.] Alas, Burns Oates, that fine Catholic house, has gone out of business, I believe: a portent. Does there survive a single major Catholic publishing house in America?

29. Read Thomas. He is one of our true masters, much misread by the priests. Class him with Freud and Weber (Max, the sociologist, *not* the painter); with James (Henry-William); with Marx (Karl-Groucho); with Barth (Karl-John).

Rennie—minding, though not proposition-wise—gags on her own vomit, when Jake's black therapist tries to liberate her from the foetus. Rennie is a natural-born follower. Pill-taking would not have solved her problem. In its conception of the significance of a foetus, part of Barth's plot is as obsolete as *Romans*: "The invisible things of God are clearly seen, being understood by the things that are made."[30] Possessed by no theory, Jake can only think of therapies. That is why, whatever violences he commits, the therapeutic's soul is not endangered. Therapeutic violence is the most flexible form of exteriority and, so, different from that interdictory violence by which defenders of soul have always endangered their own.

In *The End of the Road,* life is unfortunate enough to be treated as if it were a Liberation school. Rennie Morgan is a follower who thinks she is a student. Unfortunately for Rennie, life is both unacademic and unfree. The relation of master and disciple is both necessary and limited. She lacks a sense of the limits of that relation. Until a certain moment of revelation, the nonstop, too serious intellectualizing of her Leader-Husband binds her in the classic double-bind of obedience: to a teacher who pretends not to be a presiding presence, and yet teaches for his own glory in the role. She goes through the charade, with Joe, of constantly rethinking her position, like an interminably earnest undergraduate, when in effect her position consists of being Joe's devoted follower. As a teacher, Joe desires merely to lead; he is entirely dependent on his student-follower-wife.

Having assigned *The End of the Road* to me, as homework for our interview, you will remember the scene in which Joe Morgan dances away his dominion. He believes he is alone with himself. But Joe Morgan, unaware, is seen by Jake and Rennie through the window, playing before the mirror of his private self, released from his ever-serious leadership role. Joe's self-proclaimed consistency—his

---

30. *Romans* 1:20. With what poverty of intellect the truth of resistance to the therapeutic doctrine of abortion proceeds. [See *The Interpreter's Bible*, my own favorite work of reference, Vol. IX (Nashville, 1954).]

assertion that his public self and private are univocal—is played out in that moment, merging truth and untruth. That concealed moment of self-revelation breaks Joe's dominion over his community of two. Rennie feels she must go her own way. But she was unprepared for her freedom. Like so many other minds, this one, undisciplined, can only be violated by ideas. Rennie has gone to life as if permanently to school. And what of her teacher?

In reason, what did the authority-figure conceal from his wife-follower? It was something quite trivial: Joe makes some funny faces at himself, in the mirror; he dances a little, as I recall, around the room. What breaks his domination is that Joe has been secreting a soul all along. He reveals it antic before the mirror, a comical thing. His concealed self is a mirror image of his relentless seriousness, all up-front. Publicly world-serious, a philosopher (Columbia Ph.D. candidate, I recollect) in bed and about it, just Joe's trivial revelation of soul, his privately enacted caper, destroys his dominion, which is equal in importance to his self.

Even Rennie, that minding creature, realizes Joe has been a non-stop self-promotion; his image was not all there was to him. He was not all up-front, as he asserted, talking everything over and out. Her very own charismatic, her recognized one against the makeshift of the world, had been a publicity man, his own client. Rennie is shocked by the revelation of his self-concealment. Joe has proclaimed that, for him, there can be no on-stage—more precisely, that he is always off-stage. The poor student of how to live has swallowed that most transgressive of all ethics, the ethic of honesty. No one who marries can be so naive. Defenseless, the student-wife is caught in the struggle between Jacob and (as it was, in the longer form) Joseph, the knowing one.

Not that the pious who married in the Christian era were less brutal than these infidel marriages nowadays. The Jesuit, Thomas Sanchez, published in 1592 a folio on marriage (described by Bayle):

We do not know the domestic privacy of the ancient pagans as we know those of the countries where auricular confession is practiced; and therefore we cannot tell whether marriage was so brutishly dishonored among the pagans as it is among the Christians; but at least it is probable that the Infidels did not surpass in this respect many persons who believe on the doctrines of the Gospel.

A brutish dishonoring of marriage is now practiced in countless therapies. Encounter groups burlesque the discipline of auricular confession. The common purpose of these burlesques is to de-inhibit what should be inhibited. Fortunately, the indulgers of the sex gospel are no more devout in their practice of the perverseness they call 'honesty' than were those who once indulged the spiritualizings of the church. We should give thanks for what remains of that elemental sophistication by which the less educated pretend to accept, from the more re-educated, the latest good news of their liberation from earlier servitudes. Piety continues to be contained by dishonesty. What humbugs our deliverers from disciplines of limit are; they can only prepare us for some supreme humbug, some new tyranny that will bless the one perfect marriage I can imagine: that between complete honesty and incredulous brutality. When such a marriage is consummated, the related parties are totally dishonored. For her honesty, Rennie is dishonored and dies. She is without self-protection. To be without self-protection invites punishment. Rennie gags to death, in her own vomit. That vomit gag is an old literary symbol, I suppose, signifying something or other. Kafka, a genius at reflecting willing victims, used the gag.[31] But victims are not born; they are re-educated, their minds too much broadened. In cultures of truth, the object of education is to narrow the mind.

In the struggle between them, Jake Horner represents a definite typological advance over Joe Morgan. Even in the sweat of Jake's

---

31. Barth is a mere interpreter of interpreters, a further spinner of established myths. What a full guilty man he must be, indebted as he is to so many predecessors. All giftedness, like Barth's, signifies guilt—although all guilt does not signify giftedness, for to become gifted, guilt must take on the form of privileged knowledge. This is to say: our guilt must be instructed. For a true culture, there must be masters of the knowledge of guilt. Without these masters, what we call 'healthy' signifies illness, and what we call 'knowledge' displays ignorance.

abortion involvement,[32] he would not compel Rennie. Jake is clear of our historic authority hang-up; he is without the predicate of creative repetition, prototypes—presiding presences. As the most advanced type in the novel, he dominates by the very emptiness of his character. It is not for Jake to preside, by his transgressive intellectualizing, even over a community of two. Such student communities are never genuine, because they recognize nothing superior to their consciousness of becoming instructed. Life is not for learning. Joe is an American pioneer, hacking out his homestead, making his fortune—except now as the riches of raised consciousness. In his pseudo-vocation, Joe will stop at nothing, not even his wife's suicide. Parodying the cult of experience with consciousness as his god-term, all Joe wants are explanations, the more the better. Joe is no husband. Joe, too, is no judge. He destroys his claim to understand by seeking only to understand, as if life were a classroom; so, too, he resolves his claim as a husband. He has failed to understand marriage. He is re-educated and a fool; one condition encourages the other.

Jake still knows the difference between life and the classroom. Inside the classroom, he exists professionally, in his earning capacity. Outside the classroom, not only has Jake nothing to teach, but he lacks a sense of indebtedness for what he knows. Jake has no idea that in life he has any debts to work off. Without this sense of his essential indebtedness, in everything he can know, a man acquires false knowledge, of false solutions: the 'problem' to be solved by our Jakes is how to get their lives started and how to keep them going. Every day becomes a crisis of sorts: this type must ask himself (or herself)—'How am I doing?', which is identical with 'Am I a going concern?'

If life is an endless end-game, then its players grow restless in principle. They marry in order to divorce, divorce in order to remarry. They re-educate themselves to change jobs or, if stuck in the same job, to know it cannot be their 'vocation.' Such a creature must become: and he can only become as a creature of movement

---

32. Notice the everyday, re-educated, businesslike, sociologeseiacal rhythms of that phrase 'abortion involvement.' Note, further, my concise 'authority hang-up,' and the earlier (p. 11) 'happiness output.'

or he is nothing. One obvious therapy becoming movement for Jake is travel; another is sexuality. Sexuality is movement. From time to time, Jake moves in a sexual fashion. No love is involved. But by trying to prevent Rennie's suicide, Jake destroys Rennie. Jake is not then at the end of the road. He hesitates to feel that a case of self-murder is so heinous that it ought to be prevented; nevertheless, he acts as if this is what he feels. Therapeutics develop a marvelous pseudo-sensibility to which I have referred. After Rennie's death, Jake understands that in the light of his lapse into decisive choice he must go to the end of the road—into permanent therapy—where no choice will be decisive. In a sense, we all know Jake exists; Jake is what we are re-educating ourselves to be.

You asked whether I am encouraged by Jake's relapse during the time of the intended suicide. Of course not; it was a relapse. You can see where existentialist decision-making, an activist ethic of honesty, leads our three actors—Joe deeper into his dissertation, Jake into permanent therapy, Rennie into death. Moreover, Jake is a fictional character. Let us not take our literary pleasures so seriously as to be encouraged, or discouraged, by them. True: as moral forms, works of art may help those moved by them to resist the assaults of experience. Demoralized, works of art (and behavioral science) help mount the assault of experience. Their present phase an endless end-game, our arts and sciences conspire with political history to produce in reality that condition of terror Burke saw concealed in the aesthetic,[33] and revealed in his con-

---

33. More precisely, as a defense against the aesthetic, an essay bounding it. [See Edmund Burke, "A Philosophical Inquiry Into The Origin of Our Ideas of The Sublime And Beautiful; With An Introductory Discourse Concerning Taste," *The Works of Edmund Burke* (London, 1897), Vol. I.] Burke understood the tragic relation between reality and the theatrical.

I imagine we shall be much mistaken, if we attribute any considerable part of our satisfaction in tragedy to the consideration that tragedy is a deceit, and its representations no realities. The nearer it approaches the reality, and the farther it removes us from all idea of fiction, the

cept of the sublime. When art seeks to become a work of life, the artist fails; his failure, transferred from art to life, produces terror instead of what is sublime. A failed artist, Hitler, became a successful politician. Incite experience to riot and it will assault precisely what art and science, as moral forms, defend. The endless expressional quest belongs to art, with its absolute systems of limit, unchallengeable within the work itself. Because life cannot be made over into a work of art, the endless expressional quest can never belong to it. What destructiveness is implied in our desire to make life extraordinary. Existence is broken enough, without inducing breakthroughs as if thus to be graced. In this way, we know that being graced turns into its opposite: a cosmos in which nobody minds.

---

more perfect is its power. But be its power of what kind it will, it never approaches to what it represents. Choose a day on which to represent the most sublime and affecting tragedy we have; appoint the most favourite actors; spare no cost upon the scenes and decorations, unite the greatest efforts of poetry, painting, and music; and when you have collected your audience, just at the moment when their minds are erect with expectation, let it be reported that a state criminal of high rank is on the point of being executed in the adjoining square; in a moment the emptiness of the theatre would demonstrate the comparative weakness of the imitative arts, and proclaim the triumph of the real sympathy. I believe that this notion of our having a simple pain in the reality, yet a delight in the representation, arises from hence, that we do not sufficiently distinguish what we would by no means choose to do, from what we should be eager enough to see if it was once done. We delight in seeing things, which, so far from doing, our heartiest wishes would be to see redressed [p. 81].

I take Burke to have been a grand theorist, one who grasped the supremacy of practice; he knew "it is by imitation far more than by precept, that we learn everything; and what we learn thus, we acquire not only more effectually, but more pleasantly. This forms our manners, our opinions, our lives" [p. 83]. The forms to which Burke refers includes his knowledge of preceptorial classes, even of exemplary men—and wolf-men. To understand the sublimity that is terror, begin with Burke on dogs and love.

The race of dogs, in many of their kinds, have generally a competent degree of strength and swiftness; and they exert these and other valuable

64

Art and other defensive achievements are the forms within which the endless expressional quest is temporarily constrained. Except in defensive achievement, genius changes into routine apostle turns, self-expressional theatricals that have less to do with art than with religious whoreship. The early nineteenth-century cult of genius and our late twentieth-century apostleships of self are now profitably confused. For example, the intellectualizing journalists of the *New York Times* proclaim some apostle as a genius, usually on Sundays. "One of the great writers of this generation," or "another Kafka," is anointed with quotations from the latest transfer from art or science to life in the endless expres-

---

qualities which they possess, greatly to our convenience and pleasure. Dogs are indeed the most social, affectionate, and amiable animals of the whole brute creation; but love approaches much nearer to contempt than is commonly imagined; and accordingly, though we caress dogs, we borrow from them an appellation of the most despicable kind, when we employ terms of reproach; and this appellation is the common mark of the last vileness and contempt in every language. Wolves have not more strength than several species of dogs; but, on account of their unmanageable fierceness, the idea of a wolf is not despicable; it is not excluded from grand descriptions and similitudes. Thus we are affected by strength, which is *natural* power. The power which arises from institution in kings and commanders, has the same connexion with terror. Sovereigns are frequently addressed with the title of *dread majesty.* And it may be observed, that young persons, little acquainted with the world, and who have not been used to approach men in power, are commonly struck with an awe which takes away the free use of their faculties. *When I prepared my seat in the street,* (says Job,) *the young men saw me, and hid themselves.* Indeed, so natural is this timidity with regard to power, and so strongly does it inhere in our constitution, that very few are able to conquer it, but by mixing much in the business of the great world, or by using no small violence to their natural dispositions. I know some people are of opinion, that no awe, no degree of terror, accompanies the idea of power; and have hazarded to affirm, that we can contemplate the idea of God himself without any such emotion" [pp. 96-97; Burke's italics].

On the meaning of pain, understand with Burke that "what generally makes pain itself . . . more painful, is, that it is considered as an emissary of [death,] this king of terrors" [p. 75]. Take these Burkean visions—of God, death, pain and punishment—into account when you read, above and below, my amiable remarks on crime and related

sional quest that journalists, as a profession, tend to confuse with art or science. They are not the only ones. "One can say anything as long as it is for man, not against him. . . . It all depends on where the rebel chooses to stand. From inside his community, he may say everything." Here is the modern terribilità. Only an apostle of self, writing for the 'values'-consumption market, could say such an ignorant, impossible thing of any genuine community. Show me a community in which "one can say anything so long as it is for man"![34] What rubbish! The only kind of man who could say everything is one who would sell everything he can say—the perfect bourgeois, father to the permanent revolutionary child.[35]

---

matters [e.g., pp. 55-56 *et pass.*]. Burke's famous conservative vision is a response to the dangers raised explicitly in his aesthetics. The beauty of his politics is in his deep knowledge of "nothing sublime, which is not some modification of power" [p. 94]. Terror: Burke understood it—"the common stock of everything that is sublime" [*ibid.*]. We present-day teachers try to avoid, even after Burke and after Freud, the meaning of nighttime things. How can we possibly understand how a Stalin could have kept millions in his hands? How can we possibly contemplate the idea of God, and its hidden contrary, pleasure, when we have lost our certain knowledge that "pain is always inflicted by a power in some way superior, because we never submit to pain willingly. So that strength, violence, pain, and terror, are ideas that rush in upon the mind together" [*ibid.*]. All the questions raised in Burke's aesthetic of terror would have to be treated in a properly ethnocentric theory of Western culture. [Cf., on theories of culture opposed to what appears in this book, that of scientific anthropology as represented in footnote 36, p. 68.]

34. Elie Wiesel, *Souls on Fire: Portents and Legends of Hasidic Masters*, trans. Marion Wiesel (New York, 1972), quoted by Charles Silberman in his review in the *New York Times Book Review*, March 5, 1972, Section 7, pp. 1 and 26.

35. Ideal-typically, the revolutionary rich generate the revolutionary as permanent child. In their boredom, the one unnecessary thing, which, according to their unbelief, they have to excess, the revolutionary rich are our only class enemy; that boredom has spread, like a cancer, throughout Western society, from the top down. Boredom among the rich is the condition of that intolerable monotony imposed upon the work and consciousness of the modern poor. As the Western

Just how profitable the apostle business has become may lose significance in the hopeful thought that the more profitable the less dangerous. Surely no mind can be violated by radical chic? Pray this is true of our polished porn, as it passes for literature. Nevertheless, because our re-educated classes are too quick to express themselves, read too much and superficially, I fear their minds, which are prepared to be violated by any idea, even the most jejune, will grow violent in their expression.

In his preface to *What Maisie Knew*, James refers to something beyond the "endless expressional question," to the "quite different question of the particular kind of truth of resistance . . . some intensity, some continuity of resistance being naturally of the essence of the subject." The therapeutic lacks his saving truth of resistance; modern art (the life-acts of apostles, producing ideas for the 'value'-consuming market) cannot restore it to him. No art can be authoritative, although in its absolute rightness and propriety, a work of art may signify what authority would be like if it existed. No culture can live under the authority of the arts and sciences, which command their own matter—and that within their own forms; aesthetic and intellectual authority are not directly transferable to the conduct of life. No culture can live except under transferable authority; this is the authority of persons themselves under the same laws that should establish the significance of our arts and sciences. In their highest obedience, humans are compelled by god-terms that will not be treated as mere heuristic devices. On the contrary, rightly used, minds in their service rather than served by them, these are terms that will not suffer to be tested or reduced; after the use of a god-term, there can be no 'because

---

poor grow richer, they will find things less monotonous and life more boring. Then they will rediscover Culture, as the rich did in the eighteenth century and ever since: Culture as escape. How will we live happily ever after when we have all gone to the seashores and been through the Uffizis? In my role as Sorel, I imagine the last general strike, for a no-hour day. Then we will all simply will to be, or not to be. Will purged at last of class, struggle married to caprice, Eros and Thanatos will act reconciled. Why not? Leisured of the world, you have nothing to lose except your garlands.

of.' God-terms are neither 'functional' nor 'mythic'; they are truths. Whatever happens scientifically, technologically or artistically, a high culture is a culture of truth. In my sense, ancient Israel constituted a high culture, although its arts, sciences and technologies were not remarkable. Anthropologists might supply other examples of high cultures and, perhaps, contribute to the correction of mistaken scientific representations of *Culture* as in, for example, the compendium by Kroeber and Kluckhohn.[36]

Because repression is truth as it is always made, desperate, the interdicts becoming unconscious as well as credal, all theories of culture, so far as they are true, must have unconsciously normative implications. It would be better to call the social sciences, more accurately, the moral sciences; then, as with the arts and other sciences, the normative implications could be treated less evasively by those who, professing to be social scientists, treat what is at once indictive and evasive.

---

36. [A. L. Kroeber and Clyde Kluckhohn, *Culture* (New York, 1963; originally published in 1952 as Vol. XLVII—No. 1 of the Papers of the Peabody Museum of American Archaeology and Ethnology, Harvard University).] The first seventy-three pages, on the "General History of the Word Culture," being history, is dismissive. How right the authors were to conclude: "All in all, it is clear that anthropologists have been concrete rather than theoretical minded about culture" [p. 307]. Further, "Values provide the only basis for the fully intelligible comprehension of culture, because the actual organization of all cultures is primarily in terms of their values" [p. 340]. Note the helpful advice given, by Kroeber and Kluckhohn, as social scientists, to humanists. "Incidentally, we believe that when the ultramontane among the humanists renounce the claim that their subject matter is superior or privileged, and adopt the more catholic and humble human attitude—that from that day the humanities will cease being on the defensive in the modern world" [p. 61]. Sound advice; good thinking. Being sound scientists, freed from any conception of high culture, Kroeber and Kluckhohn do not have to do more than quote poor Werner Jaeger's silly, unscientific, defensive complaint that " 'the an-

I want to make one thing clear: interdicts are not the same as repressions; social and psychological differ. A repression is never a precept; an interdict is never anti-credal. If we are aware of our repressions, then we are not repressed. If we are not obedient to the interdicts, then we are not cultured. It is from the interdicts that repressions gather their energy; only then can repressions subserve interdicts. Interdicts are the primary forms of high culture, not the arts and sciences. Neither literary studies nor scientific constitute cultures, in either number, one or two.

Penetrative enough, the interdicts develop psychologically and yet weaken as denials of entry into consciousness of what is not to be done. Freud tells us that as soon as an "idea which is fundamentally offensive exceeds a certain degree of strength, the [intrapsychic] conflict takes on actuality, and it is precisely activation of the idea that leads to its repression."[37] As the interdicts fail, repressions show themselves in symptoms. But repressions cannot occur except in responsive defense of the established but failing interdicts from which they derive. What gives an "idea" its "fundamentally offensive" character cannot be generated in the repression itself. A culture in which its interdictory motifs were entirely stable would not need to call in repressions, which, in Freud's conception, must lead to symptomatic behavior. On the other hand, the great historical rationalizations of interdictory contents appear to lead to transgressive behavior. Analysis, too, is a form of rationalization. Where transgressive behavior is redefined as merely symptomatic, there the science of symptoms itself implies a failure of the

---

thropological concept of culture . . . has made out of a concept of value a mere descriptive category which . . . has entirely lost its true obligatory sense' " [p. 60]. These scientists of culture are not so cavalier in their dismissals, however, when they come to Eliot. "Anthropologists are not likely to be very happy with Eliot's emphasis on an élite and his reconciliation of the humanistic and social science views . . ." [p. 62]. Eliot stands in his corner, rebuked, during the entire anthropological field-theory period in the history of the intellectualizing suppression of high culture.

37. Freud, "Repression," *General Psychological Theory* ("Collected Papers," ed. Philip Rieff [New York, 1963]), p. 109.

symbolic containing that science to follow through its constitutive moral demands.

By its very depth of penetration, a symbolic splits in two; unattended images of rejection develop devious ways of accepting precisely what the interdict condemns. Reason or Science is not a way round this unsteadiness of high culture. Reason is merely the highest of the passions; intellect will serve its affects; science serves its institutions. The interdicts, in their particularity, determine what are the affects that intellect will subserve. It is impossible to construct a rational model of the interdictory-remissive form. A 'rational' culture can only refer to a rationalization of the symbolic, some particular variety of justification.

As the moral sciences and the arts must signify, so law codifies the interdicts and their remissions, which are the elementary forms within which god-terms articulate the forms themselves. All such forms are imposed. Authority remains superior to that which it authorizes. No order can exist that is not taken seriously and remains, in some respects, beyond criticism.[38] That the most compelling and yet avoidable interdicts are those buried deep in character implies their exterior existence. Culture is no more reducible to a psychology than psychology to a culture; just this double reduction has given modern culture its risible affectivity. We are learning to laugh most heartily at what are the least laughing matters. From inside his objective culture, yet estranged from it by affects that are the constraint of his possibilities, a man cannot say everything—indeed, he can say scarcely anything of all there is to say.

The purpose of culture is to fight off what-is-not. Death is what-is-not, the final opening of possibility that it is the purpose of culture to close. A culture that engages itself to the interminable opening of possibility issues its own death warrant: apostles and advertisers of the opening of possibility—as 'Life' or 'Progress' or "Better Living Through Chemistry"—have adopted the trans-

---

38. The mind boggles at the ignorance of sociologists who reveal, as if in criticism, that our culture installs its own 'values' and not others; that culture 'acculturates.' If only ours did: then we would have, reconstituted, a true culture.

gressive rather than the interdictory style as their own; and so, even more certainly than the apostles of our preceding church civilization invited violence as their disciplinary means, in defense of the interdicts, the apostles of a cultureless society invite violence as an emancipatory means, toward a pathetic indiscipline. Under such shifting conditions, all justifications exposed as ideologies, the discipline necessary for collective existence must become more entirely outward than ever before in our history. The swarming apostles of Life are harbingers of death. Our bio-revolutionary apostles are in league with our commercial geniuses, death dealers in the sacred game, which can only be made right by virtue of constantly reconstructed limits. Because moderns think they are so wonderfully malleable, they require fresh constraining orders, truths at once credal and repressive, to limit the dangers of their infinite presumption. Perhaps, as the old interdicts reorganize our culture, its future members can do without some of the repressions received in the latter-days of failure within the era dominated by the Christian churches. I say, *perhaps*, hopefully, for the churches were monstrously adroit at lowering and fragmenting interdictory intensities.[39] Compromise your mind, for a moment,

---

39. On this adroitness, under proper modesties mixed with new pretensions, see Father Gregory Kenny's *Sex and the Young Catholic* [(Chicago, n.d.), p. 19]:

> Realistically speaking, the fact of ordination does not make a priest a master of moral theology nor does it necessarily give him insight into the generation gap nor guarantee that he will keep up to date on theological thinking and psychological counseling. Moreover, the confessional—dark, silent, formal—is a very bad counseling situation where two strangers face each other, but do not see each other, do not know each other, and find out little about each other.
>
> A sound rule is to confess only what you are certain about, to confess only those matters sexual and otherwise of which you can responsibly say, "I really know I have sinned." Even in traditional theology this is all you are obliged to confess: only what in your mind is definitely a mortal sin. So, confess whatever *you* judge to be a mortal sin; right or wrong, it is your judgment that counts. Tell only this necessary minimum. [Kenny's italics]

For a very fine specimen clerical casuistry of remissions, note the remarks of "two spokesmen for the Roman Catholic Archdiocese of

with the existence of pious slavers. A painful example. In eighteenth-century Barbados, slaves owned by Codrington College had the word SOCIETY inscribed by a branding iron across their chests. SOCIETY stood for The Society For The Propagation of the Gospel.

In *The End of the Road* Jake Horner lacks that particular kind of interdictory intensity which James tried to translate into the self-defensive knowledge (i.e., the moral sense) of his splendid little creature, Maisie. By his art, which conceals precisely as it reveals, and directs by indirection, James recreates a specimen moral form. True knowledge is privileged; even in a child it is inseparable from those self-concealments by which a culture and its members are sustained. Mrs. Wix is quite uncertain, to the very end, what Maisie knew. Nor can Maisie say what she knew. She is rightly engaged in protecting herself. Her moral sense is not to be intellectualized. The interdicts prevent all easy sayings, or falsify them. As a true god conceals himself, so our ancients demanded the name of their god be known in silence; mention of it was transgressive.

By *interdicts* I have intended[40] those declared gifts of self-concealment that, faced with the frequent duplicities of their effect in practice, privileged knowledge dare only elaborate indirectly, toward chafing defensive recognitions; *interdicts* are of what is

---

New York," when asked about the cannibalism of survivors of a plane crash in the Andes. Cannibalism is permitted, the professors of theology declared, "if there is no feasible alternative for survival." [*New York Times*, December 28, 1972, p. 8.] Survival: that is the meal ticket of all acceptable immoralities. Only survive. Cannibalism is to the remissive space of the higher Andes as four-letter words once were to men's locker rooms; of course, there may always be those virtuosi of an impoverished life who do not allow cursing even in locker rooms. [Cf. p. 185.]

40. As distinct from *achieved*; my theoretical work has some considerable distance ahead of it. Moreover, I wish no System and aspire to be anything except the author of a Systematics. I am no churchman, of one or more. Nor, as a sociologist, do I await my Newton. He will never appear, except as a rationalizer of what is not.

not to be done. These are negative gifts, successfully to resist the strain of observation and the assault of experience, of which the arts are only one provender. Negative gifts, declared inhibitions of what will be done, cannot allow themselves to be taught, directly, in a classroom. Here is one way in which we teachers dare not, if we would teach, pretend to be apostles. Nor can our scientists be more daring. Pity the humanely intentioned scientists. Because there is nothing interdictory about them, the scientists are helpless against themselves; they can only intensify the strains of observation. Equally remissive, our *artists/apostles* are equally helpless; they can only mount more and cheaper assaults of experience.[41] In the obediences that they demand of us, the interdicts appear too difficult; therefore they appear too simple to resist the assaults of experience—simpler and the less resistant to any strain as experience is the more intellectualized. *Remissions* are positive acceptances: what is not done—yet, within the culture and in particular circumstances, done. Dreaming is the harmless paradigm of remissive action. What used to be called 'worldliness' is an acceptance of remissiveness, first of all in oneself. A remissive actor is one wide awake, in the world as it is and ever shall be.

To get at the meaning of intellectualization, being wide awake even while pretending a dream, I shall illustrate these assaults of experience, in their gathering cheapness, from a terrible play I saw in London last year, using notes scribbled on my program, to the annoyance of the cultural pietists surrounding me in the pews at the Aldwych.[42] In 'Old Times' (Pinter), the would-be

----

41. Cultural pietists are spiritual gluttons; they swallow whatever they are fed; the arts are not transubstantiations. We are obliged not to make of art what it is not, religion. Such art is religion made over into paradigmatic remissiveness.
42. That those assaults will be greater in quantity and cheaper expresses the context within which therapy triumphs over character: the context is the triumph of the camera over the canvas, film over painting—motion picture over still-life, so to speak. All our schools of 'Communications,' devoted as they are to the mass media, are analyzable as devices for bombarding the senses with endless stimuli that deaden mindfulness by making us all over into 'Personalities'—de-

genius-'director' ("My name is Orson Welles") announces the final triumph of art as stage-settings for the great battle of the boudoir (that place where the interdicts are conventionally supposed to yield most easily). There Deeley, the director, is proud to announce that the bed-shrines, the main props on stage, can be arranged in any pattern ("It's the castors that do it"). We scholars know what old artifacts of transgressive movement are these rearrangeable bed-shrines, atop which sit, Buddha-like, female god-terms, the Other Woman; she is the understanding angel of *love/death* by which the interdicts are to be annihilated.[43] The Saint-

---

manding, appealing, doing whatever there is to be done in order to get ourselves recognized. In a culture at once more confident and modest in its understandings, such 'Personalities' were rightly called abnormal, after they ceased to be called sinners. But that was before 'abnormal' itself joined 'sinner' between quotation marks.

43. If I were in authority, the first thing I would decree is that Silvia Pinal is to play all Other Women; Fernando Rey might be all directors; on second thought, I might just be willing to embrace that part myself. Buñuel is out. Luis (I call Buñuel Luis, or Lu, this liberty with his name taken in the American fashion, in which the more distant your knowledge of a man, the more familiar your name-calling of him: my own mother rarely fell into calling me 'Phil,' but in America perfect strangers often do so before the first Scotch or in chummely-whummely business letters)—Luis, as I call Buñuel because he is personally unknown to me, is, in his art, the supreme spinner of perverse, infinitely reproducible images for the blind eye. What on earth is not on-stage for Luis? What is to be remembered? More precisely, what is to be remembered with respect? Nothing. Everything is, at once, theatrical and possible; except respectful memories. Because in Luis's films his people can remember nothing with respect, the perverse is the last refuge of those among his people who have a sense of beauty; his other people are simply perverse. Luis thus shows us the democratic tendencies of surrealism. He is the mere critic as artist, conjuring whatever might be present against the authority of the past. Great as he is, in this way, Luis must know now, in his old age, how little his work, and himself in it, amounts to; he accepts that nothingness, no doubt. Those Buñuel movies, to which I have gone as others once went to church, for the show—those movies are irresistible: perfumed

Simonians, for example, were trying out every doctrinal sexposition soon after the turn of the nineteenth century. Saint-Simon and his positivist successors helped greatly to turn sociological theory toward its deadly praise of whatever is not and whatever cannot be—a 'New Christianity,' for example.[44]

Excuses can easily be made for Saint-Simon, Enfantin and their fellow-travelers; they lived in the last century, during the

---

entertainments of false guilt. The space in which a Buñuel movie is shown ought to have censers puffing perfumed smoke at the audience, and each of its seats ought to be isolated among its own mass of delicate plastic manicon tendrils, with garlands of pierced empty eggshells; this interior decoration of the movie house could be done quite cheaply. Even so, Buñuel movies are not perfect works of modern art, however we may decorate their images. Buñuel movies suffer from an ill-concealed analogy, drawn through the film itself, between those movies as moralizing entertainments, amounting to nothing and yet terrifying, and, on the other hand, what used to be known, by Latin free-thinkers, not to mention more northerly protestants, as the 'moralizing whore of Rome.' Nowanights, what reeks in a more attractive way of rancor and death than a Roman church? A Buñuel movie. You may attend one or both, in which case my humble apology. I would not offend any man's religion.

44. Perhaps our radical student movement should have a memorial essay written to honor its deadliness; call that essay "The New Joodeyism." What Self-serving hutzpah to speak of 'Judaism' as if the faith of Israel were disembodied by its progress into the Christian era, when, after millennial resistances, synagogue began to imitate church. What Christians still sometimes grasp as faith cannot survive the end of Israel; Israel cannot survive the end of faith. The fate of our high culture is inseparable from the relation between the past of faith and the future of Israel. 'Judaism' represents contemporary Jews to themselves as they are, still in their massive fugue, fleeing that interdictory genius for which the gentile world, like the Jews themselves, cannot be expected to show gratitude. One major form of ingratitude is the act of forgetting. A disproportionate number of young Jews are members of various angry brigades, a just reward to their doting parents for having forgotten the God of their Fathers; this forgetfulness is so acute that it does not include a language of denial.

peak rush-hour of the Western gods. Nowadays, there is no excuse.[45] The rush-hour has ended. We are safely arrived at our therapists, some of whom are also licensed as sociologists. There is a deadly role combination, if ever I saw one. Nevertheless, it is understandable that after the rush-hour of the gods there should be an increased production of therapists, just as, in the knowledge industry, there should be an increased production of problem-solving sociologists; of course, these problem-solvers are bound to create problems and themselves, as a guiding cadre, become a cultural problem.

You officers of the third force in defense of culture will not be tempted, I trust, to dismiss as metaphor my reference to our angels of understanding as a problem. In their numbers and spread, beyond our schools into the more and more heavily capitalized bureaucracies of the welfare state, of business enterprise, and of the mass media, the social scientists, as a guiding cadre, organizing the new liveliness, are a major sociological problem: as para-therapists, they represent everything a priestly theorist cannot be and everything a prophet cannot announce. A true prophet is called to conserve what is being destroyed. Problem-solvers parody prophecy; they call themselves to destroy what may be possible still to conserve.

For the production of therapeutics, therapists are necessary—and paratherapists of all kinds. Even in relatively shatterproof social orders, such as Japan's, whose members appear to have grown bored with their Western-induced affluent rush-hour of the

---

45. *The Coming Crisis of Western Sociology*, by Alvin W. Gould-ner (New York, 1970), is one recent example of the lingering death of sociological theory, of what it-is-not: the book consists of elaborate assertions that theory is the taking of endlessly critical positions. He titles those endlessly critical positions 'reflexive sociology.' But such theories are empty: they can draw no hermeneutic circles and yet depend upon those circles in order to break them. Thus the nineteenth-century religion of criticism continues as sociological theory: the theorist mistakes hostility for breakthroughs. His own breakthroughs can create circles of the merely hostile: nothing authoritative to which to submit.

gods and may soon return to the struggle for power, one cult may survive into the age of universally accepted power drives: the P. L. Kyodan ('Church of Perfect Liberty')—with its slogans 'Life is Art,' and 'A man's life is a series of self-expressions,' its total technology of fun and health as religion. Disciplined as they are by an ancient social order in modern dress, the Japanese can out-do us Americans at our own plaything.

The American social order is neither ancient nor stable; Americans have experienced no specially crowded rush hour of the gods; the revivalist period ended long ago. Such spiritual traffic jams as Japan knew for a generation after my war were expertly dispersed, in our own culture, by the late Protestant faith in criticism. Nietzsche was traffic manager, raised to the intensity of genius. But he declined to be an apostle of understanding. Here was a critic who warned away all followers. Our apostles of their own criticism behave differently. Going about their lucrative business of saying everything, stars in their new very heaven, they can recommend themselves to the new earthlings. Their recommendations are followed. Thousands among our young have taken the paratherapists seriously and, moreover, take their courses in order to relieve—in school, of all places, and in courses, of all things—frustrations. Under this tutelage in soullessness, of use and movement identical with faith and apathy, the therapeutic, as a characterless type, appears loyal solely to the promise of the next possibility. So far have we been taken down the road by the cultists of experiences.

What is Jake? Neither Jew nor Greek, Left nor Right, and certainly not Christian or rationalist progressive. He is nothing in particular. The Morgans wonder whether Jake exists. Because Jake is a special kind of virtual reality, Barth can begin his novel with the classical intellectualizing copout of the therapeutic interpreter, who, while he can be emancipated by any interpretation, can be bound by none. Barth's opening sentence is a master stroke: "In a sense, I am Jacob Horner."[46] Whenever it was that Jacob

---

46. 'Jacob Horner': how sociologically precise. Jake is probably an ex-Jew, but well beyond the earlier conditions of being an ex-Jew— *e.g.*, a Party member, a rootless cosmopolitan, anything you please. An

broke through to Jake, he had to concern himself chiefly with whether he was still all right; the problem of his name becomes a clinical apprehension about his state of mind, which is identical with the insoluble problem of his identity. A sociological definition of a Jew: he who resists—i.e., resists the very problem of his identity.

What unsociological nonsense it was for Marx to write, trespassing (unwitting) on the problem of identity, with special respect to money, that the "name of a thing is something distinct from the qualities of that thing. I know nothing of a man, by knowing that his name is Jacob." I say we know that that man, Jacob, to whom Marx referred, is, most probably, an ex-Jew. But the sociological pressure remains, its residuum enough to cause *Jacob/Jake* his historical identity crisis. The trace of historical memory has not yet been wiped off proper names; some scent of the past still goes with the name.

In Marxist theory, memory-traces mean 'value-relation,' which Marx associated, particularly in its terminal stage, with the making and having of money. How ardently Marx desired the destruction of historical memory, and its metamorphoses, which he termed 'ideal existence.' The name 'Jacob' occurs, to this day, under the authority of its ideal existence, although, in this day more acutely than ever, only 'in a sense.'

Marx's ardor for the destruction of ideal existences, which do more than survive in the cycle of primal history because they can only survive as presiding presences, is hidden in his denial of reality to the 'sabbath Jew.'[47] For Marx, the real Jew is an entirely

---

ex-Jew is someone who, having stopped going to synagogue, declines to go to church. The therapeutic has advanced beyond such negations. Why not synagogue *and* church? Party *and* commune? Jackboots *and* long hair? Masculine *and* feminine? Why not Walt Whitman as Lincoln's assassin?

47. See Marx, "On The Jewish Question," *Early Writings,* trans. and ed. T. B. Bottomore, foreword by Erich Fromm (New York, 1964; Marx's italics):

> Let us consider the real Jew: not the *sabbath Jew* . . . but the *everyday Jew.*

contemporary man and, therefore, entirely sabbathless. The meta-morphosis *Jew/bourgeois* of Marxist theory, assessed in my so-ciology, is, in reality, a symptom of the contemporary identity crisis through which, Marx thought, classed men would evolve into Man, without class. In Nietzsche, the metamorphosis *Judeo/Christian* becomes yet another grandly articulated gesture by the re-educated classes to erase their historical memories.

Let us not seek the secret of the Jew in his religion, but let us seek the secret of the religion in the real Jew.

What is the profane basis of Judaism? *Practical* need, *self-interest.* What is the worldly cult of the Jew? *Huckstering.* What is his worldly god? *Money.*

Very well: then in emancipating itself from *huckstering* and *money,* and thus from real and practical Judaism, our age would emancipate itself.

An organization of society which would abolish the preconditions and thus the very possibility of huckstering, would make the Jew im-possible. His religious consciousness would evaporate like some insipid vapour in the real, life-giving air of society. On the other hand, when the Jew recognizes his *practical* nature as invalid and endeavours to abolish it, he begins to deviate from his former path of development, works for general *human emancipation* and turns against the *supreme practical* expression of human self-estrangement.

We discern in Judaism, therefore, a universal *anti-social* element of the *present time,* whose historical development, zealously aided in its harmful aspects by the Jews, has now attained its culminating point, a point at which it must necessarily begin to disintegrate.

In the final analysis, the *emancipation of* the Jews is the eman-cipation of mankind from *Judaism.* [P. 34]

. . . .

It is because the essence of the Jew was universally realized and secularized in civil society, that civil society could not convince the Jew of the *unreality* of his *religious* essence, which is precisely the ideal representation of practical need. It is not only, therefore, in the Pen-tateuch and the Talmud, but also in contemporary society, that we find the essence of the present-day Jew; not as an abstract essence, but as one which is supremely empirical, not only as a limitation of the Jew, but as the Jewish narrowness of society.

As soon as society succeeds in abolishing the *empirical* essence of Judaism—huckstering and its conditions—the Jew becomes *impossible,* because his consciousness no longer has an object. The subjective basis of Judaism—practical need—assumes a human form, and the conflict

79

Among our famous artists and social designers of contemporary 'values' schlock, metamorphoses of therapy grow less and less grandly articulated, downright crude. In the temporal open space between Jew and some hated after-Jew, there preach impresarios of unconscious Jew-bashing, innocent purveyors of a tradition

---

between the individual, sensuous existence of man and his species-existence, is abolished.

The *social* emancipation of the Jew is the *emancipation of society from Judaism.* [P. 40]

What radically contemporary Jew can fail to deconvert himself into a Marxist and, for the sake of society succeeding, at last, commit what may be called (politely) 'identity suicide'? Marx's denial of reality to the sabbath Jew is widely shared among Jews; it is the open secret of their 'faith.' It is this denial of reality to the sabbath in them, by contemporary Jews, that makes them sick with hatred of the terrible historical fact of their birth, against which all their re-educated self-interpretations—Marxist, Freudian, whatever bizarre suicides their integrity can be made to suffer—struggle. The struggle—call it, in many cases, 'Judaism'—makes these radically contemporary Jews the least educable Jew-haters, in the classroom or outside. Of course, there are many brilliantly radical contemporaries who are not Jews and still manage to be Jew-haters, in their very defense of the Jews. See, for example, J.-P. Sartre, *Anti-Semite and Jew* (New York, 1948). Fromm's foreword to the Bottomore edition is beneath comment (see pp. iv-v). Against all these disgusting untruths stands the great question of old Gedali, "the little proprietor in smoked glasses": " 'The Revolution—we will say "yes" to it, but are we to say "no" to the Sabbath?' " Read on:

"Yes, I cry to the Revolution. Yes, I cry to it, but it hides its face from Gedali and sends out on front nought but shooting . . ."

"The sunlight doesn't enter eyes that are closed," I answered the old man. "But we will cut open those closed eyes . . ."

"A Pole closed my eyes," whispered the old man, in a voice that was barely audible. "The Poles are bad-tempered dogs. They take the Jew and pluck out his beard, the curs! And now they are being beaten, the bad-tempered dogs. That is splendid, that is the Revolution. And then those who have beaten the Poles say to me: 'Hand your phonograph over to the State, Gedali . . .' 'I am fond of music, Pani,' I say to the Revolution. 'You don't know what you are fond of, Gedali.

they would excoriate if they knew about it.[48] One of the latest bashers uses the metamorphosis *Judeo-Christian/Mother Nature-destroyer*. Another uses the metamorphosis *Jew/Science*. If one or the other of you is, as I suspect, a Jew, however unwilling, then be glad you are still held by your name,[49] responsible for prac-

---

I'll shoot you and then you'll know. I cannot do without shooting, because I am the Revolution.' "

"She cannot do without shooting, Gedali," I told the old man, "because she is the Revolution."

"But the Poles, kind sir, shot because they were the Counter-Revolution. You shoot because you are the Revolution. But surely the Revolution means joy. And joy does not like orphans in the house. Good men do good deeds. The Revolution is the good deed of good men. But good men do not kill. So it is bad people that are making the Revolution. But the Poles are bad people too. Then how is Gedali to tell which is Revolution and which is Counter-Revolution? I used to study the Talmud, I love Rashi's Commentaries and the books of Maimonides. And there are yet other understanding folk in Zhitomir. And here we are, all of us learned people, falling on our faces and crying out in a loud voice: 'Woe unto us, where is the joy-giving Revolution?' " [Isaac Babel, "Gedali," *The Collected Stories*, trans. and ed. Walter Morison with an introduction by Lionel Trilling (New York, 1960), pp. 70-71.]

Later, on page 136 of this book, I ask you the essential question about proprietorship: what is it you keep and do not keep?

48. I know for a fact, being one to all of them, that some of their best friends are Jews. Of course, it goes without saying that among the bashers are a large proportion of ex-Jews, re-educated, fairly rich wretches.

49. Think of holding onto a 'Jewish' name or a 'black' one. What 'funny' name-changes go on among American Jews and blacks. I like the old joke about the Jew who changes his name to Jones, and then to Smith, so that he can say what his name was before he changed it. Jews and blacks: their very different problems bracket the ambiguity of living in the great American present. One, unwillingly, serves the inherited interdictory motifs; the other, sometimes too willing, serves the inherited remissive motifs. O rich Jews! O poor blacks! What this country needs is a good black Jew in authority; then we Americans will have come through the racist therapies to the other side. Such a figure would be the real and ultimate minority, a superior man—superior,

tically everything, under the metamorphosis *good/evil*, by a lot of pipsqueak successors of poor, unsteady-in-his-faithlessness Nietzsche. A sabbath Jew knows enough never to look so far forward that he loses the sight of the past. Is it a fact that Marilyn Monroe was a Jewess, and that Sammy Davis is another? What was Marilyn Monroe's real name, the one distinct from her qualities?

In the ass-end of our time, pipsqueaks now wired for sound, The Revolution returns (as it should, for revolution means return) to young Marx, descendant of rabbis on both sides, impresario

---

despite his lack of connection. One thing The Man would do, early during his period of authority, would be, I trust, to ban the most awkward phrase from the language of re-educated sentimentality: 'Only connect.' The American dream: of a man who makes it on the authority of his personal superiority; what our younger Americans have missed because they no longer do the reading that stimulates the dream. Who, in my generation, has forgotten *Yank Brown at Yale*? 'Yank Brown'— *superb student/master punter*, with a mother to support. It has been decreed, by the Yalies themselves: no more Yank Browns. For a Bushnell, if he could exist, Yale would invent a coffin. Still, I believe that if Yale really did exist, Amerika would give it a fair trial before merging it, according to its death wish, with New Haven State—which seems only fair compensation to the people of New Haven for their centuries of servitude.

But perhaps Yale is not going to abolish itself, after all. In his Annual Report for 1971-72, Kingman Brewster appears determined that Yale shall survive as a university against the best efforts of its subverters. Brewster reported as follows:

> Faculty members, once they have proved their potential during a period of junior probation, should not feel beholden to *anyone* [Brewster's italics], especially Department Chairmen, Deans, Provosts, or Presidents, for favor, let alone for survival. In David Riesman's phrase, teachers and scholars should, insofar as possible, be truly 'inner directed' —guided by their own intellectual curiosity, insight, and conscience. In the development of their ideas they should not be looking over their shoulders either in hope of favor or in fear of disfavor from anyone other than the judgment of an informed and critical posterity.

Against Brewster's reassertion of traditional wisdom, there are the mindless subversions of both the technicians and the revolutionaries. I

82

of the world-historical metamorphosis: *Money/Jew*. The brilliance of Marx's vision of the money symbolic of 'value' is inseparable from his incarnation of that bad reality, the Jew. It is time that all those Mother Nature-destroying scientific capitalists know exactly who their spiritual father was, and how to get rid of him—or, at least, how to mouth the ineffable Name, for the re-education of The People—and for the money there is to be made in the mouthing. Marx knew how, and wrote an infamous passage on the name, although not for the money. *Capital* did not sell. Nevertheless,

> The capitalist knows that all commodities, however scurvy they may look, or however badly they may smell, are in faith and in truth money, inwardly circumcised Jews, and what is

---

shall quote from the infamous Cranch Report, for the reorganization of Cornell University. In addition to proposing an annual evaluation of every faculty member, with annual counseling on the "compatibility" of his goals with those "broader university goals which promote the common good," this dream of top management gives detailed procedures for termination of tenure on the grounds of being "inadequate in the performance of his University responsibilities." Chairman Mao will approve, I think. Most damning of all, perhaps, is the report reference to Departmental Chairman as "first-line management at Cornell." No need to worry: "Every faculty member is entitled to the opportunity of an annual meeting to discuss his objectives with the person who determines his salary." Here is a simple case of the convergence between the technicians and the revolutionaries; only we teachers and scholars, and the university itself, are threatened by such reforms.

A great scholar and teacher, a true Jew of culture, Huizinga, understood the enemy now deep within our sacred precinct—and, indeed, its new executive class—very well. In his letter to Julien Benda, Huizinga wrote: "Der Feind, gegen den wir kämpfen, bleibt immer unser grausamer Herr: der Geist der Technik. Unterschätzen wir seine Kräfte nicht" [Huizinga, *Geschichte und Kultur* ("Gesammelte Aufsätze," ed. Kurt Köster [Stuttgart, 1954]), p. 363].

Like the advertising men at DuPont, the technicians who have taken over the universities consider that the highest reach of culture is what Huizinga refers to as the "puerile standard-of-living" conceptions of "so-called modern civilization" [*ibid.*, pp. 361-362].

more, a wonderful means where out of money to make more money.[50]

Surely we need more Marxized research, chrematistic rather than oeconomic, in the revolutionary art of making Jew-making money make money. A suggested world-posthistorical metamorphosis: *permanent revolution/boundless greed* (no ethnic reference necessary, except to species-Man). Did you know that the eleventh commandment exists ideally? It is the second law of thermodynamics and, what is worst, those Jew-Christian-bourgeois-scientists are running down the universe. No wonder that we type-Man People have trouble childizing ourselves. Cosmic law and order are conspiring against us. We Jacks know the reason why we are not all right. There has been someone up there who does not Love us; in consequence, we cannot move fast enough—it is the old *God/Man* credibility gap what has done us in. God does not yet believe in Man. (Exterminate the brute.)

As for that *Jake/Man*: his particular historical truths of resistance have been translated into neuroses of immobility. I am reminded of Freud's 'Dora,' who, in Freud's brilliant yet barbaric interpretation, was only just moral enough to resist, but not reject, as the fruit of her resistance, playing the incestuous erotic game she wanted to play: with her father's mistress, with whom she was (unawares) in love, and with her father's mistress' husband, who had touched her with the rod of his desire. In his famous footnote, perhaps the most honest ever published, Freud tells us: "I happen to know Herr K., for he was the same person who had visited me with the patient's father, and he was still quite young and of prepossessing appearance."[51]

---

50. Cf., Marx, *The Process of Capitalist Production* ("Capital: A Critique of Political Economy," Vol. I, trans. Samuel Moore and Edward Aveling, ed. Frederick Engels, revised and amplified by Ernest Untermann [Chicago, 1906], p. 172; see also, pp. 113-172 *et pass.*)

51. [Freud, *Dora: An Analysis of a Case of Hysteria* ("Collected Papers," ed. Philip Rieff [New York, 1963]), p. 44.] Do not expect, from Freud as author, to learn Dora's real name, as distinct from her neurotic qualities. Imagine the poor woman going around New York,

Alas, poor Dora: there were no longer truths strong enough in her resistances to fight off, unsupported, the assaults of experience. Dora had no protector against the deadly competitive erotic circles that drew themselves around her. Unlike Maisie's author, the spiritual author of Dora could think of everything except to support those resistant, self-perpetuating truths by which Dora's neurotic, self-divided and socially isolated resistances were once chartered. Freud's special mission was to point out to Dora the fact (which is changeable, like all facts—changeable, not least, by the authority of his interpretation) that her truths had become neurotic, mere resistances signaling their opponents, her desires. These failures to aid her concealments constituted an indignity

---

married, and to some extent reclaimed by the realities of life, years after she had copped out of Freud's therapy: "I'm Dora," the unnamed Dora announces. No one listens. Her name is inseparable from her case history. Jones tells us, in a footnote, that "she was the sister of another socialist leader, but I cannot disclose her name" [Ernest Jones, *The Formative Years and the Great Discoveries 1856-1900* ("The Life and Works of Sigmund Freud," Vol. I [New York, 1953]), p. 362]. Very well; I accept the rules of the game. I, too, cannot disclose her name. Dora's ideal existence has triumphed, as case history, over her real one. Dora must remain forever indistinguishable from her qualities as case history. Reluctantly published (Freud withdrew the manuscript from his publisher at least once, in conscience), Dora has the honor of being nothing more or less than the first of Freud's great case histories. Indistinguishable from her qualities, Dora achieved what she could not achieve in therapy, symbolic compliance. As 'Dora,' she remains forever a compliant member of the culture Freud's imagination peopled. In all cultures, so far as they remain vital, it is our ideal existence, as members of the culture, which triumphs. Under this formulation we may understand how literature itself is not only a cultural artifact, but represents that culture in its highest constraints upon us as individuals indistinct from our names and their qualities. Autonomous individualities do not exist, except in the impossible culture at the end of history. Without a clue to the meaning of ideal existences [see, above, p. 78 *et pass.*], Jones could not have known what theoretical truth was hidden in the following sentence: "One sees, therefore, that the Dora analysis is really a continuation of *The Interpretation of Dreams*" [*ibid.*, p. 363].

Dora could not long tolerate; she left Freud and his analysis, rather than suffer yet another deconversion experience.[52]

Freud offered Dora the strangest and most dubious of all the varieties of meaning: meaning without authority, an acuteness of observation upon which she could act indifferent well and thus accept the assault of experience. Why not Herr K.? Why not Frau K.? Their sacred charms breed evil questions; having asked, we may ask another: Why not Freud? It was mainly for technical reasons of therapeutic procedure that Freud answered this question in the negative; so he says. It is conceivable that Freud gave such answers because he was not enough of an ex-Jew.

By his very effort to end the Mosaic revolution, the formative event, as he knew, in his primal history, Freud could not conclude that Jewish morals were self-evident still. Other therapists are not bound by the primal history in which Freud still belonged, withal his struggle against it. I shall return shortly to what is at stake for us, as theorists, in Freud's attempted break through his primal history, an attempt about which he made a rather strangled announcement in a preface, dated Rome, September 1913. In his book-version of the four essays composing *Totem and Taboo,* what Freud announced as an "assured and exhaustive attempt" at the solution of the "problem of taboo" was neither assured nor exhaustive. Freud admitted that "social and technical advances in human history have affected taboos far less than the totem."[53] Finally, it was the social and psychological imperatives of the Mosaic revelation, continuing to operate as it did among Jews in a compulsive fashion and rejecting certain unconscious motives, that Freud blamed for his attempt to break with his primal history. Yet he himself asserted that his break left him still, psychologically, a Jew in the "very essence"[54] of that ancient condition, which has resisted all deep down change, until practically the end of Freud's own era—and ours. For Freud shares with us the wish to have our

52. Deconversion experiences are central to the self-improving case histories of therapeutics.

53. Freud, *Totem and Taboo*, Standard Edition (London, 1955), XIII, p. xiv.

54. *Ibid.,* p. xv.

past and eat it too: the wish to break through and remain the same in "very essence." Here is the chief among neurotic facts of the immediate past.

Fellow teachers of resistance: do not wait in suspense for the neurotic facts to reverse themselves. I do not doubt that they can be reversed—and I would prefer them so, because I prefer a more humane, less dynamic world, deeply graven interdicts etched in superior and trustworthy characters. Do not count on me; I am not one of those characters; moreover, I do not know who they are and prefer not to know those who would tell me, strait out, they are the ones whom I, too, merely seek—never to find. I am at one, with all you heterodoxologists. For me, too, orthodoxies of all sorts smell of the narrowness that they permit in their characters. Beyond all orthodoxies, rejected, the therapeutic is already widely accepted, beyond my power to stop. I am not an apostle and so cannot re-direct the modern wish to obey some leader in a cult of disobedience toward a new learning of old obediences. My ideal type consumes my meanings, which can have no authority on their own; the therapeutic can treat all meanings as equally authoritative. He is even capable of spraying himself with the smelliest little ortho-doxies, ancient and modern, one treating with another in general assemblies of views.

Name an orthodoxy that is now accepted, in the world we teachers inhabit, as right and correct. Can there be an orthodoxy of constant and common departures from what has been com-monly accepted? Do not refer back to an orthodoxy eternally new that Kierkegaard claimed for an apostle; that was his paradox-relation, not ours. None among us can claim this kind of command, except to mock it. Genius is not at issue; the heterodoxies of genius require generations to assimilate. A swiftly understood genius is a creature of publicity machines. In the face of such deliberate cultiva-tions of uncertainty as characterize the higher learning in America, our best course remains the one in which we introduce our students to the option of studied ways in which to hang back, somewhere near the caution of what was once known.

True teaching can acquire its strictly limited, easily challenged authority of resistance only after it develops institutionally in teaching orders. Where are our teaching orders? (I doubt that even the Society of Jesus, an organization long trained in flexible exteriorities, can accommodate the triumph of the therapeutic.) Outside teaching orders, taking all dogma as an insult to my intelligence, I am (and you are) incapable of reversing the facts. Our academic institutions lack a presiding presence. Our expert devotions, endlessly critical, can never be commanding. We are stuck with our faith in criticism, only marginally different from popular versions of the endless expressional quest or liberated understandings. A true critic, I think, would be one who teaches in an institutional order critically opposed to the established ease of questioning. If we were true critics, then our work could not be taken up and laid down as it is, one enlightenment crowding another, and certainly we could never be hired for what we are not: each of us his own 'Perfesser,' at his piano, tinkling interminable blues for the masses of traumatized now gainfully employed in the cat house of intellect. These people are not clinically ill. They are the next worst thing: culturally disorganized.

Think well of the therapeutic; he gets high marks for his catholicity of consciousness, which is a *dis-ease/ease* of conscience. Having been broadened, as if in therapy, Man assumes a horizontal position, mind spread to receive the experience of the world. This infinitely human backslider assumes he has proved something because vertical positions have proved painfully uncomfortable. With easy access to all meanings and possessed by none, my counter-ideal type, growing fastest in America but not here alone, edges nearer and nearer a condition of life entirely free from the sacred and its prohibitions.

America has been the revolutionary place to escape the sacred, from prohibitions applied selectively, in Europe, to lower social strata by the upper—for the sake of their common interest in social stability. Americans are upward mobile in original spirit; our ancestors, remote and near, came to this land in order to make their fortunes and then achieve culture as the pursuit of pleasure, like the European rich. It was for this sociological and historical reason, I suspect, that Freudian doctrine was drawn to this shore.

To become more efficient in the pursuit of pleasure, to legitimate that pursuit under the title of a psycho-biological science which had no demonstrable connection with the spiritualizings of past antinomian movements, a Freudian bio-ethic was adopted by the educated classes; for a time, that adoption may have helped the re-educated express the complex of cultural disturbance and political complaint that now, after Freud and yet with his instruments of vision, is even more commonly observed among them.

You told me, during the interview, that you were drawn to one passage in *The Triumph of the Therapeutic*—drawn to it enough to discuss with your students what I meant when I wrote:

> Freud taught lessons which Americans, prepared by their own national experience, learn easily: survive, resign yourself to living within your moral means, suffer no gratuitous failures in a futile search for ethical heights that no longer exist—if they ever did. Freud proclaims the superior wisdom of choosing the second best.

It is no small achievement to choose the second best. Conscience survives very well where it is conditioned to accept second bests. First you make your fortune—more or less; more is best, of course; there, in one word, *more*, you have our civic religion. In making your fortune, you appeased a consummately American conscience.

It required not the Marxist example of the Jews, but the Tocquevillean example of the Americans, "to prove that the 'sabbathless pursuit of wealth' could be . . . intensely prevalent [even] where there were no aristocratic distinctions to tempt to it."[55] Now, beyond the classical chrematistic era of self-understanding, we Americans, in the psychological era, reject the assumption that to improve your condition is never to enjoy it; rather, to enjoy it means getting out of that condition as quickly as possible. Improvement means escape. Marx called the bourgeois Capital personified. It was as capital personified that the bourgeois understood

---

55. J. S. Mill, "M. de Tocqueville on Democracy In America," *Dissertation and Discussions*, Vol. II (Boston, 1865), p. 144.

that to improve his condition was never to enjoy it. In the era of psychological self-understanding, capital assured, the therapeutic knows that to improve his moral condition he must enjoy it and, moreover, to enjoy that condition he must "get out of it as quickly as possible; or if that cannot be done, and until it is done, to seem to have got out of it."[56] We can see hordes of vulgar psychological overspenders, nowadays, hypocrites of behavioral luxury; they really do not have the *money/energy.*

The bourgeois competitors noticed by Tocqueville, Marx and Mill have evolved into cultural psychopaths. Those psychopaths, masses of 'deviants' whose deviancy is a luxury they know bourgeois Culture can afford them, are remarkably successful in their amateur acts.[57] Drop-outs are in; more professional, homosexual prostitutes preside over decent familied streets, charging what the traffic will bear, their presence protected by our Manchester liberals of social conscience. Deviating on down, American culture remains a success story, at once economic and psychological, but with a Keynesian emphasis on spending. To be a success, in the world, is always to have the wisdom to choose the second best, first. Our civic religion is quite this-worldly, even in its later, swinging expressiveness. Now what we radical Americans want is a successful conscience, super-egos victorious; ourselves and the world set right. The radically righteous young advertise their counterculture as their parents advertised their wealth; they are hucksters of the critical good. What critic nowadays is not a celebrity? We who are rich enough buy innumerable Don Juans of criticism, layers of blame on The System, themselves struggling captivatingly within it, exemplars of reflexive 'life-styles.' Not least in their celebrity, our revolutionary gurus are preposterous. Imagine Kierkegaard's unrecognized one in America. *Time* would feature him as the Unrecognized Man of the Year.

---

56. *Ibid.*, p. 144.

57. The success of the American, based upon his consciousness of getting rich, is not exclusive to American culture and should not be confused with the Calvinist Superwhitey favored by our radical contemporaries in their imaginings. French versions of that success may be re-read most pleasurably in Marx's favorite novelist, Balzac.

Do not think our therapists carry in their kit bags a cure for power. There is no cure; and our paratherapists who act as if they were sick with hatred of power, are sick only with hatred of their own powerlessness. The miraculous may have been driven out of the material world, but the possibilities of what is preposterous occurring in the political world are thereby enhanced. We will have our miracles and our mysteries. Enchantment is alive and well in the struggle for power, and in perverse rhetorics of right order, i.e., in having first what should be last. Enchanters such as Ivan Illich or Margaret Mead proclaim precisely the preposterous:[58] disenchanted versions of miracle and mystery. Their piac-

---

58. One of the most preposterous proclamations of all is that of 'black culture.' It is a political put-on, a kind of Zionism without Zion and its cultural history. There is American culture, to which blacks belong, mainly as remissive figures in its mythology; there are various African cultures, but no black culture, no more than there is working-class culture. If either black or working-class culture once existed, both have been destroyed. The naturalism of the belch, beer can in hand, seated before the idiot box, does not constitute a working-class culture. 'Black culture' is the negative transference to whites, a slogan of political and psychological warfare. Excepting the political put-ons, of a warring class or race, the bloods in command at last, culture runs deep and true among the blacks, they are, in their generous spirituality, practically the only Christians in America. Without their inherited spirituality, American blacks are exactly like the rest of us Americans, spiritually disinherited, rancorous, deeply worried at any sign of inferiority. 'Black culture' is the worst kind of Americanism, a rancorous hiding, behind empty self-assertion and apartheid, of the typically American fear of inferiority. Nothing can weaken the minds and twist the spirits of young blacks more efficiently than their phony, exclusive Swahili halls of residence in the university. Already the black B has succeeded the gentleman's C as a mark of sniggering condescension in the university—except this historic time around the sniggering is from those who pass out the black B rather than from those who used to receive their gentleman's C. We teachers are creating a caste of crippled black pets (who are expected to bite the feeding hand, of course). The model for this corrupting and grotesque creation is political: the blacks as wards of the state, their militants largely on the state payroll, along with their feckless. Meanwhile, on the streets, the young black dropout

ular inversions of right order involve, for example, youth as the teacher of age—in general, any formula of rancor that puts last that which should be first. Thomas Mann foretold what was behind Ivan Illich's preposterous rhetoric of a universal deschooling. (Do not think Ivan Illich writes for South American Indians; he writes for American students and their craven parents.) In *The Magic Mountain*, Mann gives us Naphta, a Jesuit of Jewish origin, who elects himself anti-priest, thus to attack "the classical ideal in education." *Naphta/Illich* attacks us teachers and our institutions, in the

> splenetic partisanship of the formal and grammatical, which was nothing else than an accessory to the interests of bourgeois class supremacy. . . . They had no idea what an utter joke our

---

becomes a major figure, shadowing a huge impasse in the American way. That figure plays out the other side of the two-faced racist image: Laughing Boy cannot be quite dead because his other side, the black phallic swordsman, has grown larger than life. D. W. Griffiths did not do a more artistic job than our militants; Caliban has been politicized, in the metamorphosis *race war/cultural revolution,* as a charismatic. More than ever before, this antitype of civility polarizes black caste and white working class. Both caste and class are trapped before a flickering, eternally contemporary sight and sound. The sales pitch, *commercial/political,*[a] is barbaric. How can anyone, without outside help, emancipate himself from the traps set in his own contemporaneity? It might help our understanding of the American impasse to look back on the protest movement. Protest began defiantly, against its own logic, aggression itself under interdictory attack by the black civil rights fighters. In its early phase, when Martin Luther King was its voice, the black-led civil rights movement carried a meaningful interdictory thrust. 'Freedom Now' had little of the transgressive public meaning it now carries.

The American nation owes the blacks a very great debt; and that debt can never be repaid in full, just as Western culture owes to Israel

---

[a] We need more study of the rise of modern political theatre. On this subject, see my "Aesthetic Functions of Modern Politics," *World Politics,* Vol. V, No. 4 (July 1953), pp. 478-502.

doctors' degrees and the whole system fostered by our educational mandarins had become. . . . The public school system was the instrument of the domination of the middle classes. One day all the world would realize that our system, which had developed out of the cloister school of the Middle Ages, was a ridiculous bureaucracy and anachronism, that nobody in the world any longer owed his education to this schooling, and that a free and public instruction through lectures, exhibitions, cinematographs and so forth, was vastly to be preferred to any school course. The humanistic horror of illiteracy simply made him laugh.

Of course, *Naphta/Illich* are correct. School is the successor repressive institution, following church, weak as it was, a disciplinary means to install meaningful interdicts as character, so to continue and deepen those constraints of displacement by which the endless self-expressional quest is transformed into culture. Meaningful interdicts must be taught; we humans are not born with them. On the contrary, the human is a born criminal. To praise the infantile

---

a very great debt, which can never be repaid in full. Guilt, however, cannot be made true by new condescensions; contrition cannot come through the creation of crippled pets. Blacks are no less eminently corruptible than whites. Why should they be? Black slobs should not be told that they are beautiful, and black criminals publicized as race leaders. Black children should and must be taught to read English and to speak English, not pidgin English. Plato, Haydn, Beethoven, Freud, Weber: these are greater than Eldridge Cleaver, even greater than Frantz Fanon, not to mention Rap Brown. Our high culture belongs to anyone who will be mastered by it. For blacks to act on the slogan 'Black is Brilliant' demands full membership in high culture, not further playings of the remissive roles assigned in our racist drama[b] to the black. With all his mistakes and fantasies (what apostle does not make and have them?), W. E. B. Du Bois remains the nearest person American culture has produced to the ideal type of militant black. I am talking here about the form of culture, not the form of government. Politics

---

[b] There are other racist dramas, showing elsewhere: in Uganda, for example.

is to praise criminality. You and I, fellow teachers, are the real police, whether we like it or not. No culture can survive without police of our sort—priests, teachers, whoever acts as a responsible draftsman of the ceaselessly redrawn hermeneutic circle, within which is the essential safety, from the danger of living outside it. The real alternative to such authorities is power in the hands of armed opponents of all authority; otherwise, there are only significant changes of authority figures. Where authority is no longer mindful, and no longer deeply felt, first by the authority-figures themselves, then all power to armed nihilists is more than likely. Mistaking the failed present condition of authority for its nature, the *Naphta/Illiches* conjure all the dead gods of the endless expressional quest, thus to justify youthful acts of hostility against culture in any old form.

Against not only the *Naphta/Illiches*, but, more urgently, against the pious fellow-travelers of a mean egalitarianism, we are engaged, within our academic enclaves, in a struggle for survivors; what and how shall we teach the underemployed of the mass-education industry? It would be imprudent for us to drag our coats in front of the Merecrafts; our bouts of nostalgia for the small

---

and culture are not identical. The nobility of a Du Bois, his personal superiority, does not imply rule by a stupid aristocracy, no more than 'Judeo-Christian tradition' implies the welfare state; established liberal apologetics of these sorts, for the secular city, will have to be more deeply interpreted before the black militants can break out of their racist bag. How ardently their white fellow travelers try to keep blacks in the racist bag, as a genii who will rise up, some night, to pull down high culture; this is what 'the fire next time' means. In the literary cathartics against culture in any form, American blacks are as they were, dishonored by their assignments as the storm troops. For the long-awaited (by racists and revolutionaries alike) turnabout in racist terror, the intellectualizing race therapists, not poverty or cultural disadvantage, are largely responsible. The personification of freedom, for the race therapists as for the racists, remains the black transgressive. So long as Caliban, polarized for purposes of race war reversed, positive transference turned negative, remains the charismatic of the white cultural revolutionary movement, racism, in whatever color, can only further falsify true guilt.

college past will 'help nothing,' as my mother used to say. Do you think the illiterate sons and daughters of the ethnics are inferior to the condescending swine before whom our gentleman-servant predecessors dared cast their false pearls?[59] No—no more inferior than we once poor schoolboys are to those of our predecessors who lived on their private incomes or tugged their forelocks whenever they spied a Trustee. Within whatever enclaves we can maintain, in our 1,300 and more schools of the higher learning,[60] we are obliged to seize every opportunity to bring into higher learning those students who have been brought into mass education by the Merecrafts, strictly for training in techniques that should take, at most, four weeks, not four years, to acquire.

Ethnics and Greeks, any body is welcome to our alliance in defense of culture. Who is not against us is with us. Those against

---

59. The old and rich Americans appear a forgetful people. Jews of culture grow more helpless against the purse strings of the state the less private purses support their traditions against the pressures of public policy. Specially in their family Foundations, both old Americans and new rich should support the conservative purposes of the academy.

60. 'The higher learning': the phrase itself makes a joke, in the academy as it is, nowadays, profoundly affected by shifting class origins of the professoriat. In the older American pattern, the professor was likely to be, more often than among ourselves, a man of private means, the best of such men could take their sweet time with their work. How many years do you guess James labored on his *Psychology*? It remains the finest piece of prose ever composed by an American academic. In the current pattern, a professor is tempted to produce quickly; he derives his class (income) and status honor from his institutional position. There is something to be said for the professor, old-style, the gentleman-scholar. He could afford to take the time, as a scholar, that his class position outside the academy bequeathed him. Our born-bourgeois predecessors, if they had something to think about, could actually take time to think about it. How many of our contemporaries can take the time, if they have the inclination? Perhaps the percentage of mindful professors has dropped as a) they are more dependent upon making it, by sheer productivity; and b) as 'activism' becomes yet another way of making it, without having the luck to be born into the right family or married into one. 'Activism,' sometimes called 'community service,' is at least as idiotic a criterion for judging an academic as 'productivity.'

us, however, have dug themselves deep into the university itself. After the big money, from 1946, they came into the university; since that time, the university has been transformed into an operational base for the operators. Even those students who do not want to become operators or projectors, either in the university or in its prototype, corporate technology, do not understand that the captains of our knowledge industry are perfectly willing to give them what they do not yet know enough not to want, gratifying therapies and circuses—candy floss in all colors, fed on demand. Close no doors—but demand the better, which is different from the most. The only elite worth educating is one constantly open to the promise of intellect.

Mass education signals our historic opportunity, not our defeat. Less is not better. Our colleges are no longer class-bound in one kind of philistinism—although, for the moment, they may be captivated by another. I am not frightened by charges of 'elitism'; those charges express no class struggle but a cultural struggle that cuts across all class lines. The well-known special law, with reference to academic institutions, is: mediocrities finish first. This means that the better the man, the harder it is to get him appointed or promoted.[61] The ambition to recruit promising young intellects, of good character, has given the academic his own right strategy, since the Middle Ages, when peasant boys, not aristos, came to Paris and Oxford precisely in order to find their way out of the peasantry. Why should they have not? And why should not our own students try to find their way out of their radical contemporaneity? The mass of students with whom we have to study are stupefied in ways perhaps more daunting than those from which peasant boys and butchers' sons of an earlier era in the history of our culture tried to escape into something better.

Greatest among the stupefactions is an almost complete ab-

---

61. Cf., on the law of mediocrities, specially if nice guys, *The Sayings of L. Durocher,* and, further, L. von Ranke on papal elections. French and German references should be made mandatory, for nationalist reasons, in American sociology. If French and German references could be made, then would reference in the English language be far behind?

sence of historical memory within the contemporary family. Our students, whether from families more affluent or less, have inherited nothing from their ancestors; they are the true disinherited. Feeling the pinch of their disinheritance, made acutely impatient by it, some of the most promising among our students are more deeply pained by dissolutions of historical memory than they can say. Indeed, precisely these dissolutions make it almost impossible for them to articulate anything; they mistake their emotional states for statements. Detecting the advanced barbarism into which they have come, our students sometimes try, crudely inverting a politics, to demand from their college what it is too cowardly and condescending to give: a teaching authority of feeling intellect. Researchers and Revolutionaries, *obvious enemies/objective friends*, are on the same side, as Problem-solvers, against study; they and their dissolutions are the problem.

Perhaps our most difficult task is to help out those students trapped between mass education and the Problem industries in which they can get flunkey jobs as functionaries of various disclosure routines. The professoriat has fled its privileged knowledge and responsibility to the interdicts—difficulties that will not be moved, however large the removal budget. But do not think that, in their flight, the projectors are giving themselves a hard time. On the contrary. Merecraft, the projector, expands his budget (not to mention overheads) and thus tightens his grip on the university. Less and less is taught by more and more managers of the false knowledge industry, or by gurus of experimental Life, who help nothing by their preachings. These intellectual nullities, whatever side they are on in the passing political show, have disclosed their real problem: authority in the classroom. They have no idea of authority and therefore everything interdictory appears too simple to match their scientific data or literary experience.

Before masses of will-be glorified clerks, with Ph.D.'s, how shall we resurrect our pride and confidence except in the knowledge that we do not educate the masses in the mass? Rather, in our enclaves, personal knowledge is transferred from person to person; a costly procedure, and not merely in money. How often, after a class, have you not felt drained and in despair? Do you imagine any good teacher has ever imagined a full day of 'teaching'? It cannot be done. Performances, yes; teaching, no. What the most promising students imagine depends upon how they are sprung loose from their verbal and numerical dexterity routines, on the one hand, and from their demoralizing entertainments, on the other. Under the present egalitarian experience swindle, even the most promising student is likely to be confused about what he wants. Therefore, we are obliged not to give him what he wants; we can only give him what we think he should have. I have a horror of the new literacy. You know what I mean—like, with 'Meaningful Values' and the like. (The new numeracy, at least in the Social Sciences, is not less a horror.) 'Values' are not tolerated in my classroom, because the more they are mouthed the less they exist. Look for 'values' where they belong, in bargain-basement sell-outs of character. In our disciplines worst of all, those of the humanities and the social sciences, 'values' are to be grabbed off the peg. You try them on to see how you look when your private parts are dressed up. It follows that 'ultimate values' or 'concerns' can only be put on by getting undressed. Undress is the final fashion. Among our fanciest dressers, the latest thing in 'value' dress is what you have just seen through. Will we see the end of fashionability parading as critical intellect? Each of our fashion designers vies with all to see who can produce the most bizarre put-on. Try to imagine saturnalia as everyday life.

Applauded by academic and media enactors of preposterous entertainments, the dancers to any beat, each alone, compete against all, and all against self-denial, under various new, impersonal names; 'instinct' is only one new name for the original therapeutic dissolution of law and order. That dissolution had an institutional name: orgy.

Our orgies are highly intellectualized, like our mass-spectator sports. We are self-conscious orgiasts. Sex manuals sell profitably, even to the sophisticated. Conflicts among the 'risen gods' are our universal popular entertainment, the football of the re-educated classes. I prefer to watch football. What old cultic exercise is not now being practiced, under some new-fangled name? Every cult, and cult object, has its rotating membership. But it is the rare old god who gives away shiny new interdicts; these are old coins, and not Rockefeller dimes distributed to cover some younger stinginess. We have long been told what is not to be done. Meaningful interdicts survive only as they are taught. To be constantly learned, by many, never once for all, they must be retaught by relatively few guiding cadres that practice what they teach and are willing to suffer, demonstrably, the consequences of their own inevitable malpractice.

Freud has given us a superb hint of a non-responsible cadre, the therapists. In his theory of the inward historical genesis of morality, Freud mimed his own ancient, dying, interdictory father-god carried like law inside the psyche of the guiding cadre, the followers of Moses. His story of culture, in its origins, both reveals and conceals the end of a moral order first settled upon us, as our inheritance, by the history of Israel. Freud raised his ambivalence to bequeathed authority into an act of analytic genius: no one has concealed that act more artfully. It is in Freud's last testament to his own prototypal history, *Moses and Monotheism*, that we discover the ultimate murderer of Moses: Freud himself. His reluctance to publicize his hidden will is understandable; he almost succeeded in denying himself this model resolution, which might also have served the purpose of reviving the authority of his own past. In his way, ambivalently, Freud's own creative sense of guilt, his deepest reaction to the achievement of an imaginative repetition of the crime specific to his primal history, the 'crime' against the authority of Moses, survived in him to the absolute end of his life.[62] In the brilliance of his imaginative repetition of the primal crime, followed, inevitably in his case, by an immensely creative sense of guilt, Freud knew he was performing *like* but not *as* a criminal of the worst, most original, kind.

Where do all our brilliantly intellectualized murderers of authority, before and after Freud, leave those of us less brilliant, less

---

62. Cf. *Totem and Taboo*, *op. cit.*, p. 159, for Freud's speculation on the origins of the concept of 'crime'; the quotes around crime are Freud's, of course.

able to exercise our transgressive capacity in acts of theory, more disposed to act out in life than to sublimate in art? Suppose what is moral is no longer self-evident, no more to the creative than to the uncreative? All creativity may be touched with criminality, as both Freud and Durkheim thought, along with many other nineteenth-century aspirants to vicar-generalship in the order of genius; but criminality is not creative. For the uncreative, a critical dissolution of respect for the interdicts must dissolve respect for themselves. Our cults of the criminal, and of drug-use, express a spreading disrespect for self in the very act of experimenting with self. For self-respect continues to depend upon, and derive from, a respect that is not for self. If the interdicts are not deeply installed, if conscience does not express, in its particular loyalties, the prototypal series of authority figures, then authority acquires no presence; where no presence presides, authority must fail all those who can achieve self-respect only as a by-product of an inner distance that is the achievement of a disciplined relation to authority. Where authority is not personal, and the personal not made credal, in institutions that are the ground of habit, there, at best gently, the prototypal series runs out in generalities and pale abstractions. We arrive at the Protestant pathos.

The less patiently intellectual may suffer a less gentle enlightenment: they are being transgressively educated; cart is put before horse, criticism before loyalty to that which is criticized. Thus godheads become mere god-terms, for use by all those who know where to go for emancipations towards the serious pursuit of their immediate pleasures. It is toward brutality that our radical contemporaries have gone in order to murder their creative sense of guilt.

Imagination is creative only when, in its true guilt, it subserves the interdicts. This is the imagination of priestly theorists—of Dostoyevsky in *The Devils,* for example. (What scientist has helped us recreate our sense of true guilt? Name one.) When imagination grows transgressive, then it expresses itself in brutalities, however technically refined. Even more terrible: among consumers of the products of such imaginative efforts, even the most technically refined brutalities are transformed into direct actings-out of what the artist has only imagined. In contemporary literature and—more important—film, transgressiveness, the form of revolution, has taken the content of sexual display. The director of an art work becomes an honorary phallic swordsman and a rhapsode of violence.[63]

It is conceivable that, with enough scientific research and literary freedom of inquiry, the old interdicts (against economic exploitation, or incest, or murder, or unchastity, for random examples) can be revived. But I doubt any revival by force of intellect. Revivals can only be carried by interdictory figures, with a keen and communicable sense of our wrong direction. We cannot recall our fathers, nor their newly specified reminders of what we are supposed not to do, without recalling a particular past, not to repeat it but to continue in its original right order. But, for Americans, all pasts are embarrassments, beyond recall except as tactical instruments of scarcely concealed rancor against present or imagined inferiorities. I have said that 'black culture' is mainly a rhetoric of rancor against the black past. What is 'wasp culture,' nowadays, except the most craven loss of nerve and memory in their upper class,[64] and, in their middle, as before, nothing but

---

63. I shall return, below (in footnote 100, p. 154, and again in footnote 103, p. 157, et pass.), to the reciprocities between sexuality made public, and violence.

64. Closely related, as I have long thought, to the political decline of their supporting parental culture, the English. Indeed, with the end of their political dominion, after World War II, the English upper classes have themselves suffered the most severe loss of nerve at home; what, then, do you expect from their American cousins, who, always more interested in money than in politics, scarcely had more than a few years in which to accustom themselves to the responsibilities of world power, which is not always profitable. On the contrary, world power can be costly, in blood and treasure. In a recent policy statement, the Labour party declared itself ready to abolish the "public school"; this amounts to an effort to wipe out, not economic inequalities, but the institutional encouragement of intellectual aspiration. Cultural egalitarianism is now the dominant strain in English socialism. More likely to be wiped out: the "grammar school."

abject snobberies based mainly upon finding some who can be considered inferior to oneself and finding none who can be considered superior.

We have long known what 'equality' means in American culture: it means relations of rancor, a smile fixed to the face, demanding your return smile. That famous American smile is a baring of teeth, as Maisie's father always bared his, weapons to enhance the competitive sense of well being; that sense is mainly erotic, and in the transgressive mode (the metamorphosis is *genital/oral*), whether exercised by those in search of more money or by those in search of more experience. In American culture, the straights and the freaks are mirror images; the one cannot do without the other. Righteousness and indignation are on both sides of our rancorous civic religion. Further, on the freaky side: many of the theobromines, recently, have been prescribed for blacks, so further to stimulate nerves and distract minds into a racist ditheism. A few young blacks actually believe those old white fantasies that they are nature's own terrorists. The black terrors have been revived as the surest white thrill, to keep whites from dying of the one condition fatal to the modern spirit, boredom, the apathetic stall that endangers the endless expressional quest.

Blacks, too, can learn boredom. It is increasingly the case, as we whites should remind ourselves, so far as we can tolerate the thought, that more and more young slum blacks have been released from their historic racist inhibitions, toward the performance of transgressive acts in their own peculiar expressional quest. Mugging is a peculiarly contemporaneous institution; it may be more explicable, in my sociological language, as transgressive behavior therapeutically justified by a perverse order of current cover words—'disadvantaged,' or 'compensatory.' Racism is racism, no matter what color the racist. In the comic account book of 'compensatory justice,' you can color the racist black. Transgressive behavior spreads in countless unrecognized piacular rites, as if to appease instinctual demands while grossly exaggerating the burden of 'white' inhibitions. We jiggle our bodies, as if dancing. How gross those gestures are; when Africa danced erotically, it also danced ceremoniously. We re-educated ones dance to rid ourselves of any lingering ceremoniousness. How graceless do we wish to become?

The scenarios on all sides call for destruction, on camera. That is another reason why I, for one, will not take sides. A plague upon both the straights and the freaks. I see no promise for any rebirths of interdictory meaning; such rebirths would be aborted by instant publicity. Everything in our culture is over-exposed. All the old ideals, and their figures of authority, are revived as goals toward which Everyman, his own director, can pursue the serious pursuit of pleasure. In this pursuit, no four-letter word is more useful than 'soul.' Its old significance has been hideously abused by our 'black' rhapsodes—rhapsodes of the strictly contemporary. Read Barth, or Pirandello, among others, to grasp the meaning of these entertaining rhapsodes, quite beyond their passing use of blackface.[65]

Neither Pirandello's little masterpiece, *The Rules of the Game*, nor Barth's *End* can be explained, of course; they are works of art, vision not polemic. Nor can I, in this loose context, pay them the close attentions they demand; you repay them that respect

---

65. The finest blackface comedian of our time, despite intense competition, remains Norman Mailer, who insults real blacks by his imitations. Mailer represents 'youth culture' in its most slavish intellectualized fantasies of the primitive. Rank to his everlasting credit the fact that Mailer, not Marcuse, wrote the ur-text of our cultural revolution, which is 'white' in its use of 'black.' "The White Negro" (1957) is not a work of theory but of tactics. Marcuse's work remains intractably theoretical; at cross-purposes with any revolution, theory carries a repressive implication. Theory admits no blind obediences. Being tactical, Mailer's work is more useful. The tactic he recommends to whites has the simplicity of genius: if we would escape the restraints of our inherited culture, then we whites must ape the black deviant—not a black physicist or a Du Bois or any other black bourgeois, but Laughing Boy and Supernigger combined in the image of radically contemporary Man. As Norm tells it: "[The] Negro . . . could rarely afford the sophisticated inhibitions of civilization, and so he kept for his survival the

in a proper place, the classroom, I know. Nevertheless, Orrill has asked me, in his letter, to amplify my earlier remarks on Barth's novel; so I shall, and remark later on Pirandello's play, although unpersuaded that it will help our understanding of the therapeutic to point him out in Jake or in his Italian colleague.

Pointing is easy; but taken out of the work inside which he exists, Jake becomes incredible. How can a character exist who neither blames nor praises himself, who is neither a rebel nor true to his god-terms, but for himself alone even when he tries to act for another? Better to be a novelist, a poet, or a seer, if

---

art of the primitive, he lived in the enormous present. . . . The hipster . . . for practical purposes could be considered a white Negro."[a]

There is no "rational solution" to the black "Problem" in America. *Credal/political* metamorphoses are theoretically, but not practically, possible: 1) the credal resolution—a return to authoritative interdicts, represented in a presiding presence, and a consequent credal reorganization of the social order; 2) the political resolution—a nationalist drawing together of conflicting interest groups under external threat in the world struggle for power. Neither threat,[b] internal nor external, runs deep enough for either solution to become practicable. Perhaps the established American, Morton-salt solution, more money, will work. But the new militants only have their appetites for affluence and power whetted by the 'buy-off' strategy of modern rich-liberal democracy, while the contempt of the militants for their unmilitant friendly enemy-sponsors further sharpens their appetites for what the unmilitant have—and for more. Reluctantly, the fashionable white Dukes of the Black-youth, Third-World troops are discovering that *they* are, indeed, the enemy. Yet the white Dukes continue in their suicidal opinion that shakedown therapy will satisfy the troops, ultimately. Freud has succeeded in teaching them nothing about the instinctual dynamics of satisfaction, however hidden those dynamics are behind demands for compensatory justice. Freud must be whirling in his grave at the addled

---

[a] Norman Mailer, "The White Negro: Superficial Reflections on the Hipster," *Advertisements For Myself* (New York, 1966), pp. 314-15. Cf., footnote 43, p. 74, for the basis of first-name calling in America. Norm tells it, for Negroes, like it never was, except for those totally demoralized by their remissive role in the white moral-demand system.

[b] I intend the implication that all metamorphoses are threatening.

you would dare a precise evocation of such an uncharacter. The less gifted—I, for one—can only show off what is, too often, gratuitous erudition, in such contexts as this, by referring to other links in the chain of interpretations by which high culture is held together, present made to connect future with past. Therapy breaks this true connection, as if the one task of the present was to emancipate future from past.

Xenophon tells an anecdote in which Socrates, the great teacher, is surprised dancing alone in his apartment, by one of his pupils, Charmides. On being caught out, doing something he does not usually do in public, Socrates, with his pupil, Charmides, has a good laugh on himself. Socrates is a teacher who, by an irony he cannot dissemble, insists he is not a leader.[66] Joe Morgan would be a leader by pretending to be a teacher. When Joe is caught out, in a private act at odds with his public image, his student-wife can only disavow him; Joe loses a charisma that was never given to

---

incorporation of his theories into the auto-destruction of authority. The main fact of our contemporary intellectual history is that would-be authority—'Right', 'Center', 'Left'—is almost entirely without vision, the support of theory.

Among the white noblesse of the Third-World troops, an Episcopal bishop almost succeeded in discovering recently, at knife-point, that he was indeed the enemy. But he managed to avoid the discovery, by appealing against intelligence under the cover term 'paranoid'—as in 'paranoid New Yorkers.' For a turning of the blind eye toward reality in hope of vision, see the following: "My ultimate concern is what can be done about the causes that bring kids into this kind of situation. I felt no hostility toward them, but was just a little shaken up and sort of concerned that they should have been in such a situation," the Bishop said.[c]

---

66. Socrates' character as a teacher must be seen in context: between his service to the state as a soldier, and his final refusal of Crito's insistences that Socrates is his leader and, therefore, must escape prison for exile, where he could continue as leader.

---

[c] "Three in Central Park Rob Bishop Moore," *New York Times,* November 23, 1972, p. 41.

him but was dependent entirely upon his wife's recognition. Socrates is a truly independent man, as great teachers are. The modern 'charismatic,' so called in our confusion about what great teaching means, is a dependent man and must collapse inwardly when he ceases to be followed. A true charismatic is victorious in defeat. Never having submitted to a higher authority, the modern charismatic can never sustain defeat. One side we can take: against all modern charismatics. They are figures of death, political representatives of low culture—the culture of experienced deinhibitions. Such 'charisma' is opposed to any historical discipline. But high culture is just that: an historical discipline, interdictory in primary form. There are secondary, formal contents of surpassing importance to the 'quality of life' in a high culture, but the primary form cannot be constituted by this work of art or that breakthrough in science. In my meaning, therefore, a technologically 'primitive' society may constitute a very high culture indeed.

Only from inside our own established but failing high culture can we teachers witness the continuing attack on the very form of that culture. I have said that in the wars of culture, for territories of conduct, there is no neutral ground. One consequence of the attack is visible in a swarming, at all levels of the social order, of 'charismatics,' at once characterless and transgressive; many are called, by their own wish, 'intellectuals.' We can see that type, in texts and in those text analogues the pious now call Life, first frequently posed as freedom fighters against their own family: which is to say, against the basic unit of civil order, the order of descent through the generations.

What is the latest word on the family from our leading re-educators? It is enough to quote from the Reith Lectures (1967) of a distinguished anthropologist, the Provost of Kings, Edmund Leach. Dr. Leach tells us the family, "with its narrow privacy and tawdry secrets" is nothing less than "the source of all our discontents." Now we know how the social scientists, with the psychosocialists and the corporate technologists, would cure us of our civilization. The modern metamorphosis *intellectual/charismatic* agitates against mind and for a fatherless society. Such a society implies the victory of a permanent youth culture, one free,

106

first of all, from the process of idealization which leads to critical obedience.

The destruction of the family[67] is the key to a regimen of technological innovation and moral 'deviancy.' In particular, it is through hostility to the cultural conservatism of the working-class family that corporate ad-mass capitalism and psycho-revolutionary socialism are working out the terms of their limited liability, joint enterprise. Dog of dogs, most grand and senior citizen, hear my plea: preserve our hard-hats from the affects of the higher re-education. My re-educated friends, with their ardor for innovation and for the perverse, are too influential as things are; they are the permanent rebels, not the young; and they are already in office, flunkey functionaries, guiding the nonworking classes—for whose welfare? This psychosocialism may destroy what remains of our received culture in order to replace it with permanent therapies.

In their struggle, the psychosocialists have many unwitting allies: the working class has had a bellyful of the cultural revolutionaries, but not of their opposite numbers, the corporate commercial technicians of Change. This is the gravest weakness in working-class family conservatism. With their poor black enemies, the white working class sits still for the flickering, eternally contemporary sights and sounds of the sales pitch, aimed, like a gun, at their heads. At times that sales pitch may have a rock-revolutionary whine. Most of the time the sales pitch is purely commercial. In all its decibel levels, which rise from deafening to absolutely deafening, the sales pitch is subverting the quietudes guaranteed by a received culture. Who wants even the revolutionary model of two years ago? Will Comrade Davis (if that is her Party name) go beyond history, as California's first *Uncle Tom/ Mooney*, or as Amerika's first *Aunt Angela/Stalin*? I do not know. Her name, and its paternity, is in the laps of the instant historians.

We teachers in the historical disciplines, instructed not least by Freud, should prepare our most patient students to probe, in a variety of real contexts, the great question in the seven last words

---

67. The organizing unit of what remains of working-class life in America, in contrast to the life of the re-educated classes.

as, truthfully, a Freudian would have heard them spoken: 'Father, father, why have we forsaken thee?' In a culture that is no longer an organization of truth and its compulsive consequences, can the roles of leader and teacher still be combined? *Lenin/Stalin* acted out his yes; Weber thought no; hence Weber's subtle, crudely misunderstood methodological doctrines of 'value' neutrality and objectivity.[68] With the roles of *teacher* and *leader* more strictly divided than ever before in our cultural history, charisma turns into celebrity. To fill the historic void, a third role is developing on a massive scale. Neither teacher nor leader, this third role challenges the meaning of the earlier and coexistent two, specially in their nearness to each other. Let us call the third role that of *therapist*.

In his minimal re-educative functions, the therapist embodies no particular interdicts; in consequence, he can prevent no particular transgressions. There is no therapeutic reason why there should not be whatever therapy that works—and every therapeutic reason why no therapist can preside. What follows, for those of us in America (and England) who are determined to stay out of the therapy business? Where shall we stay out? Without a single institution still insisting intelligently on the almightiest need, for those inhibitions that will grace behavior in public places, American society (and its satellites) is now undergoing massive preparatory exercises toward the working of infinite therapeutic reasons. Those reasons will be fantasy inventions, more and more fantastic varieties of censorships so subtle that only a therapeutic will detect them, as part of his shakedown toward ever more self-fulfilling

---

68. Weber has been misunderstood, and abused, not only by the heavily capitalized entrepreneurs of the knowledge industry, but on the other side, also by our humanist gurus. With the impossibility of joining the roles of leader and teacher in a cultureless society, one without received truths and their repressions of possibility, compare Marcuse's effort as a social theorist to elaborate the dubious Freudian dichotomy between the concepts of repression and sublimation. In his attack on repression, Marcuse must also attack sublimation—and certainly all idealizations. But authority cannot exist unless it is possessed in an idealization to which it is willing to submit, although never uncritically.

permissions, in the name of his humanity. Yet we know it is to our humanity that everything is not permitted. It is under this negation that men have always come to terms with God, which is not the same as mending one's fortune, although we still feel the impulse of that magical conjunction. Against this magic, feeling intellect tells us not to act out false guilt. High culture, for which we teachers must stand if we are to stand against anything, is an establishment of bounds, a fixing of doors and bars in place[69] —and yet, no imprisonment. Does it still take neurotic genius to imagine our high culture as a penal colony? Or is Kafka's criticism now a "genuine fake"? Perhaps critical genius has spread into entertainment 'value.'

For their entertainment shock 'value,' certain historical analogues of the current preparations to disestablish bounds may be mentioned; for example, in Rome, plebians as well as aristocrats learned to enjoy watching animals tortured in massive outdoor arenas. Roman fun-culture began when elephants were imported for politically inspired theatre; along with the elephants came highly specialized performers, experts at throwing javelins accur-

---

69. [Job 22:21; 38:10.] Note that the deceitful Jacob, even his guilty prayer (Gen. 32:9-10), conflates coming to terms with God and good fortune; in much of the story cycle involving Jacob, the ancestor of God's people, Jacob's guilt is false and what is at stake in his self-deceitfulness is the blessing. In a considerable number of readings, I have not come close to figuring it out, not least, perhaps, because a) I study these matters alone, which is not in the tradition of Israel; b) these matters are not to be figured out. Job, on the other hand, seems clearer to me; he is a weighty man, and when he appears in public, the youth in particular show a proper fear (from which respect will never be divorced) in his presence. Accept fear, in truth; then you will know proper respect. A great teacher is a fearful presence. There is no respect without fear. Because Job is a weighty man, even in his misfortunes he commands respect. The original Jacob has never gained my respect, despite his ancestral eminence. I consider Jacob a supremely clever cultivator of fortunes, in terms of which he came to terms with God. But, as I say, I may not have studied the matter closely enough. Old Testaments are not my fach. But more on that puzzling Jew, Jacob, with whom I have scarcely begun to grapple, in footnote 131, p. 203.

ately into the eyes of the great beasts. Romans of all classes learned to enjoy the sight of elephants with their eyes gouged out, blood gushing, trumpeting wildly in pain. Such spectacles prepared for yet another stage in the Roman cult of experience, when Romans watched the ultimate staging of 'Oh, Calcutta': the delicious spectacle of near-naked men and women mauled and eaten by beasts. From these developments of state-sponsored theatre, we can learn a great deal about the development of Roman culture.

Within the next decade, I expect that there will be animals tortured and killed on-stage and in our more progressive films. The cultivated classes are already deschooled enough to support such life-artistries. So long as it remains our habit to confuse art with life, what appears on-stage will appear off; and what appears off-stage will be staged. Everything is settled, except the time and place of the event. Perhaps it has happened already, in a private theatre, as part of some psycho-drama; have I missed the appropriate film? The best strategy of resistance to the event, at this time, would be to take our pleasures and sciences less seriously—and subscribe to societies for the prevention of cruelty to animals. This does not imply that we are to take our present political men and public entertainers more seriously. God forbid that we subscribe to societies for the increase of cruelty to humans, as if politics were a staged spectacular.

Socrates never took himself so seriously that he failed to recognize the tensions within himself as an erotic and a teaching presence; there is no evidence that he was Xanthippe's teacher. In contrast, Joe Morgan tried to resolve the saving tension between erotic and pedagogic in the same man. How right it is that Socrates is naturally ugly; he can never become entirely pleased with himself. Looking at himself in the mirror, Joe is pleased. Yet, Rennie has led him, all the way, without realizing it; modern masses must be followed by their leaders. But it is the followers who suffer, in order to feed the egos of their leaders. The older roles, of leader and teacher, can only be combined again—against that of therapist—in a culture of truth, where, by repetition, interdicts continue to acquire the freshness of deep down attachments. Slowly prepared, as slowly accepted, only then can truths become forms of resistance to the assaults of experience and also to our own intellects, rightly limiting the emancipative sharpness of our own observations. Where the interdicts are alive, there teachers must tremble at the very thought of passing themselves off as leaders—and leaders, if they have a proper inner distance from their political selves, know how little they have to teach. To fight is not to teach. Emancipation is not truth, which is more complex than any emancipative symbolic, if it is to recruit followers, can afford to be. War-prophets are nearer the leader than the teacher-type. No philosopher would make a good king. An ideal leader, like a good teacher, his distances preserved, would never depend upon the recognition of his followers (what we, in America, referring to reality as the use of cosmetics in front of mirrors, call his 'image'). But, in a theatrical culture, therapeutic role-playing becomes the major form of existence; reality becomes some temporarily preferred style, a pose the more preposterous the more likely to be adopted. Historical reality becomes a theatre of transgressions. That is what the existentialists mean, without knowing it, when they declare all decisive action 'absurd'; thus they spread their apologetic, in the spirit of terrible Tertullian, for the enactment of whatever is morally endangering.

I have said that *there are no aggressions except as transgressions*; that is Rieff's first sociological law,[70] applicable to all public

---

70. Rieff's first law of private life reads: *You only live once, if then.* Further exploring Rieff's first sociological law, of public life, the tragic fact seems to be that militant faiths (to be distinguished from therapies of militancy) have built in their transgressive operations as elaborately justified defenses of their own interdictory institutions; but, here, the militancy of the Communist state-party apparatus ought not to be confused with any church militancy. The two types of militancy are quite different, yet there is always a potential of connection between the militant and his opposite number, the military man. Trotsky's mythic image was so compelling because he combined, in his swift dramatic career, the apparently clashing roles of emancipative militant and disciplined military man. It is the fate of the successful militant to put on a uniform, and to exchange his credal discipline for an organizational one. The pathos of the Trotskyist movement was that it was truly a credal discipline, and therefore at war with its own organizational discipline. What the Trotskyist despised most in the Stalinist was his com-

life. Against that first law, of public life, the most cultivated classes—our most progressive intellectual, scientific and aesthetic cadres—have been schooled to trust the interdicts only as dead god-terms: their death is the price of our trust. Here lies the Enlightenment. For the sake of law and order, justice and reverence inseparable from their god-terms, we mere teachers, Jews of culture, influential and eternally powerless, have no choice except

---

plete sell-out of credal discipline for organizational; yet the confusion of inner and outer, creed and institution, is devastating in Trotskyist theory, deriving as it does from the Marxist optimism that there is no inherent tension between inner meaning and outer expression.

Trotsky remains the legendary non-Jewish Jew, like Marx, essentially interested in what there is to defeat, not in what there is to win. I fully expect our home-bred revolutionary gurus to rehabilitate one of the big winners in the world-historical *Masses/One* elimination tournament, Stalin, as a great chief who did his thing in order to get The People together. The white militants have taken up their positions outside, and against, what they mean to denounce as well as describe under the title "White Civilization"; in particular those denunciations are against ideals in all their disguises—and, in the self-hatred of the white militants, against all white chiefs. At last, in the Third (i.e., 'colored') World, the revolutionary gurus have found a place that is beyond good and evil. It is 'whiteness,' the abstraction of Life color, that is to blame for everything that is not beyond good and evil. The struggle for power within the Third World is acclaimed as the healthy expression of repressed instinct, while in our world that struggle is denounced as the unhealthy repression of instinct. Revolutionary rhetoric changes into therapeutic: proletarian, black and id become a triune deity of vengeance against white, repressive ideals. It is this triune deity that dominates Pop culture. For a number of years, thanks to a French movie, Algiers became the New Jerusalem, even for those who had never had word from the old. You see how, in *Algiers*, as the churches were once the Bible of pious illiterates, so now the mass media, staffed largely by paratherapists, self-selected for their mission, express the instinctual and organize the higher pathology. Everyone knows there is a link between publicity and pathology. Temporarily, I trust, the publicists of principled transgressive behavior have won their long struggle against capital punishment. The logic of their struggle, and their victory, has depended upon a widespread acceptance of the criminal ritually burdened with his role as a Cain figure. In his role, the criminal

to think defensively: how to keep ourselves from being over-whelmed by that unique complex of orgy and routine which constitutes modernization and its totalitarian character type, using the language of trust against authority—without which trust can-not exist.

Do not assume that totalitarian characters must always appear buttoned up, in military uniform. On the contrary, they may appear as armed bohemians or gay liberationists—sometimes all three in one, like Captain Roehm. Nor, when he hears the word *culture*, need a totalitarian character reach for his gun. To become himself, the totalitarian character need only reach the end of the Western road, achieve his absence of inwardness—so to be able, at any given moment, to keep moving, even to reverse directions. We have premonitions of this uniquely alterable character in many older reactionaries and radicals, and more recently in young mem-bers of the counterculture who pop in and out of various bags, whether in the name of The People or of Self.

Few modern artists have been able to make this uniquely alter-able character speak articulately for himself; it is a difficult art to forge a character who, in exposing himself, reveals nothing. In real life, such characters are almost entirely inarticulate, or only speak sloganese. One artist who had a premonition of the thera-peutic, in my meaning, was Pirandello. I wish you could see *The Rules of the Game*.[71] Leone Gala, rentier therapeutic, the original

---

becomes the *victim/hero* of The System, driven to a propaganda of the deed against it for the sake of The System itself. What reactionary idiot does not know, after Introductory Sociology, that (a) the System makes us all criminals; (b) that the criminal is he who is caught, for the sake of our continued success in remaining uncaught. Thus the late twentieth-century metamorphosis, liberal and pre-therapeutic, *hidden* (*or ab-stract*) *criminality/normality*. What is then confessed, normally, is *false guilt*, the form of testimony against The System. [See, further, my probe of criticism and perversion, pp. 182-183.]

71. I was lucky enough to see *Rules* played by the greatest actor of the English-speaking stage, Paul Scofield. It was Scofield who taught me what to see in Pirandello's character and in the play. This is not to say what Scofield intended. I have no idea what Scofield (or Pirandello,

nineteenth-century edition of our more egalitarian but less dominating type, beautifully articulates his final achievement, his great alternative to being a mere dying animal: 'What I have achieved is perfect emptiness.' Of course, Gala first appeared fifty-six years ago. He quotes Bergson; that dates him. Never mind: we cannot fix the therapeutic with sacred things, a time of birth or rebirth; the necessary thing is his perfect emptiness—the entire profanity of his character, its unique alterability. Because nothing sacred remains about the therapeutic as an ideal type, modern totalitarianism will find uses for all those who now appear to oppose each other— the cultured and the countercultured.

Whatever masks the therapeutic must be his face. His achievement—his greatness—must be transgressive. In Gala's case, he manages the death of his wife's lover, not in revenge, but as part of a game neither his wife nor her lover are yet empty enough to play as well as he. In a parallel way, the achievements of modern art are deceptive. The professional sitters to psychological self-portraits expose themselves naked; naked, they reveal nothing. In contrast, no interdictory figure can be characterless; on the contrary, he must have character[72] and, by that possession, conceal

---

for that matter) had in mind. Their intentions do not determine what is to be learned from their work. Just for the record: until you assigned it to me as preparation for our Skidmore show, I had not even heard of *The End of The Road.*

72. *Character* was once understood as graven, deeply etched, changeable rarely and least of all in extreme situations, when the resistances against quick change were mobilized most compellingly; we true contemporaries have no character. Character is formed—good and bad, strong and weak—against temptation. The sociological predicate of character is discipline; the psychological predicate of discipline is deprivation, which is not at all the same thing as poverty. Absolute poverty is a doctrine fit only for a god, or a godson and his immediate apostles, as John XXII suspected. I doubt that what Geertz calls "steadfast faith" (a most protestant phrase, even Calvinist) has ever existed except as moral strength, which is not linked, in the Protestant tradition, to poverty—on the contrary, culture and character, so far as they are both successful (i.e., stable), are inseparable. But the graven quality of character and culture has been transformed into pejorative metaphors of rigidity.

114

even as he reveals. Therapeutics are plastic personalities; when they are seen through, there is nothing to see.

In his perfect emptiness, a therapeutic may sound like a preacher for life. For this reason alone, modern criminality sounds like the achievement of high bio-ethical tone. Socrates and Christ are established as patron saints at once of the deviant and charismatic. Transgressive action is thus induced more by manipulation of super-ego symbolism than by id release. In *The Mind of the Moralist*, I tried to get at the meaning, for us, of id release by the scholarly tactic of pitting John Dewey's conceptualization of habit against Freud's instinct theory. But id implies more than "the formal necessity of social response, and some measure of inhibition," as both terms, 'instinct' and 'impulse' must imply in both Dewey's and Freud's usages.[73] Generalized in contemporary usage, as a metabiological entity Freud never posited, id[74] refers to the opening of cultural possibility in the positive sense, of transgres-

---

73. See, further, *Freud: The Mind of the Moralist* (2nd rev. ed.; New York, 1961), pp. 31-32.

74. Or anti-yid, as it is called by certain Rieffist revisionists, whom I take this opportunity to disavow. Also disavowed: those Rieffists who go about interdicting everything. I never use my jargon in front of students, nor permit my students to use it, or any other. We are scarcely on speaking terms, termwise. One main difficulty among students in my discipline is that they are Terminists without knowing what they are. Though no more on the side of the Ancients than on any other side, I have to insist in every class, on a showdown with the Terminists in order to break down their constant use of terms to cover-over reality without thereby revealing any part of it. It is an unenviable job, not least because many of their teachers, equally unknowing, are themselves Terminists. Sociological theory can be taught in three ways: 1) by unpacking a theoretical effort, as I have tried to describe this ancient art at the very beginning of the book. This method is doing theory within the discipline of a theory; 2) by doing the history of theories. Erudition is necessary in our disciplines but, however great, erudition becomes gratuitous if not false, without the exegetical capacity; 3) finally, one may teach sociological theory from readings of one's own manuscript; this is a right and proper prerogative of a scholar-teacher. But unless students are already disciplined under categories 1) and 2), the pedagogic use of 3) turns against pedagogy itself.

siveness. Modern social theory too easily translated id into political criminality and that into new 'authority' figurations. In their different ways, each with considerable ambivalence, Durkheim and Weber both sanctioned this wildly one-sided translation.

Under the spell of this one-sidedness, lacking any grasp of their ambivalences, a significant change is occurring in related and popular professions crucial to this era, law and sociology; both are becoming 'reflexive,' critical of all inherited interdictory motifs. This reflexiveness is resolutely antinomian, and has led to the easy teachings mentioned most recently in footnote 70 (p. 111): that all are made criminal; that, therefore, 'normality' is merely the most hidden 'criminality.' Barth helps us to understand what is at stake in this great antinomian movement toward decriminalization. Like Leone Gala, Jake Horner is beyond criminality. His part in the clinical murder of Rennie Morgan parallels Gala's in that of Guido, the reluctant observer of obsolete codes of honorable conduct. Jake needs more therapy; in either case, there is no question of punishment. At the end of their road, therapeutics, beyond the reverence that must exist before justice can be done, shall not be put to death. Already the legal and sociological thrust away from punishment to rehabilitation is well developed; beyond rehabilitation is therapy; beyond one therapy is another therapy. Therapy is the end; from therapy, fully worked through, there appears no way except back.

To move backward, along the old road, is not possible. We know that old ideals do not simply repeat themselves; they are reborn. Should they be reborn? Have we departed from positions so far better than those toward which we are moving? Beyond saying 'Inquire,' who dares say 'Return'? Prophetic orders and their compelling god-terms have ceased to recall us; therefore, it may be said that they have ceased to exist. We exist only inside orders from which we can depart; that is the sociological sense in which all 'gods' may be said to exist. Our contemporaries discovered long ago that the prophets were really our forerunners, quite progressive chaps, perhaps revolutionary, as Jesus was. Thus Marx is in 'the prophetic tradition.' Again: what rubbish! Critical praxis has no descent from prophetic recalling. In a contrast every talmudist will recognize, the Talmud is an infinitely rich document,

116

the assenting continuation of infinitely rich documents; the Talmud is not critical commentary. True criticism is constituted, first, by repeating what is already authoritatively known. The great teacher is he who, because he carries in himself what is already known, can transfer it to his student; that inwardness is his absolute and irreducible authority. If a student fails to re-cognize that authority, then he is not a student. A teacher is not a teacher in the degree that privileged knowledge is not in himself. 'Charisma,' that which cannot be criticized, always gathers around the rich. What money means in the world outside, privileged knowledge should mean in the academy. In a true academy, the teacher is not to be criticized, except as he has not become authoritative enough, in himself, re-peating to his successors of what was repeated to him, the knowl-edge that is in repetition.

I need scarcely remind you of Marx's dictum that all criticism begins in the criticism of repetition, which Marx rightly called re-ligion; too successful, this criticism ends as therapeutic enactment. In a therapeutic anticulture, there can be no interdictory figures; modern greatness is innovative (*technological/'charismatic'*) or transgressive (*'charismatic'/technological*); innovation and trans-gression are new-old names for the different spheres of criminal activities. Therapists will be the main functionaries of life-experi-mental, infinitely changeable anticultures; all pasts collected and available for quotation, as well as for psychodramatic participant observation—what I have called order-hopping—these functionaries will operate to facilitate communication. The one thing they will not carry is a message in the prophetic sense: a moment in which faith and truth are created together; they do not exist apart.

Truth and faith grow particular and intense enough to meet, and to create each other, in the achievement of interdictory form. Men of such achievement may be prophets; they may be poetic, even poets. The creative moment has its chance when such a man is "capable of being in uncertainties, mysteries, doubts, without any irritable reaching after fact and reason."[75] The man of *truth/faith* does not reach; he is reached. Other uses of fact and reason pro-

---

75. *The Letters of John Keats*, ed. Maurice Buxton Forman (3rd rev. ed.; London, 1947), No. 32, p. 72.

duce that irritability which leads to doing what is not to be done. In their irritability with what is not to be done, makers of facts and reasons invade the interdictory forms remissively. The most unanswerable of intellectual questions is: Why not? Our credal and scientific organizations contain intellectuals who have misunderstood their main business. That business is not so to reformulate the negative capability, for ordinary use by us ordinary men, that in the heart of every moment of truth and faith, facts and reasons enter to make both dubious. The true poet, the faithful prophet, is possessed by a privileged knowledge which "obliterates considerations" while the rest of us doll up our unsteadiness in facts and reasons. Our intellectualizing rationalizations of a disenchanted world imply that negative capability is a thing of the past.

Truth and faith are never quite steadfast enough for our own good. Interdictory forms generate their own remissive energies. It seems probable, to me, that Cain knew what was not to be done. Moreover, perhaps Abel, too, knew what he was about. Some modern scholars have made Abel out to be a sacrificial victim, with Cain chosen to vivify the oldest and most common good, now rendered dubious: fertility. We modern eggs are so sophisticated that we accept as historical (or cosmological)[76] fact

---

76. The most famous modern acceptance of cosmological fact is that of Bertrand Russell, in "A Free Man's Worship" [*Mysticism and Logic* (London, 1918), pp. 46-57]. Russell's entropology, his freezing coldness, was no less personal than it was cosmological; without more than an official tear, he scrambled a few eggs himself, usually in the course of his higher humane purposes. For a portrait of the philosopher as he accepted himself, a Don Giovanni with pyorrhoea, see Russell's *Autobiography 1872-1914* [(Boston, 1967), pp. 328-330]. "I spent two nights under her parents' roof [as their house guest], and the second I spent with her. Her three sisters mounted guard to give warning if either of the parents [the father, an eminent gynecologist, was "in morals a frigid Puritan"] approached. She was very delightful." The philosopher and the Bryn Mawr girl from Chicago agreed that she was to follow him back to England, with marriage in mind "later on if [his] divorce could be obtained." Russell wrote to Lady Ottoline (Morrell), advising his return and that he had been cured of pyorrhoea. Lady

that we are to become scrambled in the super omelet. A modern Abel would collect facts and reasons for his murder. Then Cain's transgression becomes part of the rule of a game that takes at least two, or a doppelgänger, to play. The supreme interdicts, by their closing of possibility, irritate us into reaching after their most

---

Ottoline (there is a stunning portrait of her, a green grotesque, in the National, London, by Simon Bussy) found the news of Russell's cure of pyorrhoea so deeply moving that it "caused her to change her mind" about continuing to bed with him. "Ottoline could still, when she chose, be a lover so delightful that to leave her seemed impossible, but for a long time past she had seldom been at her best with me." During the course of their resumed relations, "Austria declared war on Serbia. Ottoline was at her best. Meanwhile, the girl in Chicago had induced her father, who remained in ignorance, to take her to Europe. . . . When she arrived I could think of nothing but the war, and as I had determined to come out publicly against it, I did not wish to complicate my position with a private scandal, which would have made anything that I might say of no account. [Being serviced by Lady Ottoline, perhaps, led to no complicating positions.] I felt it therefore impossible to carry out what we had planned [i.e., marriage]. She [i.e., the girl] stayed in England and I had relations with her from time to time, but the shock of the war killed my passion for her, and I broke her heart. Ultimately [i.e., in logical distinction from penultimately] she fell a victim [not only to the war system but] to a rare disease, which first paralyzed her, and then made her insane. In her insanity she told her father all that had happened." Russell last "saw" the girl in 1924. "I understand that since then she had no lucid intervals. . . . If the war had not intervened, the plan which we formed in Chicago might have brought great happiness to us both. I feel still the sorrow of this tragedy." In its depth of feeling, that last of Russell's sentences on "the girl" stands out as the most preprandial in world literature; I can see Russell now, dashing it off, for his book, before rushing out to a luncheon meeting, determined to try again to stave off the various penultimate catastrophes which the human race, vast numbers of whom remain in ignorance, continue to commit; the ultimate catastrophe, of the planet turning cold as Russell, is, of course, inevitable. [On the relations between science and culture, as revealed by Russell, see footnote 125, pp. 194-195.] Even Russell's unconscious was more arrogant than most, generating bizarre words of self-praise. Imagine calling yourself "a rare disease." Nothing rare about it.

extreme remissions. All, and sole, blame to the interdicts. All power (the interdicts blamed) to transgressive man, his facts and reasons mobilized to free him from the cycle of his primal history. It is only when authority can no longer repeat itself that a man, limited and particular in his history, buys the splendid illusion of the progressive at the end of his tether: that he has become Man.

Seen in early Marxist terms, Jake Horner is virtually a species being; he is without any particular class or ethnohistorical knot of character. For all practical purposes, the therapeutic is the first free human, unrelated to any dominating presence or class; he is the universal Man who comes after neuroses succeed souls and ethics—after shows succeed sacraments. To a therapeutic, the tragic metamorphosis *normal/abnormal* applies no more than *good/evil*. In his pedagogic relations to the therapeutic, the therapist is a professional agitator of perfect emptiness, offering the attraction of one content after another;[77] the therapist is a scientific entertainer, successor to—and incorporator of—the bourgeois projector. The end of any road must be an end to something else. This 'something else' is culture as it has existed; the method of the end is therapy. Therapy is that form which degrades all contents, for use by those who will succeed the late nineteenth- and early twentieth-century psychologizers, themselves successors to moralizers, themselves regular successor types to all primitive spiritualizers.

In our time, theatre, too, may become a social science. Such an advance, beyond the unseriousness of art to a superior make-believe, the socio-drama of everyday life, would be yet another final solution to a problem left to us solution-spotters by our predecessors, the Christian cultists, remissive spiritualizers of Jewish law and order, for the sake of deeper interdictory thrusts by Jesus: what constitutes greatness? A therapist would be just 'great' in a sense special and functional: for the relief of his client from the prototypal series of relations to figures of authority.

Older and obsolete versions of the problem, what constitutes greatness, are hidden in such innocent remarks as Buber's: "To claim to be the Messiah is fundamentally incompatible with

---

77. But not logically after; there will be a plenitude of logics.

Messiahship." We long-time students of grace know how truly Buber once spoke—if he meant, by messiah, a transgressive behaviorist. But Jesus was a tremendous re-cognizer of the interdicts. He tells us that he came explicitly to deepen law, which he thought had grown too external, not to abolish it. Our modern claimants are mere products of messiahship situations, of the distress caused by failing interdicts. How health-giving it is to have so many messiahs, proclaiming unambiguously, as Jesus never did, their fundamental compatibility with messiahship—totally reversing the meaning of messiahship, which is inseparable from interdictory re-cognition. We ordinary, everyday transgressors—we can all be messiahs now. Nothing is easier; we need only publicize our transgressions with our distress. If we can add stress to distress (things must get worse before they can get better), then the most transgressive may even become professional counselors to others on how to get beyond the old messiah role. Barth's black doctor is a messiah transmogrified into a therapist. Why not Caliban as Prospero? It cannot matter, no more to Barth as novelist than to Weber as sociologist, whether the black doctor is a hoaxer or not. In these proclamations, both artistic and scientific, we can read the historical transition from nineteenth-century religions of criticism to late twentieth-century therapies.

Therapy may include reversals of roles, returns to old ideals. Why not 'ideals'? Nothing can come after therapy except therapy. 'Traditions' may exist so long as authority relations are resolved in a progress of returns. In his first and finest historical role thus far, as psychoanalyst, the therapist intended to abolish himself as an authority figure in the prototypal series; his role perfected, the therapist-patient will be any figure against whom one cannot commit a transgression, because in such a self-defeating figure we can first accept the condition that makes all unbelief unnecessary: that there is no one (nor his theory) to transgress.

In the absence of presiding presences against whom to transgress, the therapeutic has nothing to compel him to guilt. Then he may properly insist that, whatever he chooses to do, proper care be taken of him. Goethe saw what is coming, the main consequence of what he called "the beautiful dream wish of mankind that things will be better some day." Therapists know the one thing necessary to therapy: that men can only get better if they are made worse. Murder, for which they are not responsible, is the highest achievement of Leone Gala and Jacob Horner. In a representative sense, they are the sick men of the future, totally uncriminal. Thus made worse, I believe, with Goethe, that we shall have to live with a vast practice of political medicine.

Speaking for myself, I, too, believe that humanity will win in the long run; I am only afraid that at the same time the world will have turned into one huge hospital where everyone is everybody else's humane nurse.

Goethe's vision is almost too precisely of professional kindnesses. The hospital personnel of Goethe's vision may not care so professionally. Consider each humane nurse, rather, as the crippled pet of some other. Then it is that 'the world stands like a dog, pleading to be played with,' each plea representing the equality and inclusiveness of relations and experiences. At once master and crippled pet of someone else, in *master/crippled pet* metamorphoses, a Gala well might be his own therapist; even so, there would be some other before whom he pleads to be played with—his cook, I imagine, within Pirandello's text. Text analogues abound. I shall not cite cases of perverted relations I have observed, as, for example, between teachers and students, in which the teacher becomes the paramour of the student; you may observe more outrageous metamorphoses wherever you are, for yourself. Or you can read of them in the *Times,* commonplace feature stories of too widely experienced juveniles and their elders still in quest of experience. The world of the therapeutic already stands like a dog, pleading to be played with every which way.

The model of everybody else's humane nurse is the relentlessly supportive parent, that deliberately self-defeating figure intent on giving his and her child a formative taste for moving on, for not getting hung-up on anything that is special and enduring. *No* is the forbidden word in the enlightened parental vocabulary. And, even when used, *No* often means *Yes*—as those contemporary barbarians, our children, soon find out. In the ever-increasing variety of orders, all personalities will be enriched, from birth, by knowing what is predicative of the one necessary thing: that interdicts were made to be compromised (remissively) and inverted (transgressively). For transgressive functioning, we shall recycle all manner of interdicts. Then we can sustain a large number of 'deviants'—as charismatics of everyday life. 'Deviance' was already presented by Durkheim as the model concept for any tradition of the new, that tradition to be regularly tested by Science, in a Comtean manner, as if Science carried its own interdictory energies, as if it had compelling reasons for dictating that just this and not that be tried.

There are pre-scientific models for the tradition of the new. Since the beginning of primal history, politicians have acted for themselves, on the principle that there is no one to transgress. In this early phase of the triumph of the therapeutic, everything, including sexual encounters and learning the alphabet, is being politicized. Politics is the classical scene in which anything goes; the one and only taboo is against getting caught; only defeat is evil. In this teaching, and in this alone (i.e., anything goes), do the great of a modernizing (i.e., auto-destructive) culture command obedience and so become charismatic. Contemporary charismatics, in art and politics, are transgressive—exemplars of the criminal deed.[78]

As the chief technical officer of a cultureless society, the therapist will go beyond any political consideration; he is not an other technician of power, or a partisan in the struggle for power. There is no side to which he will not change; his role demands even more flexibility than that of the politician. There will follow a new politics: as a professionally humane nurse, the therapist must see to it that no one feels defeated. Hospital-theatres are not old-fashioned political theatres. A therapist accepts no limits. He may be cruel to cure. In the new setting, all the directed can learn from the directors what they have never known before: not only that there is no one to transgress, but also that the directors, in their transgressiveness, are non-directive. At the end, political criminals, in their victory over old authority, will not go straight and present new interdicts, or take over, for their own status in-

---

78. Of course, Gandhi was no modern, as he tried to show in 1) his celibacy; and 2) his spinning wheel.

terest, the old ones. When new victors do not go straight, then there will be no one to obey; then at last there will be no one to command. It is in this condition alone that humans are free.

There is an intimation of this final freedom in Jake's lack of respect for the Doctor. Not that the Doctor cares; the rationalist dichotomy between magic and science no longer holds. That the Doctor is a charlatan in no way impairs his functioning, for his aim is to resolve authority, not reproduce it. The therapist is not the therapeutic's moral authority. Nor is he a teacher, idealized in the classical sense—a *classic*, someone after whom to model oneself. The classic professor was engaged in the transmission (and creation by interpretative linking to his predecessors and successors) of privileged knowledge. In contrast, the therapist is no model; he is a nonmaster, a tactician on how to exempt the self from those relations of reverence without which there is no justice. Like his opposite numbers, the entrepreneurs of research, the therapist has nothing to teach. Staffed by paratherapists, universities may yet develop as therapeutic communities, or as personality Research and Development units probing toward that impossible culture in which 'good' acts are no less causally determined than 'bad.'

Of course, the university does not exist, except in my imagination; fewer and fewer teachers, able to probe the workings of reverence and justice, yet also able, by their presence, to preserve both, are being created. Yet such teachers, classics, are wanted, ardently, not least by the radical students, who realize they are not attending a true university and long for its special kind of intellectual authority. To see so many would-be students, lost, on every campus, for want of teachers, describes our universities. Now, mainly as knowledge factories, they pump out research that legitimates, as Science, the destruction of reverence and justice. Such research has become a plague on culture. It supplies research money to professors who have nothing to teach, and jobs for graduate students who are thus co-opted into the Problem-solving racket. If totalitarianism does come to America, then it will come sponsored by your friendly Research and Human Development Corporation; by then, with business Responsibility fully developed, I expect the Corporation will be renamed 'Institute.' A shrewd broker would

124

take my advice and invest my money in Human Development. Let us found a firm: 'Infinite Resources' is the name for us.

I know where to look for shareholders. A certain number of therapists, as functionaries bent upon the destruction of all aristocracies of the feeling intellect, have found their place alongside massive numbers of research entrepreneurs, in the multiversity. They, too, do research, training thousands to become functionaries of the huge hospital-state apparatus. Without massive numbers of these therapeutic functionaries to train, the behavioral sciences would shrink to humane proportions, as they should. There is still too much research-grant money around. Without that grant money, the technique-mystics and the therapist trainers would have to practice their infinite problem-solvings in cults rather than in colleges.

Eased still by enough money for both sides, the alliance between the two emergent classes of problem-solvers—statistical and therapeutic—is holding up even against the dramatizations of hostility generated by that alliance. Since neither transmits that privileged knowledge which is of reverence and justice, both sides in this pseudo-dispute weaken what remains of the university. Distributed among hospital and computer mystiques, the new multiversity has little to promise that cannot be delivered, more swiftly and dramatically, by more obviously political and theatrical institutions. If there are no special disciplines to transfer by deeply personal teaching, protected from false promises of problems solvable if enough money is supplied for research on them, then the university is without justification. A cultureless society may need its automated mystiques of problem-solving; but Litton or IBM can do the job better, for HEW or the Department of Defense, under contract. Why endanger what remains of higher learning for the sake of money supplied by the state? There must be other ways to supply money and jobs for the hordes of socio- and psycho-technicians. The disciplines of the intellect that constitute higher schooling are inherently undemocratic and need both long preparation and regular exercise in a protected institution uniquely unchanging in its object. If, in a thoroughly rationalized culture, no knowledge need be privileged and no superiority personal, then the university has no sacred object, no intellect relating to the interdicts and their remissions specially to be cultivated in its precinct, no special objectivity. Under these assumptions, let the university be open, so that any so inclined can acquire the patter that pleases them. This openness would not disturb systematic training in X-ray techniques, nursing, engineering, accounting, dentistry and many other necessary skills that I greatly respect. We need more, not fewer, admirable practitioners. Those practitioners should not be confused by the re-educated, who pretend to teach them 'Culture' and other uncertainties. To treat the university as an 'ivory tower' is to make it a museum, for tourists of our traditions.

As for the older book-learnings, perhaps the future cultureless knowledge will be contained in retrieval systems,[79] with therapists handling belief problems by calesthenics of all beliefs for therapeutic purposes, thus to maintain action potential or motive input-output. How fortunate future generations will be: they will be incapable of being deceived, for they will have nothing in which to disbelieve.

Both types of functionaries, the political-technical and the psychotherapeutic, will themselves have to become interchangeable with their clients. One man's nurse is another man's patient. We can already see a convergence of therapists and patients, of actors and audiences; what will follow, politically, is a convergence of transgressive leadership and democracy, dominated by anti-credal elites who cannot be trapped by their own practice because they preach everything.

The Marxist movement supplied us the last great institutional example in Western history of a credal elite, a guiding cadre which would practice what it preached and intended not to preach everything. In this special sense, Marxism, analyzed within my sociological theory of culture, was a conservative movement; indeed, all doctrinal movements are conservative—culturally.[80] But the in-

---

79. Some academics (not many) have assured me that libraries, of books, are obsolete. All the information in books can be computerized, and what else do books contain?

80. How some 'radicals' yearn for the resurrection of Doctors who will practice as they preach, in authoritative guiding cadres!

stitutional history of the Marxist movement ended with the Party as the Prince; then, finally, Marxism concentrated itself in a transgressive figure assimilating all credal motifs into his own person. Marxism was the historic end of the road in Western culture. All future elites are likely to be anti-credal. Instead of party secretaries, perhaps there will be directors of action input-output stations, on the one hand, and therapists of need-communities, on the other; beyond the multiversity, as an institution, perhaps you shall see, if you live long enough, a genuinely new institution, combining excitement about new issues with endless problem-solving—all for use in producing infinitely varied senses of well-being.

Problem-solving action is the special sphere of anti-creeds. Problem-solving derives from the psychotechnical transformation of politics, which was the public sphere of transgressive behavior, as sexuality was the private sphere. The translation of sexuality into the public sphere augurs a basic change in the political order. The dynamism of a cultureless society will require outward order but no inward one. There will be discipline on a massive scale, but nothing that would once have been understood as morality. Emancipated from the transgressive sense, first in the erotic sphere, a new dynamism of transgressive behavior (seen from within my unalterable god-terms) awaits only a more evaginative psychotechnics, so that infinite plasticity[81] can be constructed to succeed graven characters at once mortified and proud in their interdictory symbolics.

Note further, as premonitory expressions of infinite plasticity, Jacob Horner and Leone Gala.[82] Both Jacob Horner and Leone Gala are non-responsible, unpunishable killers, in victim-induced murders. Considered typologically, the earlier construct, Leone

---

81. Now often called 'meaningless' by backward-looking intellectual aristos—who may even consider themselves anti-technological and revolutionary.

82. Just the right name, that, in Pirandello's *Il giuoco delle parti*, which is just the right title for a play (the best I know on the subject) characterizing the emergent therapeutic in his earliest class position as a rentier-intellectual—intellectualizing entirely about his self.

Gala, is an advance over the later Jacob Horner. Pirandello wrote his play in 1916,[83] while *The End of the Road* first appeared in 1958. Pirandello is the greater theorist because Gala is already his own therapist. The doctor, in *The Rules of the Game*, is reduced to the familiar type of naive old positivist sawbones, with his bag of shiny surgical instruments and no more idea than Watson of what is going on in his friend's mind. Gala has long since solved the mystery of his life. To keep up the pretense that he has something more to learn, Gala engages in a parody of an aristocratic agon with his invincibly ignorant, scarcely literate chef; that agon runs parallel to the play, showing the audience how anyone has an equal and instantaneous right to any part, or role, however unprepared they are to act it, so long as there are others to interpret it according to need.

There are two unfortunate others in the play, Gala's wife and Guido, their lover. The shared misfortune of wife and lover, the disease of the neurotic who precedes the therapeutic, as the character type of our culture, is that both are insecurely anchored to

---

83. That same year, in Zurich, dada named itself. Gala and dada are sound brothers, a euphony of determined efforts to befuddle the guides of historical memory. In their befuddlement, the guides are expected to destroy themselves. Do not mistake the fooleries of the Gala-dadaists; they have thought it out. Their historical mission is to witness destruction. Their descendants continue to construct a fun anticulture which is absolutely killing, very funny, with the bourgeois as paying victims. For the birthdate of dada, I am indebted to Roger Shattuck. There may be an earlier birthdating for the coinage, about 1843, for Professor Shattuck and other scholars to consider:

> The first question in the earliest and most compendious instruction the child receives, is, as everyone knows, this: what will the child have? The answer is: da-da. And with such reflections life begins, and yet men deny original sin. And to whom does the child owe its first drubbings, whom other than the parents? [Kierkegaard, *Either/Or*, trans, D. F. and L. M. Swenson (Princeton, 1949), p. 15.]

Between 1843 and 1916, dada suffered its reversal. After 1916, the parents were to owe their drubbings to the child. And yet men continue to deny, more loudly than ever, the originality of sin. The last question remains: what will the adult not have?

their parts. Insecure, yet anchored, they are not free to change their parts nor to hold Gala to his: that of the injured husband. The wife, Silia, in particular, can only reveal what she is not, her unexperienced freedoms. "The impossible is what I want!" She reeks of perfume, rancor and death. Her freedom ("I mean free to do as I like, as if there were no one else!") would be entirely transgressive, an elimination of everyone else; but in her the part is mere fantasy. She will not defeat a real and expert player, her 'husband,' at his own game. Gala has achieved the one and only ambition of the therapeutic: to be what he is not. This is the meaning of Gala's superbly exercised death-wish.

This mere exercise may help us understand why Gala's type promises more horror, not less—and without agonizing about horrors. As his own therapist (he is rich enough, materially and intellectually, to play both roles), Gala is beyond mere transgressiveness. He merely plays "the game of life" and understands "the way to win it." As an anti-credal man, without anchors, Gala has nothing to teach; entirely cooperative, even yielding, he knows how to "defend" himself "from others" and "above all from [himself], from the pain which life inevitably inflicts on everyone." In studied pursuit (using books and cooking utensils) of pleasure, Gala takes all god-terms lightly; he has no difficulty in waiving the rules of what he knows can be a deadly game. That is his pleasure: "the pleasure, not of living for yourself, but of watching yourself in action." Gala is the new man of leisure. If he were a professor,[84] or had to make a living, he would be on a permanent field-trip, as some few brave and lonely explorers of this science that knows no limits already are.

All styles of watching yourself in infinite action long have been available to the rich, materially and intellectually. De Sade wrote for the revolutionary rich, not for the naive poor, who would merely displace old authorities by new. In the past, only the rich could afford to be godless, or, in De Sade's fantasies, consider themselves as gods. What is uniquely revolutionary about the new

---

84. It is Daniel Bell, I believe, who first referred to academic work as the leisure of the theory class.

reflexiveness is that the poor are now learning what the game is all about and how to win it—by a form of fighting called 'honesty,' in which it is revealed that no rule is really binding.

Interpretation is indirect criticism; the freedom of the therapeutic allows him to act out all interpretations, so to destroy the specially compelling yet indirect character of any. Under the democratic imperative of acting out, for the first time in the history of our culture, the poor have a fighting chance to become as sophisticated as the rich. I call that genuine progress, toward the only possible equality. As a species man, well ahead of his time, Pirandello's rich therapeutic specializes in feeding himself; he savors (and is capable of digesting) all 'values,' compelled by none,[85] a Christ in his knowledge of how to succumb to the third temptation without becoming lord of any kingdom. As a sucker of raw eggs (more important, as a connoisseur of everything cooked), Gala knows how to toss about the delicate, pierced, experienced shell of his emptiness, without breaking it. Creator of victim-induced violence (Jake's Rennie, Gala's Guido), the therapeutic appears a supremely irenic figure. In the next culture, peace will be war—each against each, in erotic combat, the original style. This style can be seen expressed in the damaged graduates of academic life. When critical interpretations are not indirect enough, they begin to gyrate in erotic circles of envy. Drawn into sponsoring and licensing circles of intellectualized envy, students go under, from the strain that transforms their mindfulness into mimicry of academic bosses, the victors in various little *fame/money* combats. Nothing ruins the mind of the graduate student so swiftly as admission into the envy relations of his teachers. Few of our students are Maisies, with a gift for concealed resistance; few come to us as weighted characters, with a ballast of teachings that will help them resist the damage of being drawn into the combats of their teachers.

How have Gala and Jacob managed to create victims who induce lethal violence against themselves? Their secret is in non-resistance; they have learned never to be against anything, but always

---

85. Imagine, at this point, fellow teachers, a resolutive theory of our culture, at the verge of the next, perhaps appearing as a book, under some such title as *The Raw and the Cooked*.

beside everything—and, in particular, to step beside themselves, as if not responsible. Their permanent therapy is the predicate of true terror, an erotics of empty threats presumed against them. They dominate by the paranoia of their emptiness. That emptiness is cunning. It leads to defensive violence. In the larger politics, such defensiveness has led already to massive exercises in what-is-not, and to states organized chiefly for death, under utterly empty leaders. Neither in mass politics nor in individual therapies are interdicts dominant. Like the masses of a totalitarian movement, Jake and Gala are beyond any truth of resistance; they are watchers of themselves in action. This theatricality, taking the god-terms lightly, puts them in control: having no personal authority, they are subject to none. Against his one possible weakness, that he will be rendered immobile, the therapeutic must pay the price of self-watching activity, without seeking closing new answers to mistaken old questions of 'Meaning,' 'Purpose,' Intention,' what have you to watch in the theatre of ideas.

Moral questions are achieving a new dramatic unity: what is there to act out? A species man will become so, first, in his moral modesty, well only when he stands beside himself. For Jake, as for Gala, nothing is authoritative. In his knowledge that there can be no meaning without authority, the therapeutic abandons both for whatever game there is to play. Politics, kind and cruel, become theatre. Jake has solved Job's problem: he authorizes no suffering. In Jake's case, though we can see that he has emptied himself, that he has no weight, Jake has some little trouble assuming his counterweights, his therapies. Far more developed as my ideal type, Gala has placed within himself, "with artistry and perfect skill, [an] exact counterweight" to his "lucid and tranquil emptiness"; Leone's one like, his analogy between art and life, is "to cook and eat well." Of course, Gala might just as well have gone into politics, or teaching. Both vocations can be forms of eating well. Gala is certainly the most refined, yet catholic, gourmand in the history of Western literature. A therapeutic lives for nothing; he can live off anything. Here is independence for you, and a great achievement. The greatness of the therapeutic, as Gala demonstrates, is in his practical skill. He is the contrary of the poet, not because he is a better man or can chatter philosophically; rather, the therapeutic becomes great, the new man, in his grasp of contemporary reality: of his own and all others' emptiness. A therapeutic is one who does not have to preach because he knows how to practice. The world again stripped of its poetic coloring, reduced to plain prose, the therapeutic sees how little it, and himself in it, amount to. But here we have ventured forward into the wide-open space of weightlessness, which Plato introduced concealed as a theory of art; you can watch closely the first normative probe into the space of weightlessness, a theoretical effort at keeping distances proper to the relations between life and art, near the end of *The Republic*, 600-601.

Plato's academic fantasy, of society made over by its schooling, is too remote from our reality. Perhaps we can watch our putative selves in a simpler case of counterweights operating deliberately to counteract weightlessness in Jake's institutional role: he is a teacher. As a teacher, he respects certain conventions; he is a teacher of grammar. In his technical capacity, as a teacher, Jake is no polytheist of experience, letting his students dribble out their words in any order they please. You cannot be a polytheist where there are no gods. If, in the special situation of the classroom, Jake teaches within the authority of a certain strict and established order, we have seen that in life outside the classroom, he belongs to no authority. Going to bed with another man's wife means no more to him than not going to bed with her. Here is no question of spiritual weakness. Jake is freed of the spirit; he has no soul to lay bare. Though he is not a politician, the therapeutic is purely political about himself; he has no ends, only means. The danger to Jake comes from the fact that he finds nothing more worth doing than anything else. For this reason, and for this reason alone, Jake needs a therapist in order to get going on something—to act out what is not inside.

Why pick on Jake? Take Silia. (I take these names in order to avoid mentioning others of my acquaintance. We cannot learn, in theory, except when finally it gets us down into cases. This establishes the continuity of theory with empirical research.) The apparent decline in the number of Silias there are to be seen through during the latter half of the twentieth century poses another problem for empirical research to be derived from a theory of culture. Old hints survive toward new knowledge in the literature of human conduct that, in their principled forgetfulness, the moral sciences neglect. Before Pirandello, the type of Silia's character was best intimated, I think, by Goethe, in his *Elective Affinities*, in the character of Luciane. As in Silia, Luciane's will is sharpened into caprice. Both girls are nonstop performers; their performances take a traceable course toward hysteria, as Freud finally reformulated that ancient idea. A premonition of what hysteria meant occurs in Goethe's analysis of Luciane as a person incapable of "distinguishing the profitable from the unprofitable"[86] performance. The excited eroticism of the Luciane-Silia character has nothing to do with the authority of love; on the contrary, their excitements are a desperate strategy against that authority.

Although he saw how ably the most excited hysteric may give her performance, Freud could not, within the tendenz of his theory, make enough of the degree to which that performance represents an attack upon the moral-demand system to which an hysteric is otherwise subject. Hysterical attacks against a defaulting authority have grown obsolete; that obsolescence is one of Freud's victories. As authority declines so do the rewards (even if only a certain family celebrity) for hysterical performances. For a performance of the kind so easily given by Luciane and Silia—their "role," in Goethe's usage, at least among women of the re-educated classes—the rewards of hysteria have been transferred to other remissive roles; the nineteenth- and early twentieth-century performances have been redefined as 'protest.' Re-educated women do not swoon. Instead, the more liberated sort rant about their captivity to defaulting father figures, Leones, who refuse to hold them captive.

As scholars, theoretical and empirical, we have a long way to go before we can grasp how it was that a cadre of public father-figures, some famous in their own time (and always worried about money, so to mention Erasmus), succeeded in imposing reasonably graceful inhibitions upon behavior, both in public and at home, that was coarse and easily excited to brutalities, from the top

---

86. Goethe, *Elective Affinities*, trans. R. J. Hollingdale (London, 1971), p. 189.

of the social hierarchy to its bottom; not even the French aristos were to the Anglican gentleman's manner born. The cult of educated civility, in all its devolutions of considered and systematic repressive teachings, had its historic chance with the defeat of the aristocracy as military power-seekers against the national power-center; in its modern refuge, among academics, the cult remains at once the most fragile and tenacious of the various alternative civilizing impositions. The humanist imposition of what was to become, among the educated classes, by the nineteenth century, a surface of mild manners and civil reticence, a humane order of proper distances between people, has been repealed by those who think only to take liberties; perhaps now we theorists can begin to explore more deeply the historic achievement of new inner distances by the humanists and their objective allies, the Protestant Reformers.[87]

We might also study early case-histories in the dissolution of humanist repression, in the ideal intuitions of a work of art, for example, by considering Luciane's deliberate acting out of her "role" as the "unconscious swooning queen" in the endless game of dominances by which people of her class kept each other busy having at each other, at close quarters. In her role, this type of performer had become almost professionally erotic; her real profession is to be "able to display all her attractions." This is what the female parts of the jet-set are about, nowadays; they are model

---

87. On the humanists as a repressive guiding cadre, teaching in detail how (and how not) to eat, how (and how not) to blow one's nose, how (and how not) to spit, and other acts of surpassing importance for the achievement of a humane order of proper distances between people, the standard resource remains Norbert Elias's *Über den Prozess der Zivilisation: Soziogenetische und Psychogenetische Untersuchungen* [2 vols.; Basel, 1939]. See, e.g., "Über das Verhalten beim Essen" [Vol. I, pp. 110-174] and "Wandlungen in der Einstellung zu den Beziehungen von Mann und Frau" [Vol. I, pp. 230-263]. See, further, "Die Dämpfung der Triebe. Psychologisierung und Rationalisierung" [Vol. 2, pp. 369-397]. Cf., for a different effort to think through our civilization as a problem, Claude Levi-Strauss, *Mythologiques:* I. *Le Cru et le cuit,* II. *Du Miel aux cendres,* III. *L'Origine des manières de table* (Paris, 1964-1968).

displayers. Silia, too, as a nonstop actress, displays all her attractions—but her display performances do not move her husband, who has seen through her erotic strategy from the moment of their 'marriage.' Gala is more than a therapeutic; he is, as I have said, a therapist as well. Can it be accident, comrades, that this pre-war aesthete (1916 means nothing personal to Gala—the war is not worth mentioning, except, possibly, to such a type, as that which is to be evaded) is an exemplary case of the rich pre-digesting their revolution of contemporaneity for the relatively poor in options? Yet war is the most radically contemporaneous of events, culture-shattering; for those few who have everything, war can be the ultimate present, the most radical change involving them with the many. Death is the authentic democracy—if the descent, or rebirth, of historical memory and its judgments can be aborted—or safely handled, like all the 'risen gods,' playthings packaged for instant use, inside quotation marks. Each god-toy is stamped, for the user's mind-blowing: "This product has no compelling or directing element in it and need not be disbelieved."

A radical aestheticizing of life, the established culture of the rich, Gala indeed, is very near the anti-creed of therapeutic action that I have tried to imagine here, as I did first in the final chapter of *The Mind of the Moralist*, then further in the two main theoretical chapters of *The Triumph of the Therapeutic*, and yet further in my essay on "The Impossible Culture."[88] Compare this man, new in his willed pursuit of whatever presents itself to pursue, to Babel's naive old Jew, Gedali, so obstinate that, though almost blind, he refuses the saving new vision that is The Revolution brought to him by a sophisticated young Jew, equipped with spectacles. Old Gedali knows, as you recollect, that The Revolution

---

88. See my introductory essay to Oscar Wilde, *The Soul of Man Under Socialism and Other Essays* [(New York, 1970), pp. vii-xxxiv]; and, further, Wilde's essay in that volume, "The Critic as Artist" [pp. 100-188]. See, further, everything I have written, and may write, of course. I cannot discuss here the meaning of speed in the culture of the rich, except to point out that everything speedy contradicts the pace of life in the academy. [On the meaning of speed, including the pharmacological, see, further, below, p. 178 *et pass.*]

respects no sabbaths; and, though weary of his resistance to the relentless move of History, Gedali remains a sabbatarian.

How are you on the trivial old question of sabbath-keeping? Is any order worthy of the name without its strict sabbaths? *No* is the first word of resistance; it remains the word that needs deepest, freshest, most constant relearning—and those learned in its ways —to articulate any culture. *No* has to be studied and interpreted almost without break, although it too must exist in a sense heavily qualified, under the sabbath rule of remissions. The Galas and Jakes of our virtual reality have gone a long way towards inverting the authority of the sabbath into the danger of immobility. The answering *No* of our credal culture has become—in its uniquely profane, anti-credal context—a questioning neurotic inhibition. Viewed from a position inside Gedali's old credal culture, Jake and his sort are the most malignant strain of all, young men who, having accepted the disenchantment of the world, would act out the functional equivalents of all enchantments: preposterous sex-pressional parodies of infinite 'values.' We are on the verge of solving the ancient problem of what is a good society. When orders of authority, uniquely unchangeable, are resolved into therapies, entirely changeable, then the 'good' will no longer be a problem—the good is resolved into the metamorphosis *input/output*. A good man is one who knows how to keep changing inclusively, which is to say—thrusting toward everything.

You may wish to call this vitalist tactic after one of its more portentous names: *existential freedom*. Such freedom involves the embrace of meaninglessness, entirely unauthorized decisions to do that which has not been recalled. Jake's decision to try to prevent Rennie's suicide, after she has conceived by his most casual act, appears entirely unauthorized. His decision for Rennie's life resembles one of Forster's casually announced deaths: what-is-not suddenly appears and takes over the action. Free as we are, why not suicide? What—more precisely, *who*—is to prevent us? Where there has been no personal justification, uniquely unchangeable and only elaborately interpretable, there is no authority.

136

Would you like to know how to recreate authority? You would have to begin again outside yourself. A true interdictory authority can only be taught to us; it cannot be thought up by us. To achieve your own role in the scheme of authority, from the outside in, you would have a director. For its enactment, Stanislavsky's theory depends upon the presence of a Stanislavsky. In the present age, theatre-wise, we are said to be in the age of the director. But every great director is already a paratherapist, the actors his patients. Bergman is an obvious example. His films respect the irreconcilable differences between creeds and therapies. In *The Seventh Seal*, Bergman tried to imagine, especially in the Equerry, the exhaustion of moral energy in a credal culture; the Christianity portrayed is sick. Bergman's other films are mainly theatricals of the emergent anti-credal culture, entirely without a message—all art and pretend agons, as between Gala and his cook-waiter.

By this time, there are no messages to receive from our arts, not even indecipherable ones; instead, there are scenarios. Who among us older folks can forget the scenarios acted out by the Nazis? That was art transferred to life, marvelous scenarios. More scenarios will be acted out, I think. The genius of mass political dramaturgy passed to the New Right in the nineteen-thirties; in the seventies, theatrical genius is entirely the prop of the New Left. Extremes meet in the age of the therapeutic, doctrinal rigor displaced by its functional equivalent—a psychotechnics of acting out. Angela Davis is billed as the lovely leading lady of the progressive American and world-historical stage.[89] To act professionally in the real world is to protest, something or other. Even verdicts in favor of one's own side must be protested; this is what it means to be a political kunstler. The emergent role-player will be capable of stepping beside himself or herself and, at the same time, roar indignantly against anything. Hitler put this acting ability in all its power to work wonders when he answered an early, earnest follower's inquiry about what to tell up-tight bourgeois[90] when they

89. Cf., on the rewards of revolutionary starletdom, footnote 126, p. 195. Further, on simony, see footnote 94, p. 147 and, more important, footnote 97, page 150.

90. The precedent, confident rather than pejorative 'value-relational,' name for our class was 'proper.'

asked what the Nazi movement stood for. "Tell them," roared Hitler, "that we are against them!" There spoke the uniquely modern revolutionary. Anything transgressive is creative. As a slogan, 'Make Love' is as transgressive as 'Make War.' It is aimed *against* an interdict and proclaims none; 'Not War' patently excludes guerrilla war and terrorist activity. Moreover, 'Make Love' is the original slogan of universal private war, each against each. These private warriors, my young radical acquaintance, who would 'Make Love Not War,' are ardent public supporters of Fatah and PLF. (And most of my young radical acquaintance are 'Jewish.') At this historical moment, you may choose this transgressive style: *sexual/political*. There are others: *economic/political*, for example. In due course, the various transgressive styles will converge in public actings-out, as they did, premonitorily, in the Nazi movement. What splendid erotic manicons those Germans were: upon being selected for the Feldkorps, my aunts committed suicide. Beautiful women they were; the eroticism of the National Socialists was the key to the deadliness of their politics. Unbounded love makes death. Admitted: I may lean a little toward the oversensitive side, on the *love/death* metamorphosis.

After 'to act or not to act' the next sociological question not to be begged is: 'What humiliations shall humans tolerate?' (Put negatively, this question would read: 'How are ordinary men to bear the future, without their stigmata?') That all have to tolerate some goes without saying; none of us shall live entirely self-assured, within stable reciprocities of respect. To be humiliated is to accept the experience of being treated disrespectfully by an other. The question appears in the degree and quality of humiliations we shall tolerate. Some humiliations may serve us well; others make us ill; all therapies include some tactic of humiliation and, therefore, are themselves hazards the ill run in attempting to get well.

Think of what it is to be totally humiliated. It is a positive absence of respect, a lowering, some sixth hour so complete in its inferior treatment of those made superior by it that the one resistance still possible at such a time, the possibility that remains, to defend your self-respect, the utopia of all resistances, is suicide. When life becomes impossible, yet unconstrained by the utopian possibility of death, then the experience of being lowered is best seen through therapies of survival. Here is the alternative utopian possibility, not survival in itself but the guiltlessness that may develop best through therapies of survival. If such therapies succeed, then a survivor would be in the position of knowing perfectly well what he ought not to have done and yet having done it; this transgressiveness would be the one possibility remaining in the field against its utopian contrary.

My aunts died promptly at their own hands; they declined absolutely to tolerate their therapy of survival, which, after all, would not have been so terrible, if you come to think about it. By way of developing a contrasting model of conduct, think for a moment of their father. In Dachau he appeared to tolerate every brand of humiliation lowered upon him without thereby seeming lowered. On his behalf, I can say of my grandfather that he did not think to resist. On the most generous interpretation of it, my grandfather's act of resistance went no further than to pray to his Sovereign for an end to his life, to be spared more. He was not spared.

Now, having come this pitiably near distance with me, try to imagine as your option neither absolute: neither suicide nor prayer. Try, rather, to imagine absence of respect accepted as a matter of principle. Under this principle of all that matters, survival, any measure of experience may become humiliating. It follows tha. the way beyond the inclusiveness of humiliation is through an acceptance—indeed, through a courting—of experiences without reference to the inherited order of their interdicts. The less precedented the experience the more therapeutic; this goes as well for intellectual experience. You cannot step twice into the same cat house of intellect. Experience fully courted need not exclude either suicide or prayer; both types of decisive act are on your checklist of options. But everything else, too, must be made possible and nothing decisive. Then, and only then, can we live in utopia and so end the intolerable humiliation that our utopias remain what they have always been: mere possibilities.

For our progress toward realizations of utopias, the checklist of experience needs indefinite lengthening. Indeed, why should we not live again after experiencing death? But, as if to check the lengthening checklist, I expect the neo-orthodoxy option to be taken up soon again, against our present efforts of realization. It happened last, as part of my own experience, immediately after World War II. Then, some of my most articulate contemporaries and I opted into neo-orthodoxies of one kind or another. Let me not exaggerate; articulate contemporaries are never that thick on the ground. (On the contrary, as every primitive once knew, they are thicker under the ground.) We may say, against the neo-orthodox to come, what Burke said in the course of his *Reflections on the Revolution in France*:

> Because half a dozen grasshoppers under a fern make a field ring with their importunate chink, whilst thousands of great cattle, reposed beneath the shadow of the British oak, chew the cud and are silent, pray do not imagine that those who make the noise are the only inhabitants of the field; that, of course, they are many in number, or that, after all, they are other than the little, shrivelled, meager, hopping, though loud and troublesome, insects of the hour.

One difference between Burke's reflection and my own is that I see fewer cattle chewing the cud silently and more who distinguish themselves trying to make grasshopping noises. By our lights, it is difficult to see in the field which are Burke's great cattle and which his insects of the hour. Who among us claims to be in repose except as an exercise, part of the developing common capacity for hopping?

As between cattle and grasshoppers in the matter and manner of intellect: the cattle remain, as Burke thought, fundamentally more intelligent. They think no more now than in Burke's time to invent a new morality; they are pleased to diddle the old—cud-chewing is, after all, laxative. The stuff of every established morality appears to run easily through the system, inside and out. Yet it is the lesser intelligence of sincere grasshoppers to carry in their hip pockets the copyright of some morality; so adamant are they in their hostility to old remissions more and more expertly practiced, that, using the experimental solidarities of their elite half-dozens, they think they have reinvented morality.

It may be wise, fellow students, to reread Mill on judging all things by your own lights. In *The Spirit of the Age* (1831), Mill warned that

> if you once persuade an ignorant or a half-instructed person, that he ought to assert his liberty of thought, discard all authority, and—I do not say *use* his own judgment, for that he can never do too much—but *trust* solely to his own judgment, and receive or reject opinions according to his own views of the evidence;—if, in short, you teach to all the lesson of *indifferency,* so earnestly, and with such admirable effect, inculcated by Locke upon *students*, for whom alone that great man wrote, the merest trifle will suffice to unsettle and perplex their minds. There is not a truth in the whole range of human affairs, however obvious and simple, the evidence of which an ingenious and artful sophist may not succeed in rendering doubtful to minds not very highly cultivated, if those minds insist upon judging of all things exclusively by their own lights. [Mill's italics.]

How banal and indifferent same these exclusive judgments become, unsettling trifles made huge by little minds.

Hopping about, from one interdictory-remissive exercise to another, our great grasshoppers have added something new to the ordinary mortality of cultures. The healing power of their paratherapies is a power that kills. When the sociological category into which our moral demands have fallen, the metamorphic category of the *interesting/boring,* is made inclusive, then it is transformed into movements at once totalitarian and democratic; these movements, huge and little, may be better understood under the category of the bizarre. What can be perverse if all interdictory-remissive orders are transitional? That way, transitional, if they exist only by passing an infinite variety of tests, the interdicts are made to be abolished. The interdicts cannot be tested; they can only be obeyed, in fastidious orders of command. The language of morals cannot be turned into a parataxis and remain language. We cannot allow for one utopian possibility: that nothing can be disordered. That allowance encourages the likelihood that nothing will be ordered. Our teaching peace cry: no dissent without a grammar of assent.

Tested as they are, even by perfectly sincere grasshoppers who wish them well, as mere parts of speech the interdicts blend into the bizarrerie of our everyday acts. I had thought of writing a famous book on this subject, under some such title as *The Bizarrerie of Contemporaneous Acts*. It was intended, from its conception, to supersede old Freud's *The Psychopathology of Everyday Life*. That book has retreated into history; I had thought to write something successive. Alack, I have decided against writing my *Bizarrerie*. The system published—symbol and organization, action and belief placed in identical order, interdictory and remissive— my successor book might be found edifying and therefore subject to unanswerable charges that it is yet another of those extravagant departures from recognized ideas and tastes which the book sets out to resist. Besides, my *Bizarrerie* would have been a commonplace book; it is hard nowadays to be just original enough to humiliate the reading public. If a book is to succeed, as the functional equivalent of a paratherapy, relatively harmless so long as it is not acted out, then it must be just humiliating enough to interest its potential market. A fine tact is needed if the author is to avoid responsibility for text-analogizing readers. Every radically contemporaneous book is a kind of lowering. Where edifications once were, there humiliations are to be. But please, do not give up on books. Buying the most radically contemporaneous book is still less costly than actually going steady with a paratherapist—some leader who teaches, heals, does practically everything well, a regular triple-threat of a backfield man.

Of those paratherapies which free action from belief,[91] the

---

91. Equally, by those same paratherapies, belief is freed from action. Carnality is ideological, a question of civilization, as well as sexual. The last great symbolist of our inherited interdicts, Kant, remarked, on carnal self-defilement:

> Just as the natural function of the love of life is to preserve the *individual,* so the natural function of sexual love is to preserve the *species*: in other words, both of these are *natural purposes*. By a natural purpose I mean such a connection of the cause with an effect that, without attributing intelligence to the cause, we must yet conceive it by analogy with an intelligent cause and so as if it produced the effect purposefully. The question now is whether the agent's use of his sexual

142

struggle for power is the second most ancient and first expresses itself in the action of Cain against Abel. The most ancient para-therapy is sexual action, expressed first by Eve, the human original, against Adam and his poor, manipulated serpent. Sexuality is the

---

power comes under a limiting law of duty with respect to his own person, or whether he can, without violating a duty to himself, use his sexual power for mere animal pleasure, without regard for its purpose.— The doctrine of Law establishes that a man cannot use *another* person for this pleasure, apart from a special limitation by a legal contract in which the two reciprocally obligate each other. But here we are asking whether, with regard to this gratification, man has a duty to himself, the violation of which is a *defilement* (not merely an abasement) of humanity in his own person. The instinct to this pleasure is called *carnal lust* (or also simply lust). The vice generated through it is called *impurity*; the virtue with regard to this sensuous impulse is called *chastity*, which is now to be set forth as a duty of man to himself. Lust is called *unnatural* if man is aroused to it, not by its real object, but by his imagination of this object, and so in a way contrary to the purpose of the desire, since he himself creates its object. For in this way the imagination brings forth an appetite contrary to nature's purpose, and indeed an appetite that is still more important than love of life itself, since it aims at the preservation of the whole species and not only of the individual.

That such an unnatural use (and so misuse) of one's sexual power is a violation of duty *to oneself* and, indeed, one which is contrary to morality in the highest degree occurs to everyone immediately, along with the thought of it, and stirs up an aversion from this thought to such an extent that we consider it indecent even to call this vice by its proper name. This does not happen in the case of self-murder, which we do not hesitate in the least to lay before the world's eyes in all its heinousness (as a *species facti*). In the case of unnatural vice it is as if man in general felt ashamed of being able to treat his own person in such a way, which degrades it beneath the beasts. Thus when it is necessary to speak, in a well-bred society, of even the permissible (but in itself, admittedly, merely animal) physical union of the two sexes in marriage, this occasions and calls for great delicacy, in order to throw a veil over it. [Kant, "On Carnal Self-Defilement," *The Doctrine of Virtue,* trans. Mary J. Gregor ("The Metaphysic of Morals," Part II [Philadelphia, 1964]), Book I ("On Perfect Duties to Oneself"), Chapter I ("Man's Duties to Himself as an Animal Being"), Article II, §7, pp. 87-88. Kant's italics.]

The barbarism of psychological man is just that, unlike any primitive men of whom I have ever heard tell by anthropologists, he throws

sphere in which anyone, unprepared, can become a passionate unbelieving actor. Except for those who struggle professionally for power, sexuality and the economy, in that order, youth before age, are the main arenas of unbelieving action[92]—in every case toward

---

no veils. The intellectualizing varieties of our carnalities are terrible to behold. Our psychological men aim to recreate the most contemporary of all institutions, the most fleeting and first: orgy. Marcuse gives us a choice between 'one-dimensional' carnality and a richer variety. His revolutionary answer is based on the doubtful assumption that the time of scarcity has ended and that we can now proceed to the translation of quantity into quality. Our desire for permanent revolution is for a permanent barbarism; such a revolution renders all others obsolete, including the Marxist. The possibility of a permanent barbarism lies before us, hidden in the twin doctrines by which 'liberated' sexuality is opposed to repressive discipline. Marcuse seems to think that a liberated sexuality would oppose a technological discipline as the modern social form of repression. I do not understand the force of this opposition. Sexuality cannot be 'liberated'; it can be more or less transgressive, in an order of truths that, by opposing 'impulse,' appears to create them. 'One-dimensional man' can only be controlled, in his infinite carnality, by a new submission to law. Marcuse offers no lawful symbolic. His is yet another carnalization of spirit, based this time around his own version of the technological mystique of a new Eden, a world free first of all from scarcity. Like others among our most progressive theorists, Marcuse is an ally of the technological mystagogues. In order to possess any truth, a theory must be of order—of authority and its descent. An 'aestheticizing' theory treats reality as a game; such lightness and play cancels out the shadowed nature of authority, at least in the theory itself.

92. Sociological theorists of action—and, in particular, of the unbelieving actions characteristic of modernity—are obliged, therefore, to work out the hidden links between power struggle, sexual struggle and economic struggle. 'Class' is scarcely more than a cover word for these different, yet touching, arenas of struggle. A 'culture-class,' i.e., a guiding cadre, toward the methodical conduct of life, may be defined as those specially charged with training credal and repressive modalities against immediacy and directness of expressive behavior. Such training —call it 'education'—must involve disciplines of judgment, as Kant, Durkheim and practically every other theorist in our canon has tried to say. How I dislike definitions. They are my least favored children,

satisfaction of needs defined as such by their immediacy. Sexuality thus defined, love becomes an overestimation of the love object, adding belief and all its votive energies to the purity of unbelief, which may be thus understood to occur with the sexual act itself. Love is the personifying of authoritative belief; sex is the paradigm of the struggle for power. A love affair becomes a sophisticated combination of unbelieving action and authoritative belief—belief calculated to sustain the struggle; here lies, buried, Sorel's 'myth,' which was, until Fanon's, the most recent major expression, in social theory, of the sentimentality underlying the Age of Reasons, now unending.

Sorel will serve us as a godfather of the modern functional irrationalizer. Like Rousseau (indeed, like Hume),[93] Sorel is a

---

made, if at all, to be abandoned—gladly abandoned. Theorists are obliged to be the unwed fathers of their ideas. This would appear to bring theorists very near to being therapists—but only so the two types can stand, one against the other, back to back. A good theorist is not interested in his ideas because they work; a good therapist is only interested in his ideas so far as they work. A therapist is free—indeed obliged—to abandon his ideas when they do not work. Since when does truth cure? Truth is no cure; it is an arrestment, a creation of closure, a narrowing that wonderfully concentrates the mind. That is why teenagers, sexually driven, are such rank sentimentalists—as Don Juan was, even as he hailed 'Liberty'—and such rotten social theorists; even when an adolescent manages to concentrate, it is mainly upon the glory of conquering what he is supposed to learn. We educators know how wasteful must be the education of the young—and how it disturbs their sentiments. Truths are a long way round to ego identity and not at all, in the result, broadening, as the young have been led to believe. One of our tasks, fellow teachers, is to persuade our colleagues to abandon 'general education,' equally, for the best, with those dexterity routines now called 'specialization.' I hope the foregoing makes a little more clear why the young are pure only in their unbelief and, moreover, what is wrong with 'youth movements.'

93. Have you studied Rousseau and Hume, hanging, as they should, almost side by side, in Ramsay's superb portraits, in the Scottish National Portrait Gallery? Rousseau: the ugliness of his beauty caught, something sinister I see in the sweetness of his entire look; Hume: most beautifully ugly, one of Ramsay's masterpieces of serenity, without a

145

child of the Enlightenment. The textbooks have miseducated us enlightened ones miserably, for generations, on the meaning of the Enlightenment. From Hume and Rousseau to Sorel, Freud and Fanon, the finest intellects in the tradition of the Enlightenment kept up their confident lack of confidence in the rational abilities of man. In contrast, by their 'Enlightenment,' received through cliché and textbook, the social servicing ex-religious elites who have dominated Western culture increasingly since their origins in the eighteenth century, insist to this day on exercising, unawares, a rationalistically-dressed sentimentalism derived from their betters, the Enlightenment theorists.

To this day, as Swift unkindly remarked of the religion of their eighteenth-century forerunners, the rationality of our social-service elites must have nothing in it "which cannot be presently comprehended by the weakest noodle." Ever since, 'Enlightenment' has meant the rationalizations of sentiment engineers—with special respect to, and for, the passions of the weakest noodles; thus reason was transformed into sentimentality. In its most extreme content, sentimentality has emerged, in modernity, as a freer, ever more youthful sexuality: the key to cultural egalitarianism and to the new revolutionary politics. Sorelian theory is eroticism made over into political movement; sexual actions are to private affairs as political movements are to public.

Jake and Rennie fall into sexual action, not love, which is a form of respect. Barth prepares us for—and follows the implications of—that act beautifully, without trying to exhibit it, move by move; he is an artist. Following Jake, Rennie too acts out the absence of any presiding presence: she cannot resist whatever becomes possible. They fall, unbelieving, into bed. Where else? Their unbelieving transaction is, identically, a sexual exchange. Joe, the thinking man, demands their reasons for falling, as if they knew (and believed in) what they were doing—or, at least, were driven by lust rather than drawn by a) the presence of sheer possibility; b) the absence of resistance to it. Don Juan, or any other

---

trace of the sinister; nothing restive. [Beyond this paragraph on the sentimentality underlying our own Age of Reasons, split off into a resentful Romanticism, see also p. 197 *et pass.* and footnote 128.]

heroic precursor of the therapeutic, would have understood how Rennie and Jake landed together in bed: it was something to do.

Two related dangers cling to life among therapeutics: a) immobility; b) a lapse into some passionate morality. All therapies are forms of mobility inducement—personal expressions of dynamics, not of truths. Questions of truth, however, cannot be intellectualized endlessly. To ask whether there will be a revival of 'Meaning,' 'Purpose,' 'Intention,' whatever you please, we must first show that these are not items showing off the supreme dexterity of intellectuals calling (in public performances, at more or less nice fees[94]) for 'Meaning,' 'Purpose,' 'Intention,' whatever pleases you. Such display-calls, hawking change in the 'values' market, are mere entertainments of the moral sense.

What an endless variety of indignation therapies now crowd the 'values' market. All these variations of anger have increased the good living to be made by failed artists and innovative scientists. I understand our accountable angers to be democratizations of the rationalizing process by which anyone can compound transgressions by further transgressions.

Transgressive behavior develops from the top of the social order down, in alliance with the bottom. In our culture, the remissive rich and the lumpenproletariat are allied. A social order enacts interdictory remissive contents, the moral form that is culture, with some more privileged than others to break the interdicts in special ways. In American culture, for example, the very rich and the lumpenproletarians are remissive figures, able to assert themselves in ways prohibited to others. The drug and sexual behavior of our higher re-educated classes imitate (and are reflected by) a uniquely lower and yet leisured class—in America, the blacks—marginal to, yet devastating in, their own social spaces; therefore, I refer not to blacks, but to demographically minor (and widely publicized) criminal elements. Our cultural revolution is a reciprocal movement: from the top down and from the bottom up.

Facing the advantages of any social order, established in its

---

94. This raises the ancient problem of simony, in its modern complications, which I cannot take up here. Note, however, the ancient connection between simony and gnostic movements.

characteristic interdictory-remissive modalities, those most articulate for both top and bottom, the symbolists of transgressive action, in order to break beyond the limits of our inherited culture, have turned to slogans of creative catastrophe, thus spreading toward the middle of the social order a total loss of confidence in the established but failing symbolic. I shall sum up the new symbolic: our culture must be made out to be the worst in order that it shall be made the best. (Jake's action mocks a failing symbolic in the usual way: he does his worst while trying to do his best.)

How on earth can the best be made—or even the better? In every social order there will be doers unto and those done to: that strange reciprocity defines politics. Political metamorphoses are the most treacherous of all. With the best wishes in the world, those who shout 'Power to The People' mean 'We (or Some) People to Power.'

It is in the nature of the modern state, whatever its means to power and whatever justifications support those means, that no state yields power to the unprofessional People. If you are playing the power game, for keeps, then you should think to work at being The People, full time, as Lenin demanded of his professionals. Amateurs of The People lack staying power; as well be a scholar without sitzfleisch.[95] It is in the nature of modern state-power that the unprofessional People can only confirm it, or, in the alternative, be organized as means for the transference of power to another group of professional (if once amateur) power-holders. Once established, no state in the modern sense, as a monopoly of legitimate violence, however it peoples its inner justifications, will yield more than the simulacra of power to its people; in his praxis of the relations between state and party, Lenin grasped perfectly the nature of the modern state as founded on physical force. In an opposite and equally perfect way, anarchist theory has under-

---

95. How interesting, to me at least, that so many would-be intellectuals, as distinguished from scholars, like so many losing revolutionary politicians, lack staying power. Trotsky lacked staying power and was nothing if not an intellectual. Double fault: not to be left unexploited by opposing players in the world-historical Wimbledon.

stood the state, as the supreme instrument, entirely unjustified, for punishment of the unprofessional People.

Anarchist theory opts for the metamorphosis *antipolitical/dissolution of power*, a disuse of violence in its political form, as if thus to turn our mortal danger and safety in the state into a mere problem, soluble as any other, if only people knew how to keep authority entirely for themselves. In this precise sense there is no anarchist theory of the state, and no anarchist theory of authority. Wherever the modern state exists, its professionals will thrust toward a monopoly of violence justified by wrong-doing; without wrong, there can be no right. Under certain symbolics, heavily politicized, that thrust toward authority always in the right is made in the name of The People. During such struggles for power, real people can only lose, more or less completely—depending upon how intense the struggle has been.[96] Where the struggle for power grows extraordinarily intense, and ordinary people suffer most, we may expect resurgences of anarchist theory, in which the state is always in the wrong. Anarchism is a variety of keeping hope, for a respite from the cruelties of power struggles, alive among the sorest losers. It is an enchanting theory, of a world not only without gods but, even more happily, without chiefs—only plain people organized to keep the devouring beast, politics, at bay. Every thoroughgoing anarchist (read Kropotkin, Proudhon, Paul Goodman) becomes culturally conservative when confronted with real politics—conservative far beyond (and opposed to) the radical Right. But these early modern labels of commitment to a directed movement—'Right' and 'Left'—have lost meaning entirely and should be used sparingly if at all, in a late-modern

---

96. The struggle between the colonies and their father nation was not at all intense; that unique group, the Founding Fathers, beginning with Washington, would have felt completely at home with Burke and, indeed, on both sides of the House of Commons; so, too, at home would have been Franklin Delano Roosevelt, Adlai Stevenson, JFK. We may witness a fresh drawing together on both sides of the Atlantic: Heath and Nixon are early warnings of rule by the corporate managerial-type already in academic office.

joking way. (It follows that if I were your teacher, then you would have to consider in what ways you could take me seriously—and, moreover, what can be serious and yet without direction.)

What is modern may be best understood by what it is not. Until modernity, interdictory and remissive motifs stipulating cultures of truth were animated by acute dangers and awful punishments, organized into a self-defensive moral order mounted by guiding cadres of authoritative interpreters. Distinctively modern, hostility to culture in any form, in its highest intensities precisely among those being prepared for membership in some guiding cadre, reflects their own historic metamorphosis of rejection, a *rationalizing/irrationalizing* resolution of self-defensive moral orders. In their search for resolutions, the new guiding cadres— scientific and literary—have found a new voice, an anarchic comical voice pitched to encourage popular contempt for the interdictory primacy of all compelling god-terms. This democratization of contempt is more significant than the spreading intolerance of relative deprivation. Behind the tired early-modern labels of class war is the renascent reality of nihilism in the guiding cadres. Nihilism is an old name, with one enactable sociological meaning: a self-destruct therapy.[97] The release of transgressive behavior— both 'authoritarian' and 'anti-authoritarian'—is itself a teaching of universal contempt, which is implicit in all gnostic movements. Captivated within their symbolics of contradiction, a democratic gnosticism for weak noodles, the new guides seek only to abolish their own function; they are, Right or Left, followers of the basest instinct, for sheer possibility.

Learning his lesson from the Leninists, who took an un-Marxist leap over the historical backwardness of the Russian people in order to gain power over them, Hitler once put the entire case of the Right in a nutshell: "Only the impossible is successful." On

---

97. Nihilism, as a more or less implicit derivation from the symbolic of a guiding cadre, is not without historical precedent: gnostic movements have ended in a variety of catastrophic events, greater goods, no doubt, but induced (as we theorists are privileged to see them, in retrospect) to cure lesser evils.

the 'Left,' in the name of an impossible progress and originality, the modern arts, premonitory, are equally deadly: to themselves. The language of spontaneity among *artists/paratherapists*, their contempt for forms that are established, elaborates the predicate of hostility, and of destruction, that is also the key to the contempt for authority—for law and order, society itself—characteristic of the avowed enemies of Art, the fascists. I have said that fascism was not a creed; it remains an opportunity, created for it by its equally anti-credal opponents and predecessors. 'Fascism' is one name for our revolutionary character type in action. The revolutionary character type of our present age is therapeutic.

No culture is without its leading character types. As a character type, whatever his politics or anti-politics, the therapeutic denies all moralizing forms, just as his counterpart, the endlessly progressive artist, claims for himself, as the essence of 'creativity,' a breaking of the received forms. Modern art, like religions, becomes breakthrough—and occurs less and less often the more often it is announced. Originality becomes publicity, genius[98] a build-up. Modern commerce assigns its comedians the revolu-

---

98. On the law-abiding character of true genius, see Kant's "Analytic of the Sublime" [(2nd Book, 1st Part, of "The Critique of Judgement"), *Kant's Critique of Aesthetic Judgement*, trans. James Creed Meredith (Oxford, 1911)]. In Section 46, titled "Fine art is the art of genius," Kant lays it down that "*genius* is the talent (natural endowment) which gives the rule to art." But a genius is himself ruled, for it is through his innate mental aptitude that "nature gives the rule to art." It is clear to Kant that "*originality* must be [the] primary property" of a work of genius. But, "since there may also be original nonsense, [the] products [of genius] must at the same time be models, i.e., be *exemplary*; and, consequently, though not themselves derived from imitation, they must serve that purpose for others, i.e., as a standard or rule of estimating" [pp. 168-169; Kant's italics]. What is at once original and exemplary sets a standard; moreover, in setting a standard, the conservation of the excellence, in style, is also set in motion. In modernity, what Kant called the "spirit of imitation" makes the market for original nonsense exemplary; the primary property of Art becomes a continuing abortion of all styles, before they can settle in. It is the *market*, not nature or genius, which gives the "rule" to 'modern' Art.

tionary role. Revolution is in the cards. After the comedians come the straight men. Will we dare laugh with (and at) them, too? Not even Charlie Chaplin could play Hitler, successfully, into a clown.

Against interdictory form, a culture organized by contempt and rancor, rather than reverence and justice, must view inhibition, the delay of gratification, all those disciplines by which self and society can be held in mutual check, as the main enemy. As revolutionaries, along the entire political spectrum, therapeutics do no honor to some *competing* morality; nor do they honor 'impulse' or 'spontaneity'; 'impulse,' 'spontaneity,' even 'gay,' are naturalistic name-covers for transgressive behavior, within our given moral-demand system. Sexual acrobatics have no more to do with the old Eve than the scientistic functionaries of a bureaucratic welfare-state have to do with the rites of priests.

As Rousseau rightly imagined, 'natural man' emerges at the end of civilization, not at its beginning; and, in the end, he will voice all sorts of views, take all manner of positions, revolutionary and counter-revolutionary, political and apolitical, monoatheist and poly, whatever serves his sense of well-being in particular situations. His 'gods' are never resurrected; they are terms, made for use and in no way commanding obedience. Where revelations were, there the writings of 'natural man' will be, at once confessional and pedagogic. At the end of culture, 'natural man' will find all positions worth taking. Why not the clenched fist, raised and closed tight around the cross, at once a gesture of benediction and violence? The therapeutic is capable of posing with the most opposed ideals; none compel or direct him to stand long in one pose. Such a stand would mean immobility, one of the two dread diseases of the therapeutic.

The most efficient way to move closer to Nature cannot be to move backward, in some 'life-style' indebted to modern imaginings of technologically unprogressive societies; rather, Nature can only be achieved by moving forward, in transgressive breakthroughs that no historical 'primitive' adopts in his own profoundly conservative way of life.[99]

99. Excepting, of course, those occasional rebel leaders—Freud considered them, typologically, parricides—who, by becoming significant

The consummate transgressive vocation for the therapeutic, as I imagine him, would be hunting—hunting people. So the therapeutic would achieve the supreme naturalism. Emerging at the end of civilization, not at its beginnings, 'natural man' is a self-conscious killer who kills for the sake of his health. For this entirely re-educated man, Nature cannot be a fantasy of pastoral life, as it was in the eighteenth century, but a cultivated nightmare of the instinctual. If the imagined place of our origins were a garden, then the imagined place of our end is a jungle.

For their grip upon the human imagination, archaic imageries of peaceable kingdoms depended upon a widespread modesty and mildness of manners; civility expressed a repressive symbolic successfully at work. At the end of civilization, 'natural man' will express a widespread assumption that repressive symbolics, ancient and modern, are bad for his Personality. Endlessly attracting attention to himself, 'natural man' becomes abnormal, in principle. Under a repressive symbolic, social order constrains ordinary men to achieve their normality. Through mildness of manner (insep-

---

man-killers, succeed to rule. Even in the 'primitive' state, politics is the art of man-killing. Freud's 'unconscious' is (as I have had my best students point out, in place, to themselves) the warring state writ small. Indeed, Freud almost thought so. But, he did not quite think so— mainly, I think, because to think precisely this would have been to abandon one of his most cherished metapsychological positions: the autonomy of unconscious processes. Even the strongest noodle, you see, may have its fixing moments of weakness. Nevertheless, we are indebted, interminably, to Freud, for saying over again, in a beautifully theoretical way, what primitives once knew: that "the warring state permits itself every . . . misdeed." Here you are, given the "terrible opportunity" to convince yourselves what Freud knew, what Weber knew, what I know: that "the state has forbidden to the individual the practice of wrong-doing, not because it desired to abolish it, but because it desires to monopolize it." [See Freud, "Reflections upon War and Death (1915)," *Character and Culture* ("Collected Papers," ed. Philip Rieff [New York, 1963]), p. 112.] Now, fellow teachers, is it power you wish to struggle for? I understand. Power is the secret wish of intellectuals, as it was of priests. But the secret has been an open one, at least since Nietzsche's time. You are obliged to resist the wish and all its disguises.

arable from the qualities that go with their names), ordinary men acquire the quality of being safe to live near. This feeling of safety constitutes civility, whether in cultures otherwise named 'primitive' or 'progressive.' Uncivilized, how else, except as a *healer/killer*, will the ordinary therapeutic achieve his normality?[100]

There is an alternative to hunting people as the norm of 'natural man' at the end of civilization: hunting oneself. Self-murder would then be a consummate achievement of everything. One of my best students suggested to me, while I was delivering one of my lecturettes[101] on 'natural man' at a pleasant luncheon

---

100. On hunting people as the act of 'natural man,' my graduate-student assistant advised me to see *Esquire* [July 1967, p. 39]. There, in the special section on violence, the editors begin as follows: "Three people are enjoying this situation [picture of a man in a gunsight]—the murderer, the victim, and you. The murderer because he is about to take the ultimate risk; the victim because he is about to experience the ultimate sensation; and you because the vicarious thrill is more potent than pornography." Note further in the same number of *Esquire* [p. 56] the following on Norman Mailer: "The visionary of violence who, in *Deer Park* and *An American Dream*, called the shots, foresaw murder as the ultimate art-form and the essential experience."

101. 'Lecturette': A bad habit among teachers who aspire to ask questions; a name, derived from 'luncheonette,' and other pre-digestive institutions, for a teaching which cannot resist backing up questions with brief lectures.

I cannot resist a brief lecture on college reform. Why not award the Ph.D. on entrance, freshman week? As for faculty rank, my friend and fellow teacher, David Daube, who gave up All Souls for the splendid body that is Berkeley, has the best idea: everyone appointed to fullest professorships and then, for each article, book, review or monograph published, demotion, with proportionate reduction in salary as well as rank. Try to imagine the blessings—the silences, the stopped presses. Of course, we would have a parallel demotional order for all public appearances, giving of interviews—only The Pontiff would not be demoted for pontificating.

Where do you stand on rank and grading? Some students really do fail, and should be failed. One of my many names, locally, is 'The Last of the Mohicans.' I am not the last. There are many more of us, fellow teachers, than is commonly thought, even in the 'multiversities.' One

one day, that I ought to read a novel by a recent, world-famous suicide, Yukio Mishima, *Sun and Steel*. I shall try to read it, on my student's advice; but as I near the condition of being old, I incline, more and more, to read only what I have read before. I do want to keep up with the latest, but not with the latest as a display-call, producing the metamorphosis *famous/money*; our famous are, to a man and woman, overpaid. Why should I subsidize the entertainers of the revolutionary rich?

Beyond more or less fame-producing display calls, by specialists in marketing the Change game, from what characterological presence (and from what social formation) can we hope for a recognized command: to interpret our one failed sensibility—of transgressions? There is some hope—if I can make accurate reference to hope when it is so heavily qualified. The opposition to the Vietnam war, even crossed as it was by various transgressive protest movements, gave reasons for hope. I have said many times over that there can be no culture without guilt; Vietnam rekindled our sense of guilt, not widely or deeply; nevertheless, that indispensable and true sensibility seemed alive again. But I fear that true guilt for which I hope was crossed by false, creating predicates which mixed criticism of warmongers, professionals of state-abstracted violence, with amplifications of transgressive behavior among anti-culturemongers. The war-critical anti-culturemongers moralized falsely about the big baddies in Washington and the little goodies in Hanoi. Even little North Vietnam was, is and ever shall be a warring state, not a moral entity; so is South Vietnam, Egypt, Israel—any state. Do you think the Swedish state, or Canadian state—even the Swiss state—would not do before it is done to?

---

of our jobs is to prepare our successors. In the nature of things, succession is the most important process; teaching is the highest level of that process, which begins in the bacterial and ends in the cultural. Glory be to our part in the process, despite the recalcitrance of our chosen successors. Some of them remain, I will admit, spoilt children. A faculty of operators is the just result of a student body of politicos, studying their 'rights.' Pray silence about 'student rights,' and from faculty about 'productivity.'

No state is a moral entity, none are holier than Thou, whatever is said for them: that is one thing we teachers must know. We cannot grow stupid about a state just because we imagine ourselves on its side (which is to say—'our side' to power). I remember the bad old days of my youth,[102] when, among my Progressive academic acquaintance, the Soviet Union could do no wrong—and, therefore, did. I was told it was downright "immoral" —and worse, "unhistorical"—not to join the Communist Party. The Red Dawn shifts ever eastward.

The most subversive form of contemporary moralizing is no longer in the Party spirit: rather, false guilt about our 'repressive' civilization is a blare of permanent protests. Jane Fonda and Vanessa Redgrave do not have messages for us; they are professional performers, displaying their attractions for one cause or another. After Vietnam, what? There will always be causes, for the joining up. I do not suggest sitting on the sidelines; I suggest only that politics is not quite like other games. It is just the fun of it that I fear. Pleasure is what you have when you have your way. Politics is getting your way. What is democratic in the connection between pleasure and politics? Having your way is essentially undemocratic; we cannot all equally have our way; nor can we prevent others from trying to get their way. The pursuit of pleasure is close to the art of politics. And in both the pursuit and the art there is the menace of cruelty as an alternative to the tactic of kindness.

Be grateful for your sense of true guilt and doubly grateful if it has not been badly damaged. Without that guilt, an elaborately cultivated strength of inhibition preventing or punishing transgressive activity, there can be neither aristocracies of the feeling intellect nor democracies of obedience. Guilt, subserving the interdicts, is inseparable from the working of high culture. The horror we name here, for methodological convenience, 'Jake' and 'Gala,'

---

102. How can anyone regret that they are not young, that it is over and done with? This is not to say that the young ought to grow up fast; rather, only that we are mistaken to stay young. How sad for our young that their elders imitate them.

is the same: a vacancy of true guilt, upon which high cultures depend for their origins and survival.

Gala and Jake are as we become: not only beyond ethics, but also beyond its early twentieth-century successor-condition, neuroses. Both fictional characters live in their own hospital-theatres, triumphant therapeutic communities of one. As great Gala says to his victim, Guido: "The facts are to blame, my friend. We are all imprisoned by facts." Here, in modern art, but also in the behavioral sciences, is the terrible irritability, the calculated acceptance, the bowing down—as if social fact itself were not the most changeable thing except as it is a social constraint. Here, symbolics of Change become the world eternally affirming itself; fact-finders join fact-blamers, both to give yet another turn to the great wheel of politics on which all have been broken who tried to stay its turn.

The tactic of our anti-credal elites, the rich revolutionaries and their young relations, the armed bohemians,[103] resolvers of all

---

103. Whatever their age, all bohemians may be defined sociologically as young, for the essential and public form of bohemian activity is sexual exhibitionism. Bohemianism defines contemporary film art, an indefinitely repeatable series of erotic strategies more and more explicitly brutal. So the big money is made at the same time that bourgeois morality stands exposed and contradicted. This makes the best of both impossible worlds. Vadim, Godard, Peckenpah: the honor scroll of directors, toward permanent revolution, is too long for analytic digestion here.

In its most public form, bohemian activity, filmed and thus viewable any number of times by vast numbers of paying acolytes, must escalate into shows of violence. Exactly repeatable shows of violence make the least resistant way in which witnessing masses of people can be prepared to do what, otherwise, they are not prepared to do. The sexual exhibitionism of contemporary films is a prelude to totalitarian politics: never mind what positional games our politicians or actor-directors may play. Positions are taken in order to change them: there follows the usual reward for reasons, in both bohemian exhibitionism and total politics. More than ever before, the least we scholars can do is to abstain from the profitable and prestigious business of giving evidence, the usual reasons for uncensored films, television and staged *sex/violence*. In order to analyze this metamorphosis in its present rampage,

relations to figures of authority, is not to resist the wheel as it turns. Who does not see through people to blame the facts behind them? As one sweet student once said to me, when I was being severe in my analysis of that armed bohemian, Hitler: "After all, he had a terrible childhood." She insisted on blaming only the facts. So long as those of us in the social sciences continue our farcical imitation of the big children of the natural sciences, and blame the facts—or blame nothing, or everything, The System—a cultureless society is our fate. Writing in 1846 (in his *Journals*), Kierkegaard told us one of the ways in which, by our admiration for a special kind of matter-of-factness, we have gone wrong: "*In the end,*" he wrote, "*all corruption will come from the natural*

---

we are obliged to reopen the question of censorship—not only by inquiring further into *sex/violence* but, equally important, into the new *media/message* of representation. A Lawrence scene filmed is discriminably different from that scene in print. Exactly and massively reproducible visual actings-out of a printed page are stimuli in which aesthetic merit and obscene effect may become one and the same; the damage is *in* the viewable act, not merely after it. We viewers are lowered; so, too, are the actors. To discriminate between what is permitted and what is censorable in mass media, we cannot assimilate those media to works of art and books, which cannot be seen in a public darkness. Film multiplies the dangers of the remissive fantasy embedded in direct and popular Realism, its connections with surrealism unexplored.

We scholars have no choice except to reexamine, as well, the meaning of even such apparent clarities on behalf of our infinite privileges as that in our national charter, the Constitution—on freedom of speech. What does it mean, for us, to have it laid down, by the fathers, that "Congress shall make no law . . . abridging the freedom of speech or of the press"? The culture in which the fathers made it clear that freedom of speech was not to be abridged was itself patently interdictory and the character generated in that culture was severely inhibited. Are we members in that same character, generated in that self-same culture? Does our sacred document address those among us who use four-letter words, of which 'Fire' may not be the 'revelant' example? The question is not precisely what the fathers had in mind: rather, in that cultural document, what territories of mindful conduct shall be protected from initiatives that take away those protections? 'Freedom' can be a cover

158

sciences."[104] A false generalization of the natural sciences has generated a fatal superiority of facts over culture itself. So long as we accept this fatal superiority, as if facts really do speak for themselves and that all important ones are other than matters of interpretation, there can be no science of limits. Without a science of limits, the domination of Science implies a cultureless society; we are bound to become the world's first barbarians. Only interpretations are to blame, my friends.

Assume for a moment that it is possible to conceive of a social order without authority, a cultureless society. Who is obliged to use physical force against wrong-doers? What would be wrong-doing? Such an order, like any other, would have to be enacted by a dominant character type. The *therapeutic* is my *ancient/modern* name[105] for this character type. He fits all political pigeon-

---

word for an unprecedented vulnerability. In that case, "no law" takes on a double meaning. Freedom conceals limits that cannot be abridged, through the remissions granted in that word, into its contrary, limitlessness. Our Constitution is a charter of limits. Only so are there freedoms which it protects; only so, in its limiting character, upon even our freedom of speech (limited, as I have implied earlier, for our safety and common civility), is the Constitution interpretable as a sacred document—*within,* not outside, its culture.

On the entire matter of our duty, as members in this moral order, in face of 'artistic' or politicized defilements of both our individuality and humanity, see above, p. 142, footnote 91, on Kant's "On Carnal Self-Defilment," and below, p. 179, footnote 116, on celibacy.

104. [Kierkegaard, *The Journals,* trans. and ed. Alexander Dru (London, 1938), No. 617, 1846, p. 181; Kierkegaard's italics.] The sentence preceding is significantly unoriginal: "Almost everything that flourishes nowadays under the name of science (particularly natural science) is not science at all but curiosity." But cf. President Brewster [footnote 49, p. 81] on "curiosity" as an academic virtue worth defending.

105. See Philo, "On The Contemplative Life Or Suppliants (The Fourth Book of the Virtues)" [*Works of Philo,* trans. F. H. Colson (London, 1941), Vol. IX, pp. 113-169]. Always, my use of the name *therapeutic* has followed Philo's, by inversion. Having discussed the Essenes, who pursued the active life, Philo turns to the *Therapeutae,* his contemplatives. They have a discipline:

holes. In such a character, wrong-doing would be a less and less meaningful category, for there can be no meaning except under authorized interpretations of unchanging interdicts. On the Left, however, it has been expected, explicitly since the early Marx, that innocence will be established when character is liberated from its inherited interdictory particularities. To be neither one thing nor another, to be universally Man, but nothing in particular—in short, to be Marx's Jake of all trades and mastered by none—this is what our re-educated ones long have tried to mean by a meaningful life. A culture of truth can only oppose such terrific innocence with modest stipulations of guilt—a sense of indebtedness and irreducible particularity.

Who are to be our truth-tellers—better say, our guilt-provokers? I do not know. I am without authority; moreover, I do

---

The interval between early morning and evening is spent entirely in spiritual exercise. They read the Holy Scriptures and seek wisdom from their ancestral philosophy by taking it as an allegory, since they think that the words of the literal text are symbols of something whose hidden nature is revealed by studying the underlying meaning.

They have also writings of men of old, the founders of their way of thinking, who left many memorials of the form used in allegorical interpretation and these they take as a kind of archetype and imitate the method in which this principle is carried out. [P. 129]

. . . .

For six days they seek wisdom by themselves in solitude in the closets mentioned above, never passing the outside door of the house or even getting a distant view of it. But every seventh day they meet together as for a general assembly and sit in order according to their age in the proper attitude, with their hands inside the robe, the right hand between the breast and the chin and the left withdrawn along the flank. Then the senior among them who also has the fullest knowledge of the doctrines which they profess comes forward and with visage and voice alike quiet and composed gives a well-reasoned and wise discourse. He does not make an exhibition of clever rhetoric like the orators or sophists of to-day but follows careful examination by careful expression of the exact meaning of the thoughts, and this does not lodge just outside the ears of the audience but passes through the hearing into the soul and there stays securely. [P. 131]

. . . .

They lay self-control to be as it were the foundation of their soul

160

not seek what cannot be sought. Authority is given or it is fraudulent; it cannot be taken by force or ambition. That was one of Weber's main errors in his theory of charisma.[106] In the absence of truth-tellers, however, waiting their reappearance, we teachers can give some preparatory thought to how we may defend ourselves against a culture destroying itself in the dynamics of contempt, dissociating justice from reverence, associating charisma with publicity and power. We must begin to know again that lawful authority is being progressively destroyed by criminal power, which is no monopoly of the 'Right' but equally of the 'Left.'

---

and on it build the other virtues. None of them would put food or drink to his lips before sunset since they hold that philosophy finds its right place in the light, the needs of the body in the darkness, and therefore they assign the day to the one and some small part of the night to the other. Some in whom the desire for studying wisdom is more deeply implanted even only after three days remember to take food. Others so luxuriate and delight in the banquet of truths which wisdom richly and lavishly supplies that they hold out for twice that time and only after six days do they bring themselves to taste such sustenance as is absolutely necessary. They have become habituated to abstinence like the grasshoppers who are said to live on air because, I suppose, their singing makes their lack of food a light matter. But to the seventh day as they consider it to be sacred and festal in the highest degree they have awarded special privileges on its due, and on it after providing for the soul refresh the body also, which they do as a matter of course with the cattle too by releasing them from their continuous labour. [Pp. 133, 135]

Go on to read Philo on Greek—even Socratic—banquets, and on the "supreme contempt" which the "disciples of Moses" have for them [p. 151 et pass.]. The Therapeutae, too, are "carried away by a heaven-sent passion of love"; they too "remain rapt and possessed like bacchanals," but in a way opposite to that of the Greeks: the Therapeutae are a "people always taught from the first to use their sight" [p. 119]. That sight is trained by "laws and oracles delivered through the mouth of prophets . . . and anything else which fosters and perfects knowledge and piety" without the encumbrance of property. "They keep the memory of God alive and never forget it . . . even in their dreams" [p. 127].

106. That theory is best interpreted under the book-laden metamorphosis *Protestant sentimentalism/modern sociology*. I have tried to

In the absence of a supreme interdictory figure, another Moses, with his disciples, a defense by Jews of culture against our democratic orgiasts[107] may be reordered, their preposterous position-taking constrained, from the outside in—by a revival of severe codes of law. It is barely possible that interdictory forms, without which relations between reverence and justice, culture and social system, cannot be maintained, may be prepared from the outside in, as if by the Stanislavsky method. Imagine reinstalled, as among true primitives, a severe code of role-limit that would carry with it severe penalties for deviation. Such a code would have to be strictly retributive. To prepare for this return, and renewal, of the interdicts, we scholars in the humane studies might begin by examining the culturally subversive idea of rehabilitation. The result might be to replace rehabilitation by repayment in kind for transgressions committed; there is an original idea.

Once the transgressive sense is exercised, it will grow more acute. Then the transgressor will again subserve authority rather than subvert it. Let there be no more *Christian/unchurched*, psychiatric chatter about the 'crime of punishment.' Such chatter is

---

make this interpretation in a cluttered eruditional warehouse of a book, complete with a passionate chapter on Lutheran jurisprudence, titled *Charisma*, not to be published until it is as tight as a drum and yet without sounding in the slightest 'charismatic'; I shall probably fail to make it so—but one thing the academy is for, precisely, are such failures. I might learn something in the attempt, over the years. Ours is a fast pace in a slow business. But this is only to say how we enchant ourselves with our breakthroughs; privately, I make about one a day. Is writing a fertility ritual? Then file away your children, where they are safe from harming. Why publish? That is a real question for all scholars of meanings; for all intellectuals, as well. The world is broken-through enough. With so many authors, who remains behind to read? Every man his own original: that is democracy sold out, and an impossible culture. Where do I return my vote? The more original the book, the less justified we are in publishing it. Do not blame the publishers for your thrustings; justifications are not their business.

107. That orgy is the one, only and original, totally democratic, institution—the common utopia of all our gurus, 'fascist' and 'liberationist'—is the key to a revival of interdictive knowledge.

another blaming of facts; only persons can be blamed and only for their transgressive acts, never for their transgressive imaginings until and unless those imaginings take public form. Even then, blame, translated into punishment, must be made strictly according to statute, Law. The indignation of a moral man can be no less transgressive than the transgressions of an indignant man.[108]

Particularly civilized men cannot afford to accept themselves as charismatics; all gifts of grace should be returned, with thanks for the affluence, recently achieved, of the giver. This culture is riddled by cheap gift-giving. 'Charisma' is a concept for moral parvenus, just as paranoia is the pathological hostility of suppliants. Rousseau and his successors have misled us and our brother contemporaries. When the nature of authority is misconceived, then the charismatic, too, is misconceived[109] as a politicized criminal. As for those who send millions to their death, mainly to feed their insatiable egos: surely death is too easy a punishment for their crimes. Perhaps modern technology can devise a rehabilitative apparatus which would inscribe the interdicts upon their bodies, so deeply that never again would they fail to understand that doing what is not to be done means death. Only when we live willingly, privileged in our knowledge, under a science of limits, have we a chance of living less harmful lives, protected from the ultimate danger: transgressive thrusts of our own invention, so inventive that they overcome our god-given, animal sense of danger.

I doubt that, in the foreseeable future, a culture of militant, opposing truths can be reorganized to teach again fear of and in Law—and respect for presiding presences.[110] To welcome, as right

---

108. A problem for psychiatry, in this theoretical context, is the fantasy indignation of the paranoid, that indignation suppressed along with problematic sexualized hostility toward imagined figures of real authority or, equally possible and to the same affect, real figures assigned imagined authority. Paranoia is an intellectualizing pathology of revolt against authority, the pathological side of charisma.

109. As he was during the era of the religion of criticism, from which we teachers have not yet emancipated ourselves; we believe that criticism is a superior way of life, if only we could lead it.

110. Cf., above, p. 108, and footnote 69. The task of a credal or-

and proper, a rich variety of lawful punishments takes a keen transgressive sense—which can only be installed by a rich variety of lawful punishments. But that circle has been broken. Men cannot know how guilty they are if they are not punished. To explore the possibilities of a return to lawful fear seems, therefore, a futile exercise.

Nevertheless, we may hope for a renascence of guilt. The therapeutic movement has not yet penetrated deep down into the culture class-order, but dominates only the strata at the transgressive top, the commercialized middle stratum, and the false (bohemian) bottom. Still to be entirely deconverted to transgressive 'life styles' are those masses of the less re-educated, including still churched and exquisitely moral blacks. Another reason for hope I have already noted: at all levels of the culture class-order, there continues to develop a more and more acute intolerance of pain and deprivations—even the least physical. Nietzsche noticed how sensitive we moderns are. In our not long abandoned, perhaps recoverable, justifying symbolics, life was not only full, with dangers of transgression, but also sanctified by compensatory punishments—most of them eminently merited; only grace was unmerited. Authority thus preserved its sanctity. The inner truth of an authoritative symbolic has not been completely evaginated; even those nearest the achievement of therapeutic emptiness know that if they are to insist on laying blame, it must be upon persons, not upon systems or facts.

Yet, pre-therapeutics knew that blaming persons was terribly dangerous, that the effects of any action may be double: both

---

ganization is to express this respect coherently and to inhibit the fantasy of each officer in the organization that he is its sole advocate. " 'Forgive me if my explanations seem rather incoherent. I do beg your pardon. You see, the Commandant always used to do the explaining.' " [Kafka, "In the Penal Colony," *The Penal Colony: Stories and Short Pieces* (New York, 1961), p. 196.] A likely story. Commandants never explain. It is we officers who do the explaining; that activity is our office. Kafka's officer is dead, in theory, before the story begins. Moreover, as any Freudian could explain, he must have concealed an intense disrespect for the old Commandant.

good and evil. It is only upon this tragic sense, of the dangers to soul inherent in any judgmental action, and not upon the endless expressional quest for the identity of self, that the interdicts may be reconstructed. The reconstruction would be facilitated by our lower thresholds of sensitivity to pain; we can also lower the threshold of fear, of those punishments by which the interdicts are recognized in their right and proper authority, withal its dangers, which must be hedged in by the severest interdicts.[111]

This is only to repeat what was once generally known: that any authority worthy of being so called is right and proper. All crimes are against authority—or they are not crimes. Rehabilitate authority: that is the one and only way to solve the problem of crime. All else is academic profit-taking and schwärmerei. 'Decriminalization' in the law masks an attack on authority. The therapeutic movement halted, a science and art of limits well begun,[112] there would be some hope for a society in which art and science are clearly distinguished from, and related to, other actions.

Any revival of authority from the outside carries a special danger, of which I am quite keenly aware and to which I refer, above and below, in my remarks on hedging in political authority by the severest interdicts: punishment must always be an instrument of those in power, as if so to establish their authority. No one, in theory or practice, has been able to separate punishment from power, on the one hand, or power from its attempts to create self-justifications, on the other. Nevertheless, power and authority are never the same; power is always enacted in a way that causes authority to react. There is an unresolvable tension

111. Note, again, how we scientists have lost knowledge by which our 'primitive' predecessors were held; we re-educated ones—we are the 'culturally deprived.'

112. There are beginnings, nowadays, although these are hard to recognize: as the performance of music becomes more and more restricted to professionals, there are fewer amateurs to endure the risks of vulgar readings of, for example, the Kreutzer sonata. We are increasingly spared the silliness of romantic adulteries and neurotic revenges. Sexuality thus again desentimentalized, the next step could be to return it under interdictory rule.

between power and authority that is only concealed by the modern concept of legitimation.

To the powers that be who are inward enough still to want authority (not their own) reconstructed: consider eliminating the prison system entirely; instead, substitute an ordeal of physical punishment—applied most strictly and first of all to transgressing officers of the established political and economic order. The supervision of such punishments would again become the right and duty of a would-be ruling class. A true ruling class, one deriving from a presiding presence, seems always improbable, for it would be obliged to use its authority against itself. On the other hand, revolution does not occur except as the aftereffect of a collapse of authority at the top of the social order. Power can be destroyed by another power. But no power, as such, acquires authority. The expression of power, as such, is terror—transgressiveness entirely free from its interdictory predicate.

The price of power justified is complete submission of the powerful to an authority that is not in their service. Reciprocally, the greatest satisfactions of the interdicts and their godheads are in punishments of the powerful. Politicians should always be treated as they once were, as putative criminals, and carefully guarded against, because the power they seek, in expropriating the apparatus of the state, is the highest reach of criminality. It is because the powerful themselves are not obliged to be fearful enough of an authority that is not their own that we cannot be hopeful enough for the general decline of crime.

Instill fear in the powerful; the powerless will follow and so revive the constitution of authority. Do not ask me how otherwise a new lawfulness can be established, specially in our commercial culture, where every transgression is a transaction; I do not know how else the crooked can be made straight except they are straitened. Fear is not a bad teacher of certain elemental lessons. Love comes after law. Positive acts are prepared by negative commandments. The modern notion that a victim has no rights represents the return of the most primitive iniquity, a worship of he who does and a contempt of he who is done to. That is the popular name of the political game: doing and not being done to. Gala, for example, plays the game consummately well; he knows when and how to play by none of the rules. Why should he? He takes none of the rules personally.

For those increasing numbers, and for their expert counters, who do not take the rules personally enough to be kept by them, we teachers shall have to reconsider, at a length greater than I can manage here, theories of punishment and its procedures. A theory of punishment should have as its aim the recovery of a missing knowledge of true guilt. Is it time to reinstate the principle that guilt is never to be doubted? No matter how great our technological capacity to produce comfort, the higher knowledge is of how to create a greater, constraining inner discomfort confident in its teaching of self-limit. In such a theory of punishment, which our ancestors understood and we seek to forget, punishment becomes retributive where it fails to be inhibitive. The modern concept of deterrence conflates retributive and inhibitive motifs to the detriment of both. The movement away from punishment is completed in modern theories of rehabilitation; that completeness expresses the triumph of false guilt, an inversion of right order. The latest cause of the re-educated, for the rehabilitation of criminals rather than their punishment, is a subversive ignorance of the cultural law: that there is no crime without punishment.

To know what is not to be done, specially for those who do what-is-not, punishment should be so administered that it generates guilt. Should that sense fail, then at least the punishment should support, by transfer, the order of interdicts codified in law. Retribution should reward those who forbear doing what is not to be done, as much as it is the punishment of those who have not tolerated that forbearance. Atonement cannot be transferred to The System without destroying it in the very measure of transfer. Those who forbear doing what is not to be done cannot be held responsible for those who do; this shift in responsibility constitutes the modern criminological rationalization of false guilt. That shift has gone too far, to the point where victims are treated dismissively, as provoking agents of the crimes against themselves. Original sin, too, emerges at the end of a civilization, shifting from the doer of what is not to be done (he may be a policeman or a street predator), to he who is done to, representative, in his non-doing, of the interdicts, whether in the torture chambers of the regime, or in the erotic arenas Don Juans stake out for their permanently revolutionary acts. Freedom has come to mean a break through the inhibiting civilities characteristic of high culture.

We theorists may wish to consider, in our appointed defense of high culture, a strategically 'primitive' use of powerfully remissive motifs, which invariably make their way back into any high culture. For example, we might encourage a scientific campaign to shut down all prisons except for those housing criminals waiting capital punishments. Executions might then be made public; this public offering to the interdicts could constitute a grand remissive occasion at which ordinary, less scientific members of the public would celebrate the terrible nearness of every interdict to its transgression. Then, after this most grand and oldest theatre, social scientists (selected by a National Commission for Social Defense) could display their criticisms of the show on televised talkathons offering ritual analyses of the 'causes' behind both happenings, the crime and its punishment. In prime time, as if to justify what has just happened, everything would be made understandable because nothing had been forgiven. The post-mortem television show would have its own ritual limit, however. No publicity.[113] Our capital-criminal's name is never to be mentioned, neither before nor after punishment. His face is never to be seen; the exact nature of his crime is never to be reported; his guilt is to be inferred, by the public, from his punishment.

It may be objected that punishment will not deter the psychopath who seeks punishment. Of course not; for psychopaths, the National Commission will know how to offer punishment free of charge, before *Family/Society* induces commitment to the crime. Further, it may be objected that severe executions of an interdict will encourage transgressive behavior by vicarious transfer. Of course; the interdictory-remissive motifs are not discrete fields of

---

113. "The accused man's diary indicated that he considered that killing Wallace would not give him the public attention he desired. One entry in the diary read: 'They never heard of Wallace. The editors will say: "Wallace dead? Who cares? You won't get more than three minutes on network news." ' " ["Nixon 'My Prime Target,' " *Daily Telegraph* (London), August 4, 1972, p. 4.]

perception or action. So long as we dichotomize them, the moral order to which they point will elude us; the reality of supposed oppositions is as false as the guilt that follows from an unwillingness to act responsibly upon that supposition. Remembered 'as ifs' bequeath their answers to present 'why nots?'; the latter perform demoniacally without the former. Ends precede means; privileged knowledge is that which keeps the relation of ends and means precedent. Our scientists and literary lights have forgotten what is known and how long ago. How barbaric is the affect of their principled forgetting. How wrong Whitehead was about Science, which should always hesitate before it creates the predicates and pills of release from the old penalties of old acts. A forgetful science—Kierkegaard called it "curiosity"—is a menace to civilization.

You bring me good news of what, I hope, is the latest:

> There are many of us, one finds especially many in the universities,[114] particularly among students, who find themselves very uncomfortable in this kind of a universe and find that they don't want to acquiesce in the kind of condition that you speak of. What is open to these people as a means of response? What ought to replace, for example, forms of personal unruliness, delinquency, futile ethical protest of one sort or another? Is there anything that people who feel compelled to express themselves in that way can do?

To explore your question, I must remind you of how culture and politics intersect. Culture articulates polar motifs, interdictory and transgressive. Keep in mind what culture does when you inquire what is the alternative to the student counterculture. I repeat what I have said often to others: immediately behind the hippies are

---

114. Let us not exaggerate the rotating reality of the numbers involved in our discontent. Of the eight and one-half million students, we are talking about some thousands, a vanguard. Sociologically more important than their numbers is that they are our own protected children, who expect to dominate and arrange their own destinies as their parents have arranged that their children dominate them.

the thugs. They occupy the remissive space opened up by the hippies, deepening it from an aesthetic into a politics. The self-absorbed therapy of the hippies clears the way for the mass-murder therapy of the thugs. Russia's revolutionary students gave way to technically trained Genghis Khans with bugging devices. Our American Nechayevs with acid will have no more civil successors; transgressive succeeds remissive. Students can bring us no hope at all until the protest style, as Love of Humanity and Power to The People, is seen through. With the vision of this horror, we will see in true light the craven aping and interminable apologies for the transgressive types at the bottom: the perverts, the underclass, all those who can do no wrong because they have been wronged. This is no Christening movement; the early Christians did not ape the publicans and sinners they tried to save.

What happened was bad enough. The Christian mystery-cult evolved into the most terrible rationalizing of transgressiveness ever to curse our culture. Nietzsche knew that Christendom's love was a covert form of making war on culture in any form, an expression of the most terrible hatred, envy, revenge. How sad that Nietzsche remained Christian enough to blame the proud, elitist culture of Israel for this curse, derived, not from Hellenism, but from ex-Jewry. Jew-hatred remains the deepest transgressive motif of Christian Love—and, in succession, of Western organizations of Humanity, including the Marxist. This terrible hatred was directed at the highest, the noblest aspects of human achievement: it challenged the order of reverence and justice. Nothings would be instant everythings by imposing a love that was entirely mendacious.

Nietzsche might have learned more than he did from the case of *Saul/Paul*, that ultimately concerned, universalizing democrat of spirituality, genius taking its supreme form as an apostle, credal organizer, founding church-father and still enemy-in-chief of the Jews. Nietzsche missed the point that Jew-hatred rests its case on non-Jewish Jews; they were non-Jewish Jews who first confirmed to the world at large a fundamental change in the classical pattern of hatred, Rome against Jerusalem. It was in rejecting their very own messiah that Israel became proud, stiff-necked, a distancing people.

For persisting in their interdictory-remissive way—despite political defeat and amidst the inducements of a more entertaining culture—the Jews were despised by the ancient Romans, who were the most political of people and knew, therefore, how to use culture as well as religion politically. There was something different, however, about the early Christian animus against the Jews. The subject of the Christian cultus was himself a non-Jewish Jew, a victory in particular over every particularity, beginning (and ending) with the particularity of the Jews. In his victory, Jesus represented the defeat of the Jews in their particularity, as Jews; this is very different from representing the defeated Jews. (Cf., the Nietzschean symbolic.) On the contrary, all that a Jew now needed to do in order to escape his defeat was to join in the victory cult of the non-Jewish Jew. What a tempting model, both of humiliation and of deceitful escapes from humiliation. Equally deceitful: assertions of Jewish 'faith' as a matter of pride in a resistance at least as necessary to the cultus as to the Jews themselves. The humiliation of Jesus went no further, according to the Christian cultus, than the irony of his sovereignty over the Jews, who had rejected Him. 'King of the Jews' intended to deprive the Jews of their spiritual kingdom. In his millennial resistance to that deprivation, the Jew became a negative and implicit performer of the positive and explicit cult. By whatever they appeared to do, the humiliation of the Jews was deepened. According to the Christian symbolic, which Romans learned to understand well enough, the Jews had not only lost; more important, as Jews, they could never win. Who can bear to be on the side of a loser as perpetual as history itself? All the world hates a loser or, at best, condescends to him. To be a loser does not imply defeat in the simple sense, during every round of history; rather, it implies having to walk through history as if on eggs. The early Christian Jew-hatred, integral to *Saul/Paul's* victory over the 'Judaizers,' expresses a fundamental egalitarian Christian rancor against the internal distancing symbolic of the chosen people and, at its full transgressive implication, against the Christ of the ex-Jews and their democratically accepted cult-followers. It is in this sense that faith in Christ—and the organization of that faith—is ineluctably anti-Jewish.

Western messianic movements toward universal equality, now

171

psychologized as a closeness of self-recognizers, share in this impression of Israel as a distancing people. The impression cannot be altogether false. As a boy, I could still see the distancing at work in my elders. Of course, I am too thoroughly re-educated to feel distant from anybody; that feeling would be downright unloving, I suppose. Love, like hate, demands the closing of distances. How that descendant of rabbis, Dr. Marx, would have growled at this end-result of socialism psychologized, the democracy of love. Nietzsche, too, despite his residual Christian sentimentalism, tried to make war on love and its traumata. Judged by the results specially among our eroticized propertied classes, Nietzsche failed miserably; the famous refusal to sacrifice intellect has been recruited into the cat house of intellect. But we must continue to make war on this politicized eroticism—on all the oppressions of liberties taken with humane distances that give voice to the totalitarian democracy of emotions and dictate the most preposterous of all egalitarian positions: the equality of results. That way lies principled irreverence and the gross injustice of an equal treatment of unequals.

Who is to teach our students that reverence and justice they should have sucked with their mother's milk, and heard at their father's feet, long before they reach us? Moreover, we ourselves—many of us in the academy—have long since forgotten our main purpose is to teach: strictly to transmit what is already known, not as a sideline of our entrepreneurial R & D or as gurus of Change. We are neither geniuses nor apostles. We should be highly trained masters of the culture, in its variety of special respects. Unless we ourselves achieve this mastery, the chain of intellect cannot be forged in varieties of respect for unequals. How can we expect true disciples, in real disciplines, when we ourselves have never met a master, but only office managers and more or less celebrated critics of whatever might be construed as reverence? (Meanwhile, justice is coupled with irreverence.) We have taken too seriously the superiority of all disestablishments; nothing entitles us to this belief in unbelief—and yet this is what we teach; a transgressive mystique under various names: *critical, original, liberating, innovative, fulfilling, christening, actualizing, ad infinitum; reflexive* is the latest.

Am I hanging back again? Have I missed the very latest name? This is what comes of listening mainly to Haydn. I shall never get past Haydn. Even so, for me, the *Hammerklavier* long has been the latest. I am still not far into it, in any of its available interpretations. This is a private matter. I am proud of my captivity in this Beethoven. He says what there is to say to me. But I cannot be sure that there is anything connected with him, or with other masters of my privacy, in what I have to say to you. That uncertainty is important, for my craft is intended merely for chainmaking. The one thing that worries me is how we moderns have contrived to lose our chains, not least by our too easily recognized talents for garlanding them. If ever I were to write a theory of culture, it would be called by one of the two following names, perhaps both: 1) *What Is Not To Be Done*; 2) *The Garland and The Chain*. It would be a down-to-earth, practical, help-hinting type book, for the Domestic Science market. I would expect big sales in the American How-To and Interior Decor markets. For those markets, what do you think of an illustrated edition? I would call it *How Not To Garland Chains*. Let me know if you can think of a snappier title.

Plato, Rousseau and Marx were three master-makers of chain images. They are dead now; nothing can bring them alive, except through our minds, in further makings of links for the chain of feeling intellect. Now, in authoritative relations of master and disciple, first our students and then we teachers who would try to have them follow us, will have to learn how to express ourselves less; we shall have to be more reserved about our protests and breakthroughs. The first thing is not to pretend either science or religion when we are playing politics. Pretend religions and unlimited sciences make the most transgressive politics.

Under the unjustified entitlements of pretend religions, all world-accepting, even the revolutionary chain-breakers (Marx was the last) are obsolete; nothing remains for them to break. The Marxist revolutionary was a sober, confident analyst of the movement of History; that movement was to have a happy ending —we know with what dreadful consequences. At the end of the Marxist road, a creature of its movement: *Lenin/Stalin.* Do not underestimate the still-recent shock of recognizing where these tough-minded, disciplined, elaborately studied and argued expectations of History led.

Beyond the irrationalizing end of *that* rationalizing road, in "The Plowman," a significant number of would-be revolutionaries have determined to be more erratic, bohemians rather than research-workers in The Movement, more engaged in demo-therapy than in practical exegeses of class conflict. Our students try acting out, in an exemplary way, all manner of freedoms; this is the behavior of therapeutics, who are everything except determined competitors for control of the machinery of politics; the powers that be have nothing to fear from therapeutics. Our first task, as specialists in the perpetuation of the feeling intellect, is to resist the twists and turns of all the illiterate body-English that passes for expressive behavior, whether or not it is directly political, among our students. The worst thing is that our students refuse to recognize the totalitarian implications of their endless expressional questioning: displaced from art into life, the failed artist becomes a successful tyrant. It has happened, although not yet here.

For less self-expression, and toward a highly personal objective discipline of masters and disciples, there would be the learning of respect for, in knowledge of, what has already happened—an acute memory of the suffering that is past, passing and to come—so to inhibit ourselves before all new posturings of sincerity, particularly in its twin complicities of self-justification and power-seeking. To revive this inhibiting art of memory, toward an excess of caution about new worlds and freer feelings, implies no condescending historicism. An historical memory of truth opposes historicism.

Because they are so young (and because there are too few among us willing to risk the superiority of being old), the radically contemporary world catches our students in their own crude, sensual music. The most celebrated Pop groups, beginning with the Beatles and climaxing in the Rolling Stones, have projected an image of youth without a past. Indeed, Pop, as 'youth culture,' has nothing whatever to do with the ancient cultures of the populace. Rather, Pop is a seeking after the bizarre, including imitations of some distant present (e.g., Hindu or Amerindian) with which to break through established but failing interdicts. Pop goes The Revolution. The cult of youth, Pop, is whatever can oppose tradition. Rolling Stones gather no moss; I assume that is what the name intends, and, moreover, that the qualities of the group are associated with their name. Are we expected to drop totemic meanings completely? This, too, is impossible, as the culture of the young reminds us.

What is the 'culture' of the young? Music always signifies. Can you listen closely and with respect to the orgiastic beats of the music of the young? Even they cannot. That is the kind of deafening noise that will muffle the cries from electronic torture chambers. Against both cultural orgiasts and electronic technicians of power we must create quiet and play the graceful music of civil respect. Then and only then will humane distances be achieved between real individuals in a just social order. Love should be as Purcell's Dido sings it, so beautifully: "Remember me. Forget my Fate."

To achieve humane distances among sovereign selves: that must be the aim of our study, rather than position-taking on interminably shifting struggles for power. Let position-taking be the discipline of parties, not of universities. We may insist again upon what we love and fear to know: what we are not. The further interpreting of that privileged knowledge may help save us from becoming free, as if gods. A renascence of this knowledge might slow the pace of our lives. Our barbaric innovators would have to run the gauntlet of deeply informed objections to the carrying-out of their experiments.

I am aware that these intimations of an alternative future appear entirely negative. It is not in my gift to be positive. If understanding is the All we are after, then our thoughts are better expressed in some show of irony; otherwise our thoughts grow penal. What on earth would you do if I tried to position you? Suppose it were in my gift to be positive? What is it you might then rightly expect me to demand of you? In its expressions, such a gift would be tantamount to making fresh interdictory demands upon you. Then, would I not appear to be against you? Without irony, a gifted theorist must find those who are not for him are against him. I prefer neutralists. I am, as you see, a neutralist myself. But suppose I said, straight out: "Give up (for me, if not to me) your name, your money, your wife." Of course, not being an interdictory figure, I can say no such things. Having no authority, I ask you to give up nothing. Having no power, I can do nothing to you. I am meaningless, in this double sense, because my meanings are not decisive; I assume they will sell, modestly, in the Meanings market. If anyone among our colleagues dared not to be meaningless, for something other than the Meanings market, a *leader/teacher*, decisive first of all for himself, then such a person could only teach those meanings in continuities that are at once personal and commanding. Let me know if you hear of such a person. I would be interested; it could lead to a book. In our books or outside the tense friendships of masters and disciples, in what is now unnamed,[115] e.g., 'network relations,' there is the risk

---

115. Often, it appears, disciples, in their movement toward credal organization, are given (or fake) the name of the master. There is an inherent contradiction in eponymics attached to certain movements— e.g., Marxist, Maoist, any movement that aspires to be scientific. Equally contradictory: therapeutic movements named after some great emancipator; the 'after' contradicts the emancipation.

At the modern convergence of masters and rather rich disciples, attracting special kinds of professionals referred to earlier,[a] drawn from ex-Jews,[b] leading to the mastery of the One[c] in the name of The People,[d] I think you may want to share in the insightfulness of V. S. Naipaul, seeing what there was to be seen in the Argentine. Naipaul refers to his meeting with young Argentinean revolutionaries:

> These lawyers had been represented to me as a group working for "civil rights." They were young, stylishly dressed, and they were meeting that morning to draft a petition against torture. The top-floor flat was scruffy and bare; visitors were scrutinised through the peep-hole; everybody whispered; and there was a lot of cigarette smoke. Intrigue, danger. But one of the lawyers was diverted by my invitation to lunch, and at lunch—he was a hearty and expensive eater—he made it clear that the torture they were protesting against wasn't to be confused with the torture in Perón's time.

---

[a] See, e.g., p. 56, footnote 27.

[b] See, e.g., p. 75, footnote 44, further, p. 78, footnote 47; p. 138, *et pass.* Jewry suffers, internally, from an overdose of re-education.

[c] See, e.g., p. 187, *et pass.*

[d] See, e.g., p.148, *et pass.*

of appealing to the interdicts in a way that expresses disrespect for the precise manner in which they must be given—and, moreover, supervised. It is bad enough that, in response to the rationalization of knowledge and belief, we, in the nascent opposition, are reduced

---

He said: "When justice is the justice of the people men sometimes commit excesses. But in the final analysis the important thing is that justice should be done in the name of the people." Who were the enemies of the people? His response was tabulated and swift. "American imperialism. And its native allies. The oligarchy, the dependent bourgeoisie, Zionism, and the 'sepoy' left. By sepoys we mean the Communist Party and socialism in general." It seemed a comprehensive list. Who were the Perónists? "Perónism is a revolutionary national movement. There is a great difference between a movement and party. We are not Stalinists, and a Perónist is anyone who calls himself a Perónist and acts like a Perónist."

The lawyer, for all his anti-Jewish feeling, was a Jew; and he came of an anti-Perónist middle-class family. In 1970 he had met Perón in Madrid, and he had been dazzled; his voice shook when he quoted Perón's words. He had said to Perón, "General, why don't you declare war on the régime and then put yourself at the head of all the true Perónists?" Perón replied: "I am the conductor of a national movement. I have to conduct the whole movement, in its totality."

"There are no internal enemies," the trade union leader said, with a smile. But at the same time he thought that torture would continue in Argentina. "A world without torture is an ideal world." And there was torture and torture. *"Depende de quién sea torturado.* It depends on who is tortured. An evildoer, that's all right. But a man who's trying to save the country—that's something else. Torture isn't only the electric prod, you know. Poverty is torture, frustration is torture." He was urbane; I had been told he was the most intellectual of the Perónist trade union leaders. He had been punctual; his office was uncluttered and neat; on his desk, below glass, there was a large photograph of the young Perón.

"Violence, in the hands of the people, isn't violence: it is justice." This statement of Perón's was printed on the front page of a recent issue of *Fe,* a Perónist paper. So, in sinister mimicry, the south twists the revolutionary jargon of the north. Where jargon turns living issues into abstractions ("Torture will disappear in Argentina," the Trotskyite said, "only with a workers' government and the downfall of the bourgeoisie"), and where jargon ends by competing with jargon, people don't have causes. They only have enemies; only the enemies are real. [V. S. Naipaul, "The King Over the Water," *Sunday Times* (London), August 6, 1972, p. 30.]

to views and games of position-taking. A culture of truth cannot be created out of views and the broadcast of positions. Broadcasts belong to the therapeutic anti-culture. Our task is to hold out, in our academic enclaves, for those students to find who seek a slower understanding.

We are not defeated; we are only out-numbered by our principal investigators. Our strategy should be to strengthen our enclaves; prepare to receive refugees from the cultureless society— those who are not actively against us. Those refugees wander all around us. How sad that there are so few enclaves prepared to receive them: sad, because an academic should know how to procrastinate, if not for his own, then for the sake of his students, against both enemies: power technicians and movement therapists. Along with our wasp nerve, we have lost our Jewish patience, our gift for procrastination, our modesty before problems and their solutions. No wonder our students raise tumults; they have been promised too many new earths. Such promises are no longer naively utopian. In the quick turnover of solutions is the discipline of a cultureless society, and overhead profit for the problem-solvers.

You quote the following passage and ask me what I intended by my metaphors of speed and locomotion:

> Psychological man may be going nowhere, but he aims to achieve a certain speed and certainty in going. Like his predecessor, the man of the market economy, he understands morality as that which is conducive to increased activity. The important thing is to keep going.

I was writing of the re-educated classes, who have the illusion they know something when they ape their guru, or know where to go to catch up on some data or retool some expertise. Until we reach a proper distance from gurus and technicians, charisma and data-retrieval, culture cannot reassert its slowing sovereignty over our actions.

Recall that to a therapeutic, the terminal sin is immobility itself, the one virtue is growth, a metaphor of upward mobility. If he keeps growing upward, then a man becomes not a god but a golem. To be self-disciplined is to achieve modesty. Disciplines

178

against immodesty merge into authority; the intellectual form of disciplines against immodesty is interpretative repetition. Interpretative repetition cannot become a therapeutic device, to keep the therapeutic going, for the aim of this discipline is the right recognition of authority, which is always interdictory, not its dissolution, which is always transgressive. Therapeutic interpretations aim at dissolutions of authority. The therapist is not a teacher nor his patient a student. I expect that, in their community, Jake and the Doctor will exchange roles—more than once. Jake was never a disciple because the Doctor was never a master.

In a cultureless society of role-changers (now misunderstanding themselves as identity-seekers), sexuality was bound to become the first object of therapy. Shorn of authority—more precisely, as love without authority—sexuality becomes movement freed of inhibitions limiting it to this position or that, this purpose or that. Here again we can observe why cultural struggle must occur so fiercely over the endless expressional quest in its sexual form;[116] the transgressive sense had to be broken first in the erotic

---

116. One little example of this cultural struggle: the issue of celibacy in the Roman church. Alas, the leaders of the church appear on the verge of losing their minds; none I have read appears to know what celibacy means. Nor are the increasing number of Roman heresiarchs more knowing; they appear on the opposite side from their bishops, but without understanding their role in breaking what remains of the transgressive sense long institutionalized in the erotic sphere so difficult to separate from their priesthood. Are you surprised at the know-nothingness of the Romans? The Roman hierarchs give no evidence that they understand, to this day, what was at stake in Dr. Luther's marriage to Katherine von Bora. In one letter to a *friend/ disciple*, an "honored and dear doctor and friend," a married man, John Rühel, Luther writes (4 May 1525):

> I almost believe that I am the cause that the devil can do such things in the world, whereby God punishes it. Well, if I ever get home I will meet my death with God's aid, and await my new masters, the murderers and robbers who tell me they will harm no one. Highway robbers always say the same: "I will do you no harm, but give me all you have or you shall die." Beautiful innocence! How fairly the devil decks himself and his murderers! Before I would yield and say what they want, I would lose my head a hundred times, God granting me his

sphere. Only then, with sexuality liberated, in life no less than in literature, can there develop a cultureless society. Since the gods of love (title them 'Eros,' 'Jesus,' any name, old or new, you care

---

grace. If I can do it before I die, I will yet take my Katie to wife to spite the devil, when I hear that they are after me. [See, further, Preserved Smith, *The Life and Letters of Martin Luther* (London, 1911), p. 162.]

Erikson does not miss the irony of ex-priest Luther's marriage—and after marriage, his acquisition, for his personal use, of the Augustinian monastery in Wittenberg. Erikson refers to the property, shared with Luther by his wife, a former nun, and their children, as an "ironic architectural setting" for the first Lutheran parsonage. Erikson makes Luther over into the man who broke through "the hypertrophy of the negative conscience" [Erik H. Erikson, *Young Man Luther* (New York, 1958), p. 195] in Western culture, an "historical force in Ranke's sense; that is, 'a moral energy . . . which dares to penetrate the world in free activity' " [*ibid.*, p. 233]. 'Moral energy' and 'free activity' are not precise enough. Put in the context of his marriage, that new security Luther used against certain credal organizations, Luther's activity seems far from 'free.' Within that security he could joke about bigamy and other impossibilities. If, as Erikson says, Luther is the "prototype of a new man, husband and father" [*ibid.*, p. 250], then we know there is a questionable sentimentality in Erikson's immediate pairing of Luther with More, as "another such man" [*ibid.*]. It is of the utmost significance that the new man, family man, will not die a martyr. Was this the right man—at once family man and penetrator of the world in free activity? How in hell was this 'right man' chosen? Erikson's mighty attempt to tell us fails because he takes Luther's side. Of the two right men, Luther and More, who is the more ironical figure? An examination question: analyze and compare Luther and More—and that third right man, Erasmus—their thoughts and actions in the erotic sphere. Of course, for years, I have collected notes for an examining book about them. Sometimes I think of combining these with my fragments on the erotic in SK. That would make a book of higher price. But, in these aging fragments, I resist the role of author in search of a book. That role is almost universal among the re-educated. Without authority, it is natural that we become authors. No one of my acquaintance is not writing at least one book. 'Publish or perish' has to do with the question of authority.

Further on the questionable moral energy which has dared to pene-

to use) no longer persist, there is one act our contemporary impersonators of love can decline to perform: i.e., say *No* to all desublimating symbolics of sexuality and its perversions. Here

---

trate the world in free activity, see the publications of an interesting symbolist in the Lutheran style, Paul Tillich; in particular his chapter "The [Heideggerian] Transmoral Conscience" [Paul Tillich, *The Protestant Era*, trans. James Luther Adams (Chicago, 1948), pp. 136-149]. "It is Luther who derives a new concept of conscience from the experience of justification through faith. . . . Luther's experience grew out of the monastic scrutiny of conscience and the threat of ultimate judgment, which he felt in its full depth and horror. Experiences like these he called *Anfechtungen*, that is, 'tempting attacks,' stemming from Satan as a tool of the divine wrath. These attacks are the most terrible thing a human being may experience. They create an incredible *Angst* ('dread'), a feeling of being inclosed in a narrow place from which there is no escape. (*Angst*, [Luther] rightly points out, is derived from *angustiae*, 'narrows.')" Yes, but: given Tillich's ending Lutheran symbolic, his completion of the Schleiermachian psychologizing in the Protestant tradition, and his own ambiguous relations to both political and sexvolution, Tillich, like Erikson, fails to see the nearness, for Luther, between his 'tempting attacks' and his resort to his Katie; the security of Luther's marriage, to spite the devil, being a family man, generates a subtle demonry, juxtaposed unconsciously by Luther in the letter quoted above. Helped by the work of Tillich, Erikson and others, we have more to learn about the breakthrough of "the hypertrophy of the negative conscience," the daring penetrations of the world in the free activities of family men, husbands and fathers. There are narrowing inner spaces yet to be explored in the concept of an existential "transmoral conscience" which "has no special demands; it speaks to us in the 'mode of silence.' It tells us only to act and to become guilty by acting, for every action is unscrupulous." What a terrible narrowing to declare that "existence as such is guilty." Equally narrowing: the doctrine that "we *must* act, and the attitude in which we *can* act is 'resoluteness.' Resoluteness transcends the moral conscience, its arguments and prohibitions." Tillich concludes, rather blandly, hands folded, as if delivering a lecture: "The way from Luther's to Heidegger's idea of a transmoral conscience was a dangerous one" [*ibid.*, p. 148]. Tillich does consider the open possibility, of guiltlessness, but slides out of the narrows with the standard ease. "*The good, transmoral conscience consists in the acceptance of the bad, moral conscience*" [*ibid.*, Tillich's

181

again are the conceptual predicates for understanding the necessity of censorship.[117]

A critical theory of desublimation conceals the rising social reality of perversion. Any doctrine of desublimated action must be, in its early stages, a symbolic of perversion: a stated disorder of desire. That disorder then becomes specially significant as transgressive behavior. Perversions do not immediately displace right order. A certain parallel development takes place: the criticism assumes it will not take effect, that the normative remains dominant. What was normative remains normative; criticism depends upon the dominance of what it criticizes—that is the key to liberalism. As Scheler remarked of the early stages of a developing perversion: "Loathsome foods still arouse loathing." It took me, for example, years of trying not to feel more than slightly ill at eating lobster and other crustaceans, or horse-steak. Only later does feeling, Scheler continues, reversing the right conceptual order, "gradually follow the impulse." Surely our 'deviants' require sociological, equally with psychiatric, analysis. Some contemporary perverts are bound to be, I think, pietistic moderns, testing their liberality. They have been taught to put their bodies on the line. Perversion becomes the culturally determined form of 'sincerity.'

---

italics]. *Acceptance*, indeed. I shall return to this acceptance world of the existentialists near the end (pp. 212-215). In the end, it was Kierkegaard who said the last word, to himself, on Luther, I think. The "closer I examine Luther the more convinced do I become that he was muddle-headed. It is a comfortable kind of reforming which consists in throwing off burdens and making life easier—that is an easy way of getting one's friends to help. True reforming always means to make life more difficult, to lay on burdens; and the true reformer is therefore always put to death as though he were the enemy of mankind" [*Journals, op. cit.*, No. 889, 1849, p. 298].

117. Cf., above, footnote 103, pp. 157-159. Further towards a theory of censorship, and for the quotations following in the next paragraph, on perversion, see Max Scheler, *Ressentiment*, ed. Lewis A. Coser; trans. W. W. Holdheim (New York, 1961), pp. 59-60 *et pass*. Note what a solid Jew-basher was our second sociological Max, Jewish mothered, Protestant fathered, sometime Catholic.

A displacement of right order by perversion occurs as transgressive behavior is praised as the enactment of a theory critical of all orders in their authority. Transgressive behavior is made the basis of an attack on right order; it is in its liberality that criticism of right order parodies, by paralleling, the early developmental stage of a perversion. Merged with endlessly critical theory, transgressive action then may establish its dominance over interdicts which are integral only to the first stage, where perversions are still recognized as perverse, rather than themselves enacted as if beyond criticism.

Our critical theorists teach their students, in one mystique or another, flesh. Like everything else, flesh must be taught—and, nowadays, as Revolution or in whatever mystique, constituting criticism itself, it is taught as if beyond criticism. Being thought culpable, spirit is untaught; the best spirit can hope for is benign neglect. Neglected, spirit may steal back, behind us; we may be caught again, before we can become watchers of ourselves in action. You see how the most forlorn idea generates hope.

In its variable mystiques, flesh has become the exemplary expression of timelessness, an ahistorical world. But, as a teaching, flesh is not beyond interdictory analysis: taught, in all its expressive varieties, flesh amounts to erotic *sado/masochistic* activism. Go where this action is, in any of our cities, and you will step straight into the enormity of the present. In our city,[118] Man and Woman, in particular so far as they have been re-educated, cry that they have been banished out of the garden and try to strip down to what they consider flesh, as if in protest against their banishment and to mimic what they think life must be like in the garden. Yet they remain banished, even as they deny meaning to the banishment as the myth of a failing symbolic. The significance of the banishment escapes them, for, in that banishment from the garden, God clothed them, and so protected them. I have tried to say, earlier,[119] that to remain alive, as humans, we are required to dress and that there is no dress without memory of how our

---

118. To call our city 'secular' is another of those forlorn ideas; worse, it is designed to generate false guilt.

119. Cf., above, on dress and undress, p. 98.

ancestors dressed. Adornment, the dressing up of existence, is inseparable from historical memory.

By this page in the book, I hope 'radical contemporaneity' will carry for you some precision of theoretical effort. One implication of our flesh mystiques is that the famous 'transvaluation of all values' has had its American climax as a 'valuation of all sexuality.' Nothing is perverse. What, in a repressive symbolic, might be called perverse, becomes flesh dominant in its transiency. We think nothing, if we are properly re-educated, of this public oversexualization; how can we mind anything when the aim of that oversexualization is precisely to make the private parts so public that we will mind nothing? Minding is not a spectator sport, and impossible to televise; not minding, in action, is precisely the opposite: viewable.

Do not underestimate the parallel implicit in the new technology of vision and the new evaginations of Western reticence. The current public gush of direct and unconcealed sexual and defecatory images dissolve humane subtlety and, in time, will dissolve the indirections of civility as well as simplicity of manner. Already, I hear the matrons using locker-room language liberally at their dinner tables—but not at my dinner table. Note, I refer here not to the speech acts of the uneducated, but to those of the re-educated. How crudely inarticulate the re-educated are becoming: they talk like their children. 'Like Wow!' seems the most refined concept current in our more spacious homes. Mystifiers of flesh, armed with some new anti-god term, such as 'desublimation,' point to transgressive behavior for relief from spirit; who among the re-educated does not understand how to raise a therapeutic affect? Transiency and liberation: the mergence of these flesh mystiques implies the metamorphosis to which I have referred earlier, public *sexuality/violence*.

In contrast, the mystics of our spiritualizing past—not only Jewish and Christian, but in other symbolics—experienced their eternal moments of transiency in the interdictory mode and never to therapeutic affect. Among Western mystics, there was no nonsense about getting high. Experienced timelessness was any-

184

thing but a radical contemporaneity; that latter idea rejects the authority of the past, which mysticism accepts. No principled forgetfulness violated the mind of the mystic. Rather, experienced timelessness constituted a refinement of the most exquisite minding, prepared in long and patient disciplines of contemplation.

Activists cannot be, at the same time, contemplatives. Yet, when the interdicts have achieved full supremacy, a release of limiting action may occur, as in the case of St. Theresa or St. Francis. Such releases cannot be into what used to be called 'temptation.' Rather, the releasing activity that follows upon interdictory and repressive achievements is what Freud called 'sublimation.' It follows that 'desublimation' is a new-fangled term of mystification to cover its real meaning, i.e., temptation. I prefer the old name; it both conceals and reveals what is dismissed in the concept 'sublimation.'

The rarest achievement of the mystic, total sublimation, is momentary, a passing condition. Temptation, the most general of anti-god terms, reappears after the victory of the mystic, even as a consequence of that victory. Bonaventura is not Francis. Jesus himself is mystically experienced only as he is traditioned. A sociological study of the Spiritual Franciscans or of the Poor Men of Lyons, soon to become the sect of the Waldenses, would reveal, in holy poverty as a doctrine, much that is not Francis or Waldo. Francis was the son of a rich merchant, and Peter Waldo himself a rich merchant. The organizations under their names, which constituted a traditioning, took the experience of nouveaux riches in their true guilt. The temptations of poor boys to the interdictory life, following a few virtuosi of the guilty new rich, closing their options, may be as subtle and dangerous as the recognized worldliness they oppose. Therefore, although both Francis and Waldo thought their yoke sweet and their burden light, a yoke is a yoke; voluntary poverty, too, creates demands which, aimed against satisfaction, themselves may also subvert culture by postulating impossible satisfactions.

You cannot maintain a true tradition of breakthroughs; 'the tradition of the new' does not exist—no more than can a world of celibates. We are first born to our parents, however then we learn to dishonor them, and their satisfactions in us, so to claim some rebirth. There is no traditioning except in the re-cognized authority of the old. There is no honor without a sense of the past; every genius is indebted to it, beyond quits.

There was no 'eternal yesterday' except in generational continuities of interpretation. Towards continuance in our teaching generations, we may be helped to learn how a mystic acts: even as the gentle Francis, he is a repeating severe celebrant of the interdicts. Those "refusing to obey the commandments of God are damned: of them it has been said by the mouth of the prophet, 'Cursed are those who fall from your precepts.' "[120] (That was gentle Francis addressing the faithful; he invoked the one true terror, of obedience; neither science nor the arts has discovered another way, equally true.)

In their opposing raptures, one aiming to abolish memory, the other aiming to complete it, even for a moment, satyr and mystic become the nearest of rivals and the most irreconcilable enemies. In contemplation, the mystic does not assert any part of himself. In copulation, the satyr asserts the lower part, the most capricious and, therefore, least trustworthy. Sublimation is *from* the sublime, not *to* it. Freud got his directions reversed, I think, mainly because his theory of authority remained, to the end of his life, attached to his therapy. The object of true transference is not its resolution. The welcome terror, of a mindful obedience, can never be recognized in the masks of terrorists, freedom fighters, mouths opened wide. Contemplatives are closed-mouthed; memory survives best

---

120. [St. Francis, "A Letter To All The Faithful" (circa 1215). See Lawrence Cunningham (ed.), *Brother Francis* (New York, 1972), p. 155.] "Furthermore," writes the gentlest saint, "let us perform fruits worthy of penitence" [p. 156]. What a full guilty man, a veritable virtuoso of guilt and a civilizing man, was Francis. Of course, Francis began at the top; thanks to his father, Francis was, like Loyola and other reformers for the sake of order, a wealthy young man. Another business we could make a go of, cashing in on the razed consciousness market: Franciscan habits for women, clinging, complete with sandals. The most expensive part of the operation would be our *New Yorker* adverts. Francis held the manner of poverty in his clothes; imagine the manner of poverty made chic.

in the silences implied in every oral tradition. No one has heard the roar of the traditioned mob, except at autos-da-fé—which were controlled by a reverential hush, perhaps only the better to hear, see and smell the burning.

Beyond Christian culture, and its particular types of violence, Conrad's image of the terrorist, open-mouthed, in the character of Mr. Kurtz, is a negative teaching of what it means to be traditioned. By Marlow's evocations of him, long before he reached the man, we know that we are journeying with Marlow toward a transgressive of tremendous personality. In *Heart of Darkness* it is the blacks who are traditioned. Broch uses the same *open-mouthed/power-driving* against traditioning metamorphoses to tremendous effect in his teaching book for moderns, *The Death of Virgil*. I consider *The Death of Virgil* the most powerful prose poem of the twentieth century.

> All about him were the gulp-muzzles, the shout-muzzles, the sing-muzzles, the gape-muzzles, the opened muzzles in the closed faces, all of them were opened, torn apart, beset with teeth behind red, brown, or pallid lips, armed with tongues. . . .

Broch transports us, obedient to his vision, into the

> moment . . . which the brooding mass-beast had awaited to release its howl of joy, and now it broke loose, without pause, without end, victorious, violent, unbridled, fear-inspiring, magnificent, fawning, the mass worshiping itself in the person of the One.

Broch makes us see the metamorphosis *masses/One*, the evil to which a radical contemporaneity can turn only its blind eye.

> Evil, a tide of evil, an immense wave of unspeakable, inexpressible, incomprehensible evil seethed in the reservoir of the plaza; fifty thousand, a hundred thousand mouths yelled the evil out of themselves.

In the enormous present, there is nothing that can make that blind eye see again. Without historical memory, the eye itself becomes that of a sharpshooter. In that time of our time, as Broch imaged it for us, trans-temporally, in *The Death of Virgil*:

> The blind eye had gazed without remembrance, without remembrance . . . as if there were nothing but a desolated, desecrated present, as if, lacking a future, a past had never existed.[121]

Conrad's personifications, in *Heart of Darkness*, mind us to the emptiness of the man of power. In the vacant immediacy of Kurtz, Marlow witnesses for us a mystifier of flesh, consuming flesh. Kurtz dies erotically, of power exhaustion. Desire has fed fully on itself. Kurtz's case was moral cancer, the total consumer consumed. European man achieved the 'natural' by carrying 'civilization' to unprogressive cultures; those cultures sometimes even appeared to welcome the 'natural man' (who, often between the sixteenth and twentieth centuries, could achieve nothing back home in Europe), perhaps even allowing him a self-deification, as in the case of Kurtz. Compare this perfection of the transgressive with the mysterious restraint Marlow believes must be at work inside his black (sometime cannibal) boatmen.

The Africans who sacrificed themselves, perhaps fascinated, to Kurtz had not that resistance which is the object of Marlow's journey toward Kurtz—precisely to test himself, his resistance, against the announced fascination of Kurtz's transgressiveness. Although their defenses are entirely incomprehensible to him, Marlow sees how his boatmen endure the ultimate temptation: of survival. They will neither kill nor eat him in order to survive. The reasons for his safety with them, however precarious, remain concealed—

---

121. [Hermann Broch, *The Death of Virgil*, trans. Jean Starr Untermeyer (New York, 1945), pp. 22-34 *et pass.*] There is one other modern prose poem worth mentioning, Simone Weil's *Iliad or the Poem of Force*. Everything Simone Weil wrote was injured by her self-hatred, I think; her self-hatred appears even in her less tense writing— *Oppression and Liberty,* for example. Yet, her meditation on the struggle for power, of which war is the supreme exercise, as the substitution of means for ends, supreme evil, is without rival—except for its superior, *The Death of Virgil*.

concealed even from Conrad, godlike as he is in his authorship. Marlow is privileged to know a moment in which the interdicts stripped bare, to their form, hold—without the passage of a word, in silence. (My paternal grandfather, the aforementioned old grad of Dachau, a presence among his junior colleagues, told me of moments in that institution when the interdicts, stripped bare, held. Tell me: did you imagine I pick my theories out of a bag of books? Books are, at best, mere life analogues; do not trust to books. But how privileged we are to enjoy the concealments of the book.)

The primacy of the interdictory form is universal; each high culture sounds out this sacred music of the mind. The metamorphoses of the interdictory form, which includes its remissions, are particular and historical, therefore complex, and the primacy never out of danger. Every last primitive knows that much; yet we sophisticates, in the face of this permanent danger, maunder, often under the name of Science: of Change. The most dangerous of these maunderings was named, as if they had discovered a solution rather than intensified the danger, by Saint-Simonians, in the City of Light during the nineteenth century: "rehabilitation of the flesh." Imagine that climactic wrestle Conrad reports in *Heart of Darkness*, between Marlow and Kurtz, *rehabilitator/waster* of flesh: what style of wrestling is it? Not Greco-Roman, or comical American. I think their wrestling was a rapture, Marlow's moment of truth—and no less transient for being his truth than Kurtz's entire orgiastic life-lie.

In the moment of his lie exhausted, thwarted by Marlow, Kurtz realizes mindlessness and utters it in a remark, at once vacuous and judgmental, that is also the author's, on what it means to consume everything, himself. His self-mystique is, finally, "a cry that was no more than a breath: 'The horror! The horror!' " The horror is something Kurtz cannot name; it is the opposite of what should not be named. Carnalizers of spirit are unreconciled to whatever limits their lives. As death-dealers, they are ever at the merest beginning of their activity. However much life they consume, the result is a wasting away.

By his quest for Kurtz, the young Marlow invited his kairotic moment of resistance against sheer possibility, a moment authoritative enough to point his life in its right direction.[122] (Conrad composes Marlow explicitly in Buddha figures, at the beginning and end of the novel.) Later, in Marlow's story of himself, the pleasure of the contemplative, after the rapture of his victory over temptation, is gained in a discipline of modest recollection. Marlow's pleasure, his victory, remains concealed even in the recounting of it.

How shall we teach our flesh-led students that if joy is to come, it comes as ideas do: by stealing up on us, the entire mind prepared by understandings concealed from mind itself. The joy of being possessed by an idea is slow in coming and swift in passing. No intellectual is a regular happy fellow, and perhaps least regularly happy in his work; part of his time, an intellectual worker is at a standstill. Yet that standstill, with its fiddling, is itself part of his preparation. Tell that to your graduate students. They will have to like the life, regular only in its discipline of containment, for both short flights and long perchings—like it or leave it. Most now being positioned for it would be wise to leave off trying to lead a life of scholarly discipline and all should leave off that ruinous fantasy, the life of a free-lance intellectual; for one thing, it is a mistake to put all your ego-eggs in one basket.

Among the unhappy few, there are even fewer who can make a profession of thinking, and writing, institutionally unattached. Of course, fellow-teachers, you and I know how many among our colleagues are institutionally unattached, neither scholars nor teachers but Operators—operating out of the University base since its relatively recent catastrophic capitalization. We have been through all that. Will the University ever again be able enough to police itself and find the limit of its institutional identity? In part, the answer depends upon whether there are enough of us, with a courage understanding enough, to teach our successors what, as

122. On 'kairos,' see Paul Tillich, *The Interpretation of History,* trans. E. L. Talmey (New York, 1936), Part II, pp. 123-175, and *The Protestant Era, op. cit.,* pp. 32-51; further, Philip Rieff, "The Meaning of History and Religion in Freud's Thought," *The Journal of Religion,* XXXI, No. 2 (April 1951), 114-131.

academics, they must see that their institutions are not to do. Moreover, within their institutions, scholar-teachers will have to take responsibility for the survival of their enclaves, while the university continues its own complex struggle for survival. We teachers cannot hope to capture the modern university for our own purposes; it must remain a 'multiversity.'

Within the 'multiversity,' in our enclaves, vital as they are to the 'multiversity' itself, we have the privilege of making our flights and perchings—and the job of disciplining our more promising students to the responsibilities, personal and institutional, of that same privilege. Within our strict discipline, we are the freest of creatures—the least encumbered and the happiest. The true world of ideas will not yield to force or ambition. You cannot politic your way to an idea. Both joy and understanding are what they are, ideal existences, delicate, sudden, unannounced just before they occur but never unprepared.

Preparations can never be made in public or by seekers of prestige in this intellectualized world. You need pay no attention to the mind that always announces itself on the verge of a big breakthrough in understanding. Those announcers are making display calls; they are impresarios of the intellectual variety show; do not mistake it for the real thing. I have referred, earlier in this epistle, to the dangers of taking too seriously our pleasures in the performances and their performers. Those performers will never reveal their big breakthroughs, because they have nothing to conceal. Between the concealments and the revelations are the announcements, publicity without end, Self astir to gather in its dividend. In their public relations, our performing colleagues cannot help but become breakaway churches of one.

In view of the intense competition among breakaways for pieces of the public, the fate of the impresarios follows: to be disavowed soon after they become established. The whirligig of fashion has suffered its intellectualization at the cost of feeling intellect; without the discipline of modesty, against openmouthedness, intellect confuses itself with ego. Are not we teaching types a vain lot? Our vanities have spread, with the higher re-education, in acosmic intellectualizations of Self among the entirely unprepared, who, at most, have hearsay knowledge, unprivileged,

191

secondhand stuff, cheaply (i.e., too quickly) bought. Intellectual gossip is no *successor/functional equivalent* of an oral tradition. The nearest analogue to divine contemplation available to us, within the academy, is to bring ourselves and our students, through a moment of understanding, a fresh subtlety stable in reference. From the strength of such moments, practiced and yet unpublished except after oral traditioning, the student will know what is simple and what is 'simplistic'[123] or falsely complicated.

What of our Scientific social teachers? In lusting after Science, moral education has put itself in a methodological strait jacket. It deliberately rejects, as an obsolete practice belonging to humane letters, the discipline of personal moments in which fresh yet stable subtleties may occur. In any right discipline, study remains the practice of understanding moments, an orderly effort towards saying precisely what you mean—which is not at all the same as being obvious. This guiding practice in the precise use of language yields, as a secondary affect, acute feelings of being alone, as in a crowded field. There is no standard remedy for these *solitude/loneliness* affects. Nevertheless, the affects would be less acute if study—I refer here not merely to sociology but to any other discipline of moral education—were what it ought to be, a common pursuit. Not more 'teamwork,' thank you, or research in 'projects': that sort of communion is too obvious a parceling out of trivialities in order that the research managers can gather in their dividends.

By 'common pursuit,' I mean something more modest than Research. There is no good study without talk—useless, unmanaged talk. (In Oxford, our sacred city, there are a few who remain virtuosi of the fine art of talk.) Dividends are not most efficiently gathered in this way; fine talk may not go with high productivity.

---

123. 'Simplistic,' as in 'charismatic.' In its changing jargons, operated by armies of functionaries, sociology, as a discipline, remains what its worst-informed critics say it is: simpliste. As scientists of the present, sociologists can only know what they are doing in terms that derive from the authority of the past. Perhaps sociology can do, in our academy, what literature has failed to do: teach in an acutely historical yet normative way—as a science that is defensive.

Such talk as we ought to permit, in the larger silence of the university, cannot be of the mindpicking sort. Talk, in the academy, cannot be conducted according to the model of briefings and debriefings. According to that model, which is dominant in the American academy nowadays, talk should only lead to dividends. We hear plenty of shop talk. Indeed, the dividends go not only to managers of the knowledge industry, but also to the more talkative critical theorists; our new campus demagogues know how to cash in on talk; Revolution—or, more graduate, Change —is their shop talk.

The managerial revolution in American society is even further advanced in the university, where the knowledge managers are sophisticated enough and the scientists tolerant enough to share their dividends with the gurus; this joint enterprise is part of the feed, back and forth, between 'multiversity' and corporate technology. We shall get back none of our inherited culture from the scientists. Despite all interdisciplinary endeavor, and a continuity of clucking with tongues about the ignorance of non-scientists about Science, the Scientists themselves remain ignorant of high culture; there is nothing, yet, they would not, in principle, *think/ enact*. Simone Weil's reckoning of their condition in the early thirties, and before, remains substantially accurate: she could count on her fingers the number of scientists who were not "entirely deprived of that general view of things which is the very essence of theoretical culture."[124] I would disagree only with her reduction of "theoretical culture" to the modernist "general view."

Modern scientists are so full of views that many of them will never know enough to feel their lack of theoretical culture. Amazement in the face of their corporate achievement continues to parallel their dismissive ignorance of the privileged knowledge of the past and what that remembrance might tell them of the present, in which, above all, their Revolution is the hottest commodity. We see various technique industries cashing in on the Scientific Revolution, and not least in the perverse world of fashion in human behavior. Our scientific colleagues will have to try even harder to grow more critical in theory of their behavior

124. Simone Weil, *Oppression and Liberty* (London, 1958), p. 13.

as scientists. That is their problem. I do not know what we can do, in any direct way, to help them. Our own ignorance of their work is mixed with envy of its radical contemporaneity. The scientists are helpless in our culture so far as we make them our model. Our ignorance of their work is equally dismissive.[125]

125. The leading philosopher of science, for those too ignorant of it, like myself, was, for more than one generation, Bertrand Russell. What a neat succession of essays, in *Mysticism and Logic* [(London, 1918), pp. 33-57]. First, the chapter on "Science and Culture," titled, more lengthily, "The Place of Science in a Liberal Education"; then, his famous declaration, "A Free Man's Worship." Both essays, on education and worship, contend against the "magical power" of "the Past." Russell makes of "the Past," with the most courteous respect, a museum piece. He does not grasp, as Yeats did, that the "artifice of eternity" is a living thing, the true present. Instead, for Russell, stripped as he was of all but a dead historical imagination, "the beauty of its [i.e., the Past's] motionless and silent pictures is like the enchanted purity of late autumn, when the leaves, though one breath would make them fall, still glow against the sky in golden glory." Very poetical, respectful. Then Russell dismisses the Past in one perfect condescension to it:

> The Past does not change or strive; like Duncan, after life's fitful fever it sleeps well; what was eager and grasping, what was petty and transitory, has faded away, the things that were beautiful and eternal shine out of it like stars in the night. Its beauty, to a soul not worthy of it, is unendurable; but to a soul which has conquered Fate it is the key of religion. [P. 55]

In the prior essay, Russell makes the dismissive point, for science and against culture, with such magnificent and commonplace naïveté that I shall quote it as a model dismissal—the Scientist with a "general view" and without "theoretical culture." We learn that there was "one defect . . . in a purely classical education—namely, a too exclusive emphasis on the past." Russell is fair-minded, even tolerant in the face of the recalcitrance of what he imagines the old educated class to have been. "By the study of what is *absolutely ended and can never be renewed, a habit of criticism towards the present* and the future is engendered. The qualities in which the present excels are qualities to which the study of the past does not direct attention." [P. 35, my italics] But Russell underestimates we men of "sensitive taste." We are not shocked

194

To grasp the mergence of critical theory and perverse action in modern America, repeat for yourself my Deweyan suggestion that impulse follows habit. Culture articulates interdictory-transgressive polarities; a social order institutes the complex of moral demands within that articulation. Impulse indicates the failure of habit, of interdictory discipline. Cultural revolutions begin in the collapse of authority, and thus in the emergence of impulse, carried from the margins of society to the center by cadres of the perverse. The articulation of a culture may be referred to the question of what groups in a society become agents of its centrality. Critical theory is an effort to deauthorize the center. In this unmasking, the carriers of impulse emerge as contenders against the established but failing moral-demand system, themselves no longer its victims, as in the first phase, but as rhapsodes of disestablishment, professional misguiders.[126]

---

by the new and growing, nor by the crude, insolent and vulgar. We do not quiver from the rough contact with the present. (On the contrary, it is my radical, contemporary friends who quiver and withdraw at, for example, the rough contact of the 'Old Testament.') Those who merely retire to the "trim gardens of a polished past" I have already dismissed: they are museum guides—but not terribly dangerous, as are those for whom "the Past" is "what is absolutely ended and can never be renewed." Russell was a great barbarian. I honor his memory.

126. Again the problem of simony arises; the more celebrated of the professional misguiders are well paid for services rendered. A tidbit from *Publishers Weekly* [October 30, 1972, p. 36] under the headline "Bernard Geis and Bantam Books Sign Angela Davis":

> Angela Davis has signed a contract with Bantam Books and Bernard Geis Associates to write a book entitled "The Education of a Revolutionary." According to Mr. Geis, Bantam is paying the former member of the faculty of the University of California a "high six-figure" advance against royalties. While there have been numerous books about Angela Davis, Mr. Geis points out that this will be the first book by her. . . . In cooperating with Bantam on the Davis book, Mr. Geis, whose company recently had been experiencing financial difficulties, said his firm was embarking on a new program of originating, editing and promoting books [although his company last year] had filed . . . under the Federal Bankruptcy Act.

American culture is now somewhere between the first and second phase, I reckon, with messed-up amateur cadres of displacement at work, in their tens of thousands, within endlessly transitional dynamics of cultic remissiveness. These amateur cadres are mainly of young people; it is questionable whether they will turn professional. But there are even younger people behind the present young. 'Youth culture' constitutes the cultic remissiveness by which old contemporaries hope to grow younger. What a bizarre idea, of vicarious salvation. 'Youth' is the messiah, incorporated. We teachers are obliged to get our schools out of the 'Youth'-cult business. Our first tactic should aim at preventing all changes in the curriculum except those that return to learning in old disciplines. Our triune division of the curriculum, for the higher education, should be readings (to include the reading of music), writings and arithmetics. All courses in 'driver education' and the like are to be taught outside school, by your local police, who, with your local firemen, are to have their salaries instantly raised ten-fold, under the concept *danger/money*. Criminology students might do well to serve a mandatory decade on a police force before taking up their criminological profession, which deals with original experiences and therefore needs a specially repressive preparation.

The original cultic experience, which critical theory only tries to imagine, and against which all interdicts must aim, is of orgy. Do not imagine orgies were ever 'natural'; nor can they ever be 'natural.' Finally, when the therapeutic strips to play satyr, he has taken off only another onion-skin. Nakedness is another ploy. A true therapeutic is perfectly capable of undressing and so claiming to reveal something at once universal and essential; this is style as Man.

All current quarrels are about style, and yet the conservative benefit of style—of finding one satisfactory enough to resist changing to another, as if one's own style were true or superior (truth

---

Here is a bankruptcy act, indeed. The Miss Davises, more or less celebrated, are a study in themselves. Call your book: *The Gratifications of Doing IT: A Psychohistorical Accounting.* Will Angela Davis succeed in bailing out Bernard Geis?

196

and superiority amount to the same thing)—has all but disappeared. Another campaign: for the abolition of the fashion industry. Under this dissolution of cultures of truth, any style can be resurrected. The hermeneutic life of the mind should be a continuation of certainties. Now that Man can step beside himself and utter a string of authoritative disclaimers—even claiming that he himself is horrified by his old look, which exists, at that instant of disclaimer, only as an eidetic image, in the eye of the beholder—we cannot hold to the moralizing mystery of something essential. Interdictory in form, true god-terms have a binding and inhibiting authority all their own—an authority based on the objectivity of that kind of profound authorship which is inseparable from close, personal understandings. We can understand truth better in a true work of art or science, which sets its own terms and cannot be successfully challenged, but only understood, in its unique authority, for which the author is responsible. That is what authority means: responsibility.

Irresponsibility means opposing authority in any form, including the doubtful authority of intellect. One of your students said she felt surrounded by holy men—Norman O. Brown, R. D. Laing, Charles Reich, *et al.* How do I assess and sort out these people as advocates of a certain kind of future?[127]

It is not true that these are holy men—a holy man cannot be a rhapsode of transgressions except as he leads us on to deep-down interdicts, repressions fresh achieved. These rhapsodes are significant, sociologically, only in their aim to break us of the transgressive sense, by a rehabilitation of flesh that mocks the Pauline spiritualization of it. Their exercises of erotic health must end in violence. They preach no new law, no new order. Their Love is all disorder, rancorous and perverse, a sentiment against authoritative form, within which selves can be civil to others. The

---

127. Speaking of that future, I understand that recent prices for a seat at a Laing performance, for example, in Philadelphia, were $5.00 for balcony seats and $6.00 for orchestra seats. This implies that the higher the price the nearer you can get to your guru. I understand that the Laing show was S.R.O.

one course these holy men teach is a course in self-destruction.

As if to specify the target of this course, the student acolytes of these holy men have concentrated upon the destruction of our temple of feeling intellect. Make no mistake: the figure under siege in our culture is not Johnny Carson, but Lionel Trilling, superior teacher and leading American Jew of culture. For us pedagogically inclined Jews of culture, England was Zion, the fantasy father-land; perhaps it was only the Pax Britannica, seen from the top of the Hawksmoor towers.[128]

---

128. Even as I write, Professor Trilling has retreated from Co-lumbia, for the year, to All Souls. The *Times Literary Supplement* for November 17, 1972 [(No. 3689), pp. 1381-1385] has just reached me. I have not had time to study in this number the text of the first annual Thomas Jefferson Lecture in the Humanities which Professor Trilling gave in Washington in April. I am glad to see, in the editorial note at the end of this essay, that the lecture was financed by the National Endowment for the Humanities; it is time that the state functionaries did a little something to protect us from themselves. The Jefferson Lec-tures, perhaps the entire National Endowment for the Humanities, are intended "to help bridge the gap between learning and public affairs." When "wisdom, knowledge and experience" are brought to bear, by major thinkers, "on contemporary concerns," it will appear that, con-cealed in such knowledge there are senses in which the gap between learning and public affairs is unbridgeable—worse, the bridges are in-herently dangerous when used for crossings.

Even on a first reading, I catch hints of strong apprehension in Pro-fessor Trilling's lecture, once it has made its more than courteous bows to Jefferson's "firm confidence . . . placed in mind" [p. 1381]. Trilling's own confidence in mind seems linked to a learned ambiguity relating to the eighteenth-century confidence in mind and, moreover, to the decisiveness of mind in political life. In their greatest penetrations—by Hume, Kant, Rousseau, Swift [cf. my probe of this question, pp. 145-146]—the most powerful eighteenth-century theorists included in their mindfulness just that "powerful cultural tendency to which we give the name Romanticism" thus "to correct" mindfulness itself. As I have said, it is only the weaker noodles of that century and after who make this correction the enemy of reason and, in consequence, the main form of our misguidance. The dichotomy between rational and roman-tic too sharply made, Trilling continues to struggle, yet cannot escape the grasp of the liberal imagination. In consequence, he must dread the

198

Authority attracts; authority long established, woven into manners that cultivate men, has the virtue of attracting those who need a shelter from the crudities of power not yet refined. High culture must stand a political test: what brakes, not counter-power, there are in it against both anarchy and the warring state. A warring culture is bent on its own resolution, in politics. A culture can be 'strong' only in a sense related, but not reducible, to

---

force of truth that may be drawn in "the analogy . . . between the authority claimed by mind, or for it, and an exigent and even repressive social authority" [p. 1384]. Immediately, Trilling must face his own thought, in general and specially in reference to our teaching orders, on what may be said to be the case for relating the authority of mind and social authority: that

> Implicit in the concept of mind is the idea of order, even of hierarchy, the subordination of some elements of thought to others. And in the carrying out of the enterprises of mind a hierarchy of persons prevails—those who are recruited to such undertakings must rise from the ranks, usually by slow stages, although some are inequitably privileged to rise faster and higher than others. In the institutionalized training of mind, some persons are given, or arrogate, the right to prescribe to others a certain degree of proficiency, to specify the means by which they are to attain it, and to test the extent to which they have done so. Such personal gratification as mind affords is likely to be of the postponed kind. Sometimes, it is true, the mind makes exhilarating leaps, but not often, and if its ethos has at times been associated with the aristocratic-military ethos, which, though deplorably aggressive, is at least spirited, a more common association is with another ethos of later growth and less vivid character, the work ethos of early capitalism, whose defining virtues are patience, the taking of pains, and the denial of spontaneous impulse. [P. 1384]

Exactly right; a firm description of our modest hierarchy of persons as it must prevail—yet so modest that Trilling (who knows of course that here he has our sacred institution exactly right) thinks to hedge a little, against this right knowledge: by referring, as if at some opposing historical distance from it, to his knowledge as "this resentful view of mind." Even Trilling's little hedge is not "wholly new." This old knowledge remains adamant, not least in its prudent attributions of what is known to the opposing force. Let those who are against us believe there is a sense in which we are with them.

In his important Eliot lectures, *In Bluebeard's Castle: Some Notes Towards The Redefinition of Culture* (New Haven, 1971), George

199

politics. I have opened the question of this relation early in this text, specially in reference to academic side-taking. I do not doubt that English high culture has declined with the decline of empire. With the dissolution of the Pax Britannica, the manners of young Oxonians grow visibly more American, specially among those who, suffering identity-shrinkage under the retreat of English authority, talk themselves into easy hostilities to its callow successor, American power; those Young England hostilities are easy and, at the same time, imitate the worst in American society because American authority does not yet exist, while its parent, English, has failed. Our power is resented not least because it does not present to the less powerful anything in it superior to its mere existence. On the other hand, American culture is more therapeutically advanced, without authority, and precisely for this reason it is not resisted in other cultures less advanced in our way. While the others hate us politically, they imitate us culturally.

I sit, some part of each year, looking out on my defaulted second Zion from its Masada, All Souls. My participant observations have taught me something about the arbitrariness and pathos of old authority when it will not stay far enough in arrears; it is there, at the old top, where revolutions, cultural and political, begin, visible everywhere except in the blind eye of the defaulter. Marx knew this; his revolutionary theory, in the name of the proletariat, was addressed to the young intellectuals at the old top, or near enough to that top for the management of inverting movements. With what art Marx wrote and schemed. He is an original. For his revolutionary purposes, the first explicit task of Marx, as theorist, was to make the bourgeoisie ridiculous in its

---

Steiner may well have pursued the strategy of conciliating those who, not having understood that they are against us, believe themselves to be our true successors. Steiner's hedge is constructed at the colon in the following sentence: "Theirs [i.e., the scientists'] is the commanding energy: in material fact, in the 'forward dreams' which define us." (P. 128) I have come to a hearing of Steiner's text too late for benefit from its chastely mounted voice, which seems to parallel the soundings of *Fellow Teachers*, toward a normative theory of culture. But in my book, as in Steiner's, commanding energy may be opposed to commanding presence and material fact opposed to hermeneutic discipline.

200

own mind's eye. His form of argument makes massive mockeries, which have become a staple of the bourgeois style. You see that there is *fame/money* now in the Revolution move. Poor Marx; he was born too soon.

So far as the privileged youth of England, as in America, continue to be taught to feel relieved by their disinheritance, authority in default raises itself to a pedagogic principle. Under the pedagogy of defaulting authority, a suicide in principle, the young can assume, without trial, the experience of being a self-deceitful Jacob: these Jacobs celebrate their fatherlessness even as they adopt new fantasy father-figures and lands. The most aggressive and least psychologically stable[129] among the re-educated young have adopted that most ambiguous fantasy father-figure of revolutionaries: History itself. Our Jacobs aspire still, as the Marxists did, to become the favorite children of History, the father enacting his own defeat in order to prepare the sons for unbroken victories; under this default of authority, victory becomes final. These young, being doctrinally young, cannot think how they can win and yet lose at the same time.

From its beginnings, Marxist theory was toned by this fantastic response to the default of a History it read too easily and with too great an interest in conclusions: however unkindly the father predicate may act, its secret struggle, hidden from itself,

---

129. Sociology, my discipline, has a special problem: the disproportionate number of disturbed young people who seek to study (i.e., change the world) under this rubric. Much of modern sociology is part of the symptoms to which its concepts are addressed. Sociology, if it succeeds, demands situations, roles, and the like. By the very spread of its own namings, modern sociology treats the world as if it exists between quotation marks. 'Value' is the main term in that treatment, money its scarcely concealed reality. Abusing the science of sociology, you may become famous in one of two ways: by investigating 'values' or by being investigated. Better be the investigator; the investment is high, but the returns greater. Investigators, like chaplains in the army, are not the sort of people to whom you want to go when you have a problem; but they are likely to seek you out. Who is not now playing an investigator and investigated? This is the sociological meaning of being both master and crippled pet.

as in 'ideology,' is to produce the conditions of its own defeat. A defeated parent, training children to reciprocate with victory, is the most helpful kind. The one and only reason that the 'proletariat' will not be defeated is that it constitutes the youngest class; after its victory, primal history will produce no more favored sons. What romance could be more childish, more self-deceitful, than that of the Jacobs? Yet our Jacobs celebrate their 'honesty' and each is inclined to pronounce himself a more ethical I than Thou. What an orgy of a dream: each kid his own authority. Imagine grandfather Abraham reduced to saying: 'Play nice.'

Under the most extreme pressure, survival in the world as it is, as in the case of Sodom, grandfather Abraham pleads brilliantly against the strictest and most complete punishment of broken interdicts. Although Israel becomes Jehovah's favorite people through, and only through, the commandments revealed— and in the establishment of a cult proper to those commandments —grandfather Abraham understands that there are saving concealments in that revelation. At least so I understand Abraham's brilliant defense, standing before the Chief Justice, pleading in the case of Sodom. That defense is not of Sodom—that goes without further saying. But Abraham grasps the tragic danger of judgment: "Wilt thou sweep away good and bad together?" There follows the grandest and most concise of all theoretical efforts in defense of culture: Abraham's supposition after supposition, qualitative and quantitative, that for the sake of first fifty and finally ten just men who may be found there, the city is not to be destroyed. This is grander than anything Plato imagines about justice, because it is so indecisive; Abraham's brilliant casuistry will never make political sense.[130]

Abraham assumes that those ten are also hidden from themselves, that they do not know they are God's favorites and are still in the doomed city, their goodness unremarked. Yet a true Jew is he who is such in externals.

This is to point out, as best I can, how complex is Abraham's call. The old rabbinical truth-tellers grasped the intricacy of Abraham's call and tried to teach it in their own interpretations

---

130. Genesis 18:23-33.

of what the original story means. One of these stories has Abraham teaching God that if he wants to maintain the world, then the interdicts cannot be maintained without specific remissions. Supreme authority, according to *Abrahamic/rabbinic* theory, cannot be simple; it must be cultivated in its judgments or the world cannot endure. Fanaticism is not superior to the absence of convictions—as we interpreters of the original Abrahamic case might reconstruct it.[131]

I am merely retelling motifs from Israel's family romance. Under the Freudian conception of family romance, we can grasp in a very different and competing way the psychodynamics of the principle that authority attracts: the romancing child invariably adopts fantasy parents from classes or characters higher than those of his biological sponsors. Who among us has not been switched, however momentarily, in the cradle? My parents were not nearly good enough for me; I was lucky to have grandfathers. Father figures do their difficult job best if sons, with them, are subject to grandfather figures, who, in their own submission to a tradition at once credal and oral, will stand for a strictly limited amount of new nonsense from their successors.

The Jacobite romance is a variation on that of the modern family, preposterous in its identification of the last and youngest as the future first and permanently young, never to be trapped in their system. Romantic egalitarianism is the most vengeful conceit of what my Jacobite students call, at the slightest brush past their immense and fragile egos, 'elitism.' Their abstract extension of the family romance, made collective, was paralleled in my own youth by the adoption of some fantasy fatherland, a true, undefaulting authority.

---

131. See, further, on this point, below, p. 210 *et pass.* In my theoretical work, I have not yet been able to cope with the prototypal Jacob metamorphosis. How to grasp the original Jacob's revolutionary bout of disrespect: imagine wrestling with God—the real and ideal God—as the central act of your 'identity crisis' and demanding to be blessed by name! Abraham knew that even argument (his or any other) has its limits. What follows from the fact that Jacob is the most successful of our founding fathers—and a rather questionable brother? How should I know? I am not learned in the tradition.

Until the default of English authority, the cultivated gentlemen of England supported, willingly or not, their junior American establishment. Now, this historic support for the wasps has entirely withdrawn. A Dean Acheson is no longer authorized, by that rentier nation, England, to be an American statesman. Even a John F. Kennedy, with his ritual stop, after Harvard, at the LSE, conformed to a pattern which is less and less mandatory for even the most Culture-conscious American power-holder. (Mr. Nixon does not appear culture-conscious, or historically minded; he is a Californian. The fantasy fatherland of Californians is California.) The fantasy fatherland of the American power-holders has become a never-never land of endlessly dynamic, rational and bureaucratic corporate enterprise, located where the sun is seen never to set, a land without shadows, ideal for children. Imagine unzer Amerika that way, a California of the mind, or a Dusseldorf, everything new, the entire state of mind as far away as you can get from our good old Europe. With what shall youthful America identify while Europe itself is committing the suicide of Americanization? Where shall Henry James go? From whence can he return, to write *The American Scene*? Better not to go, except on visits; this is the scene. We have to fight it out, our own special way, here, in this vast horror, without feeling holy in the slightest about our decision.

Our holy men, pretending they are not quite at home here, are equally ridden by fantasies that respond to the default of home authority and its father predicates. The chief fantasy figure of the make-believe holy men is an anti-father figure: the politicized criminal.[132] Mock messiahs, children of rich parents who think themselves forerunners, just good enough to tie the sandals of

---

132. Note that in the most saleable of American films, the son, Michael, is a total success: by taking over the "family" in its death-throes and transforming it into corporate enterprise. The original godfather is a dying old man who, in a moment of incaution, sacrifices himself to the mindless frivolity of the grandchild. Remembering Marlon Brando, Michael's son—name him Adams Corleone—is bound to become Senator, then President; his presidential campaign will be called Camelot Two; in America, tradition is script continuity.

the young, receive from their biological sponsors and guru elders a new baptismal teaching: that vandals and psychopaths, the young in mind, barbarians all, have the historic privilege of showing the way to act against the burdens of propriety (and, if only in a showy—i.e., exemplary—sense, against property). The rich can afford cultural revolution; they keep a careful grip on their capital.

Privileged vandalism, the revolutionary action of the rich children of the Western world, has been directed mainly against a powerless institution, the university. The struggle against authority is against us; we are the civilized who are stuck with and in our good forms and conservations. How can these celebrated men, by whom we feel rather as if surrounded, be holy when they have not even a Chekhovian lightheartedness about the condition of being stuck? Our holy men know very well how to get to Havana, Algiers, Moscow, Hanoi, San Fran—wherever the scene is. I prefer Philadelphia, hometown of W. C. Fields and his Joke, where scenes are simply not made, however hard the young and trendier rich may try. We do have The Orchestra, The University and many fine hospitals. But, then, you do get The Orchestra in Saratoga Springs.

If we are to help build student resistance to the holy men, who would abolish the ordinariness of life, the Philadelphia of the mind, then we must create it against the endless expressional quest: first, in our intellectual capacity, by helping to clear the intellectual atmosphere of the guru's loving ultimate concern, and of the violence such concern does to our separate and often opposing particularities. To resist the holy men you mentioned, and many others still to come, is to resist prophets of transgressiveness; know your prophets—at least the false ones.[133]

Speaking of prophets reminded you of Herbert Marcuse.

I wonder whether you might relate Marcuse's conception of one-dimensionality to your own ideas of psychological Man.

---

133. How sad, how symptomatic, that so few students nowadays have even the foggiest idea of what has been achieved, within any of their (lost) traditions, on the matter of telling false prophets from true.

They do appear to have a number of things in common. Suppose we talk somewhat about Marcuse's whole notion of aestheticizing reality. He has said that since the world is essentially as we know it to be, a place in which reason has barbarized sensuality and virtually eliminated the possibility of its authentic expression, what we need to establish is a kind of freedom from the established reality. This involves an aestheticization which in Marcuse's terms at least would make reality a thing of lightness and of play. The reality would lose its seriousness. I wonder whether you consider such a development possible, and if so, desirable.

A culture so bent upon its own destruction as to make Marcuse's authentic expressiveness possible will make it terrible as well. That aestheticizing reality, as a thing of lightness and play: it will make murder and incest, too, acts of lightness and play. Marcuse does not comprehend the sentimentality thrusting behind enlightened reason; it is reason for the weakest noodles that barbarizes sensuality. The god Eros was playful, cunning, cruel and unmanageable; Hesiod thought Eros damaged the mind. Long since, the acts of the original and dangerous god, disguised finally as harmless little Cupid, were used up; the god, abandoned, ceased functioning. The acts of Eros may be said to be carried on, equivocally, in our crimes of passion: acts of stupidity to be deterred least when the erotic is imagined theopathetically, as nowadays, complete with rituals of public enactment. Those rituals are mind-damaging; they are based on the assumption that there is in them no problem of sublimity.

The most original figure of lightness and play is the satyr of Reason, who opposes the Jew of culture. Culturally, truth is the renunciation of sheer movement, of lightness and play; aestheticizing reality can make truth less grim, but jokes can be quite cruel, specially when perpetrated by the young. The joy of games depends upon there being something that is not a game—something grave to relieve the tedious jollity. Marcuse's country is no place for old men and slow movements. I consider it is most often the slow movement that is most beautiful, not the scherzo. That country is a destructive fantasy of the real loveliness, of a place

206

ruled by the ideal (rather than real) young. Critical theory leads to an intellectualized eroticism, to immediate and crudely mistaken applications of book-learning, to that 'romanticism of the intellectually interesting' we teachers must always resist. Marcuse expresses one aspect of the American disorder: in the absence of presiding presences, in their proper age, he would hand over authority to a youthful version of himself—beautifully cultivated even when grossly mistaken, witty, a virtuoso of intellect. But the real young are not old Marcuses made immortal by sexual energy. Until they are inducted into the order of the old, graven with a tragic sense of a world that will not yield to their wishes, the real young remain desperate dying animals, too young to assume responsibility, and hiding from reality behind the skirt of their ethics of conscience. One version of the problem to which old Marcuse and old Erikson, the original misunderstood identity-quester, testify, is our refusal to grow old gracefully: we appear to have lost that precious gift. Yet Marcuse and Erikson are two of the too few graceful old men I know of, in the Western world today.

Marcuse's ancient mistake is to associate the good with desire —more precisely, with the incitement of desire. Rather, to recognize desire is to recognize its relation to power. That double recognition leads to every true good, as a discovered limit of desire. The good is always true and beautiful by opposing the inseparable dynamics of desire and power. Authority emerges out of the crucible in which desires are tempered. What is good can only emerge in interdictory form. From among the lessons to be learnt still in the history of our culture, we have forgotten that no good can be achieved except as the supersession of desire and the limit of power. It is in this latter sense alone, as a modal naming of interdicts, that authority is itself right and necessary. All true ethics are ethics of self-deprivation, modeled in a commanding interdictory character. In all other forms, authority abolishes itself, without the help of some critical theory, as a transgressive quest for power, based on a model of unsatisfiable Man, in endless thrusts toward what is not himself. The 'surplus value' of desire is death.

The questing student self need not use the language of romance. As society becomes cultureless, without presiding presences repeated prototypally in parenthood,[134] authority resolves into technical tests; to act technically does not imply renouncing or condemning anything as unenactable. The moral life begins with renunciation; the therapeutic life begins with the renunciation of renunciation. So it is that certain contemporary false prophets call upon us to become ahistorical infants—that is, to act contrary to our historically achieved renunciations. (Bomber technicians, in B-52's, are called upon to act in precisely the same way.) I, for one, will not choose sides nor be chosen; I will stay out; and I will not be guruized, in the attempt to stay out. But how do any of us stay out? Anyone can be guruized; there is nothing to it—and nothing lasting. Our gurus incarnate the quick turnover of ideas; they have nothing in common, except the name, with the classic and highly authoritative Indian teacher. To teach ourselves how not to be played in the ideas market, perhaps the best we can do is practice the art of silence, specially in this period of over-publication and shouting controversialists. After learning the art of silence, then we can relearn the lost art of conversation, so to become conversable men.

In a therapeutic movement, irresponsible therapists abound; their first love is controversy. Naïveté in combat, not simply the will to win but the notion that the victory is justified, protects every great movement from more justified suspicions of the consequences encouraged by the movement. The social scientists are exactly right to announce that they spy, not far off, new world communes thirsty for Love, this-worldly in their acosmic love and, in consequence, entirely without standards of exclusion. It is in such communities, the transgressive component made dominant in the dissolution of the interdictory, that all orders will co-exist argumentatively and offer themselves, not exclusively, for enactment.

---

134. It is the prototypal cycle of authority that generates order in the family. Therefore, no strict and affectionate discipline can apply to children without applying, first and more rigorously, to their parents. From the rigor of that self-application, authority descends through the generations and so allows children, in the family order, to correct their parents; for it is the parents, first, who must be an obedient people; then it is that children have someone to obey.

As utilities of order-hopping, even the Christian cults may take on new life in a hortatory way. How tolerant, indeed how encouraging, of differences our Jacobs will be. That hortatory way amounts to a supreme indifference.

Competing new cults are being founded every day. I cannot begin to count charismatics as they pop up, nor their organizations. Practically every psychotechnician attracts or builds up his own little organization; that build-up is, after all, the technique of 'charisma' and the profit of therapy. Among ex-Protestants, there have been whole schools of naïve therapists, preachers of one method or another, considering their therapies, in an evolutionary way, as somehow the messiah method brought up to date. These methodists seem to me historically and sociologically explicable: they are the outriders of the therapists. Every movement needs its cover, its reconcilers of once deadly enemies. These apologists, for a movement without credal character, are much like the late nineteenth-century liberal Protestants, who were bound to reconcile Religion and Science. The quasi-clerical outriders of the therapeutic movement herd the strays, and the recalcitrant, those who have fallen behind or hang back.

The modern intellectual is he who does not hang back. I have already tried to sketch some connections "between the intellectual, on the one hand, and the analytic individual, perhaps the therapeutic as well, and practical politics." I note, first, your reference to *intellectual* as if it were a free-floating category. Intellectuals belong in and to teaching institutions, I think, or their critiques become therapies. The modern connection between intellectuals and therapists is so close that you are exactly right to ask, further: "Is there a *function* in the political domain for a therapeutic or for an intellectual?" I have italicized your use of the playful god-term, *function*. Functionalism is a doctrine of effective performances, by which whatever happens is confirmed by validations from the socio-scientific magistry; these magistrates of Science make up an awkward, constantly changing, cover language of justifications. Because politics are a struggle for power, with the fascination of terror their ultimate aesthetic, it is entirely appropriate to refer, since the work of Machiavelli, to the *function* of certain intellectualizing types in modern politics. To intellectualize politics is to help maintain the terror implicit in it.

'Political religions' have been composed as one such recent term of maintenance. Here is an intellectual concealment that reveals something very different from what our magistrates, the functionalists, themselves conceive. This peculiar maintenance is best seen in relation to the recent and, historically, quite misunderstood totalitarian movements; what our colleagues, and the re-educated classes do not wish to understand is that totalitarian movements (Nazi, Fascist, Communist, and so farther) are not fanatical—in the eighteenth-century meaning of 'fanatick.' Because communists and fascists are anything but men of deep and settled convictions, they can be the more easily functionalized in our understandings, and made false to the terror of their acts, by being transferred conceptually under some deceptively familiar label such as 'political religion.' One of the most trustworthy guides to our time and its past, Hannah Arendt, put it profoundly: "The consistent elimination of conviction as a motive for action" she considered a "matter of record" since the great terror under Stalin. "The aim of totalitarian education has never been to instill convictions, but to destroy the capacity to form any."[135] That capacity destroyed, action is released from motive. Terror and therapy, East and West, converge in something genuinely new—neither politics nor religion in any sense earlier received within the orders of Western societies. Toward that convergence, Marx and Freud generated remissive motifs, as Sciences of historical movement or of unconsciousness, that cannot be overestimated.

There is no reason why the therapeutic should not get along perfectly well in a totalitarian order. Take a wrapping of onion skins without a center, an actor of many parts, including 'devoted follower,' put him in an interminable struggle of expropriations, and you have the guiltless totalitarian—democratic, authoritarian, everything that could be wished—a perfectly plastic man; unconvictable. If his side should lose, such a figure has an infinite capacity for changing sides. I am reminded of the actors on the TV

---

135. Hannah Arendt, "Ideology and Terror: A Novel Form of Government," *Review of Politics*, XV (1953), 314.

screen who have a black eye to testify their loyalty: they have demonstrated that they would "rather fight than switch." We know that they are equally capable of switching. In his agonizing old-time character, Nerzhin,[136] Solzhenitsyn may have missed the point: "What was lacking in most of them was that personal *point of view* which becomes more precious than life itself."[137] The therapeutic raises the holding of personal points of view to a method; *Jake/Gala* are willing and able to adopt any point of view you like, to treat food fads and ancient taboos as equal partners in the all-too-human game of life itself.

So we have circled round the consumer of all ideals, subscriber to all criticism, perfect in his Arnoldian roundedness and balance, quite up to holding personal points of view, even of sacrificing himself to them—so long as he has access to the 'existential awareness' that it was only a 'point of view' that brought him up thus to sacrifice. Why not self-sacrifice, too? Sorel would have understood my anti-ideal type perfectly. It was Sorel who preached "absolute revolution," because he knew that "all that is best in the modern mind is derived from this 'torment of the infinite.' "[138] You cannot make absolute revolution without breaking every last one of those empty historical eggs (including the Marxist); all have been sucked out and can expect no better fate. Call this the 'justifiable victim' theory.

Imagine, if you will, a vast scene and, in it, Gala, once a mere aesthetic activist, the duel he will not fight politicized, himself a survivor (because he understands that it is only a game and that he can manage the rules) whoever wins and loses. The Priests (Guido) will fight; they need their myths and meanings. (As a

---

136. In *The First Circle* (New York, 1968), p. 389.

137. "Personal point of view," as an implicit successor and equivalent to "theoretical culture," relates to the Tolstoyean rather than Abrahamic teaching that "no one in the world is just and no one guilty" [*ibid.*, p. 400]. This Christian sentimentality reduces the tragedy and heightens terror in a world thus accustomed to seeing the good destroyed because no one is bad.

138. Georges Sorel, *Reflections on Violence*, trans. T. E. Hulme (New York, 1961), p. 46.

woman, Rennie Morgan better takes on the function, in my very European and extended metaphor, of The People.) Politicized, the therapeutic will need to produce naïfs, dogs, those over whom he can lord it, as first Joe and then, consummately, Jake, lord it over Rennie—or as Gala lords it over his wife and their lover, both mere barking dogs.

Do you see some connection, here, with the existentialists? There is; but the connection must be carefully made and followed along both its branches. The counter-argument, against this book and for teaching as therapy, appears to come not from Freud but from Kierkegaard. That genius, who would have liked to be an apostle, concludes:

> The more difficult it is made for him to take himself out of existence by way of recollection, the more profound is the inwardness that his existence may have in existence; and when it is made impossible for him, when he is held so fast in existence that the back door of recollection is forever closed to him, then his inwardness will be the most profound possible.[139]

Of course, Kierkegaard is right: we cannot go backward. I agree. But to go forward then means, for the remotest Kierkegaard, that the achievement of inwardness can only come by working through therapies in order to get back beyond them. Himself unable to move backward, Kierkegaard was anticredal. Yet, by 'existence,' Kierkegaard meant nothing like radical contemporaneity. That subjectivity is untruth; its eternal beginners are condemned to remain big children, callow in their ethical aspirations, because those aspirations are more like exhalations, from the erotic and aesthetic spheres of struggle between thrusting selves. An individual, in social existence, needs distance between himself and others; a lawful social order keeps others from pressing in too close. It is authority that surrounds subjectivity and protects its truth.

We remoter Kierkegaards: we cannot live in faith for a moment except under the paradox of an historically distant authority.

---

139. Soren Kierkegaard, *Concluding Unscientific Postscript*, trans. David Swenson (Princeton, 1941), pp. 186-87.

Smile your best Kierkegaardian smile at the bizarre apologetics of some radically contemporary religionists, who, following the *reconciliatory/dichotomizing* model of the heresiarch who made it biggest of all, the most brilliant writer of dialectical prose alive today, *Saul/Paul,* discover their updated Jesus: black militant, freak, Pop star in direct succession to successful ad-man, even (of all closed possibilities, this is the one that cannot be opened) Jew. As like imagine Jesus was a Danish religious intellectual of the mid-nineteenth century, a twisted slip of a scrivener. Such metamorphoses are advert slogans of the original *horse/god.* You cannot horse around with the son of god, Man. No, sire. In the living moments of Kierkegaard's passing, not steadfast, faith, he could not divorce faith from the supremely distant interdictory figure of his own case-historical consciousness: Christ, *messiah/ man,* the "eternal truth" who has "come into being in time."[140] The true, artful story of Kierkegaard, if it were to be *re-told/-tailed* for our edification, would have to treat his father, Regina and (last but not least) Christ as the three corners of a triangled box from within which, using something like the Fosbury flop, head and back first, Kierkegaard tried to leap free; moreover, he experienced his jumps under pseudonyms—very important if you assume them so to take yourself up, healthy, beyond the fatality of your name.

If our leading radical contemporaries, first in the historical field, the Mod Prods, want to follow the authentic Kierkegaardian connection, then they cannot treat Existenz as the functional equivalent of therapy. Whatever they still mind, our ex-Protestants keep smiling. Or, are they baring their teeth? Both. They are happy enough in their professions, as outriders of the therapeutic movement. Let us not disturb them; the Mod Prods, our old Americans rejuvenated, can be tolerated except when they try the metamorphosis *culture/politics.* Christ and politics will not mix; but our methodists, with their moral messages to the nation, a people disgraced by their immoralities, are not living Christians; they are

---

140. [*Ibid.,* p. 187.] In a casebook of charismatics, Jesus must come first, of course; without Jesus, the concept 'charisma' would not have come into being.

simplistic paratherapists, pretending to heave a significant post-coital sigh, a pregnant tristesse, in honor of our relaxed new to-getherness. The Eros symbolic presses us altogether too close together. Make distances, not love; there is no more responsible way to protect our freedoms.

Now to follow the therapeutic connection with Existenz along its second branch: to the point where it meets the existentialists as pure role-players, gathering a 'meaning' or an 'authenticity' as they act. Role-players do not require resonances of the old preaching lingo, with its overtones of repression, to get themselves started on something. For pure role-players, learning their lessons from the dynamics of erotic caprice, action politicizes and direct action politicizes directly. J.-P. Sartre[141] is the theorist of Man in the street, who aspires to the dictatorship of his class, for an indefinite period of transitionality. Among role-players, leaps of faith be-come strategies for gambling. In trying to pick a winner,[142] Sartre, like any professional gambler, spreads his bets. He has picked, without contradiction, Soviet 'Communism' *and* 'Revolution' (not the same thing) *and* Fanon's mythic 'Black' *and* the 'Tout' of the counterculture. All such thrusts towards authenticity as Sartre's are fatal games, signalling the absence of authority and never its in-hibiting presence; it is during such an absence that everything becomes possible and nothing true. Authenticity is an act, all that is worst in the modern mind at play with its precious torments of the infinite.[143] In his role-playing, the therapeutic cannot be a

---

141. Sartre is another of those armchair prophets, like Sorel, against whom Max Weber warned us long ago. Better the conditional devotions of faith (if there were still churches and synagogues, to which there could be a return) than this unconditional revolutionary prophecy, with its cruel show of excitements, for the eschatology market.

142. Trying to pick a winner was the last thing Kierkegaard was trying to do; as any Christian knows, the Messiah is not a winner and does not pick winners.

143. It is no accident, comrades, that the 'infinite' was the god-term of Schleiermacher and other Protestants who made the critical turn into modernity, at the beginning of the nineteenth century; Schleiermacher completed the Lutheran psychologizing of the Christian

civilized man. Civilization is, in its most personal aspect, the role played without thought of change.

This spacious new authenticity of role-playing is the opposite of old spirituality, not its evolved expression. We know what a revival of spirituality would cost us. The sense of guilt again true, spirituality would return us to our culture at the price of making restitution before the transgressive act occurs, thus the better to suppress those acts as sheer possibilities. Such a tremendous inversion of will does not often penetrate a social order nor for very long before it is displaced by more tolerable sublimations, remissive openings of possibility. I see no signs of a coming inversion of will. There is no end ahead of our cultivation of caprice. Only the weakest noodles, those with the lowest respect for truth, claim prescience. We are still at the end of an era; the new beginnings, as I see them, long established, are therapeutic rather than spiritual in character. The popular teaching is entirely of experienced deconversions from what we have all but ceased to know.

I tried to make clear to myself, in *The Mind of the Moralist*, why our great master Freud is best interpreted as the chief figure at the endless transitionality of our era. I shall not go into all that again. Here, I need only remind you that, in his personal adherence

---

godhead into a god-term, a spiritualization of dangerous thoughts, but, in the Protestant era, now ended, strictly for use outside—in a professional, even intellectual way—from within the security of being a family man. Out of Protestant psychologizing came that smart condition of the modern intelligentsia, adultery of the head. From adultery of the head, penetrating the world in free activity, the Protestant principle penetrated downwards. There is a subtle but distinct difference between the intellectual as interpreter and the intellectual as adulterer. This is not the place to trace the line from Luther and his Katie to what became, in principle, the age of adultery. For the intellectual, adultery became the form of spiritual aspiration. Moreover, as he is moved from affair to affair, the intellectual expects each to end in his disappointment. For the security of the family, the Communist adulterer substitutes the security of the Party; anything goes, so long as he has the Party to go back to. After the 'family man' and 'husband' as adulterer, then what type of actor shall we see?

to the constraints implicit in his primal history,[144] combined with his refusal to make of therapeutic procedures a model of public behavior, Freud was not a protestant in principle, against interpretation. Against the remissive motifs generated even in his own thought and movement, Freud appears our last grand theorist, gifted with a capacity to defend high culture in its failures, against infinite openings of possibility. It has been Freud's fate to be debased into a herald of the therapeutic, so grossly in America that he is now further debased by therapeutic rejections of him as a renegade, sold out to culture. As I have said, perhaps the fate of our minor master Fanon, linked to Freud as he is, to be reduced to a rhapsode of the terrorist act as racial therapy, is more deserved. Even so, when will the militants discover that Fanon was another one of those finks who could think? He is reduced, as he feared, to smallness of mind, when made to serve their positions. Both minds, the great one and his remote Parisian disciple, remain better than their popular success encourages us to understand; one of our duties as teachers is to protect the minds through which we must make our way from the horror of their *success/failure*. Anti-mind thrives: more swiftly than ever before in the history of defeats suffered by our Freuds when they tried not to take sides. At least our Freud was never so vulgar as their Marx; Freud was never enchanted with *historical/political* evolution.

I do not know what next. I do know what every seeing man knows: that it is mainly from the top down that therapeutic and terrorist penetrate modern culture. I expect the two types to merge, medicine and politics, into a political medicine, the therapeutic dominant and not more indebted to Freud than to any other theorist of therapy.

Cleared for action without interdict, the therapeutic is our ultimate terrorist, the leading man in the auto-destructive scenario of a cultureless society. In his *Notes Toward A Definition of Culture*, Eliot admitted he was baffled by the phenomenon of hostility to culture in any form. In these remarks I have tried to ease my

---

144. On the difficult matter of Freud as what I have called, in the past, "a psychological Jew," cf. *The Mind of the Moralist, op. cit.*, p. 283 *et pass.*

own bafflement—not yours. But then, you may be on one of the many other sides to the question of how to defend our culture—or, perhaps how not to defend it. If we teachers are to cultivate afresh, first among ourselves, the vision without which our culture must die, then that defense cannot be rightly in the form of invective, except in our late modern joking way, upon what Milton called "the insolency of tumults." Tumults there will be, even when interdicts are at their persuasive height, as in certain evangelical, and often withdrawn, sects. Our defenses must be different, neither sectarian nor quarrelsome. In our schools, we can never hope to withdraw inwardly from society far enough for the practice of our theory; what a release for us that we are not the ones to lead a return. We are not backward-looking; we do not propose restorations, for an equality of reasons the participating parts of which I have tried to bring into their special prominence, each successive and overlapping.

Here I am at the end of the coda in this fugue,[145] my *personal/theoretical* performance played out. Because in our sacred institutions we teachers are now over-organized, and demoralized, the three of us, having met once, probably shall never meet again to explore whatever there may be consequent, as a counter-subject, in my answer here to the subject you raised. Another public episode, as on the evening of 26th March, 1971? Not again. I try, within the limit of prudence, never to attend such meetings. In our episode, because we were not linked in a chain of interpretations, we could not have achieved a pedagogic discipline, on the model of contrapuntal imitation. We should not mistake for continuity what is only our thrust toward opportunity. All I could learn from another

---

145. I have referred, earlier [see footnote 44, p. 75], to fugue in its psychiatric meaning, in which the actor may appear to perform in his usual manner and yet, afterward, is without articulate remembrance of the time or of his conduct during that time. We end on the problematics of remembrance. Remembrance articulate: Wie ich einen Ausgang finde / Liegt nicht schwer mir in dem Sinn.

217

such meeting is where you stand, not what you think. Where you stand is no concern of mine, as a teacher. We shall not exchange views, I trust, for the exchange is really a self-display. Here, of course, for the same reason, I must make no stand.

The Codrington Library
All Souls College
Oxford

Summer, 1972

The University of Pennsylvania
Philadelphia

Autumn, 1972

Acknowledgments

To Martha Pamplin Rosso, my secretary, but for whom nothing I write would be often enough rewritten, until it is, as a matter of conscience or chance, filed away, destroyed or published. A 'final' draft is whatever manuscript escapes my grasp. Mrs. Rosso's hard and exact work supplies me, and any student of mine who cares to notice, with a superior lesson in professional competence; equally, her patience with the tedious little tasks of both the scholarly and institutional life. The main aim of any book, as I see it, is to help the author learn a little more precisely what it is he is trying to say. Mrs. Rosso is harried by words, chosen and unchosen, each trying to gain their respective weights and tension enough to become a link; how admirably she copes, day after day, I cannot begin to say. Sometimes, I suspect, the words, and their strife, follow her home.

To Jack Dash Harris, my graduate-student assistant, who made the index. Mr. Harris, by questioning, helped me make certain passages behave themselves. He checked the references and, in general, is responsible for the accuracy of page citations and quotations.

One of the best of my graduate students, Samuel Heilman, deep as he is in the writing of his doctoral dissertation, took time to give the book a first reading. I have tried to work the most critical moments of Mr. Heilman's reading into the text, either by deletion or by amplification.

Index

Abel, 118, 119, 143
Abnormal, 74n, 153
Abraham, 202, 203, 203n
Academy(ies), 8, 9, 17, 21, 52, 95n, 117, 135n, 162n, 172, 192, 192n, 193; American, 193; true, 117
Acheson, Dean, 204
Acting out, 7, 14, 100, 130, 137, 174; public, 138; visual, 158n
Action, 142, 142n; infinite, 129; judgmental, 165; original, 44; perverse, 195; remissive, 73; revolutionary, 205; sexual, 143, 146; therapeutic, 135; transgressive, 115, 148, 183; unbelieving, 144n
Adam, 143
Aesthetic(s), 27, 46, 63, 63n, 66n, 170; ultimate, 209
Age, 92, 144; of adultery, 215n; of the director, 137; of prophecy, 15; of reasons, 145, 146n; of science, 41; of the therapeutic, 48, 137
Aggression, 5, 92n, 111; release of, 35
Ambivalence, 25, 99, 116
America, 35, 40, 43n, 50, 58n, 87, 88, 91n, 104n, 108, 111, 124, 195, 201, 204, 216

American(s), 38, 54n, 77, 81n, 88, 89, 92n, 95n, 101, 104n, 137, 213; alliance, 37; black, 43n; disorder, 207; dream, 82n; establishment, 204; fashion, 74n; films, 204n; imperialism, 177n; language, 45; radical, 90; scene, 46
Analogues: historical, 109; life, 189; text, 4, 34, 106, 122
Analysis(es), 5, 21, 69, 158, 168, 182, 183; of faiths, 35
Anarchism, 149
Anticultures, 128n; therapeutic, 117, 178
Apostle(s), 27, 32, 65, 67, 71, 73, 77, 93n, 114n, 170, 172, 212; of the body, 43; business, 67; of life, 71; of self, 66; of understanding, 77
Arendt, Hannah, 210, 210n
Aristocracy(ies), 94n, 125, 134, 156; intellectual, 6
Arnold, 14n
Art(s), 3, 20, 44, 50, 52n, 63, 64, 65, 66, 68, 69, 70, 72–74, 77, 100, 103, 106, 110, 123, 134, 137, 158n, 174, 186, 197; of concealment, 9; of conversation, 208; of critical concealments, 18; of critical interpre-

221

Art(s) (*cont'd*)
tation, 18; of criticism, 18; film,
157n; of genius, 151n; hermeneutic, 16; of interpreting, 37;
and life, 131; of limits, 36, 165;
of man-killing, 153n; modern,
52n, 67, 75n, 114, 151, 151n,
157; pedagogic, 10; of politics,
156; of the primitive, 104n;
revolutionary, 84; scholar's, 2n;
of silence, 208; and the social
order, 21; theory of, 132; unseriousness of, 120
Artist(s), 13n, 64, 80, 101, 113,
146; failed, 64, 147; of life, 15;
modern, 113; progressive, 151;
'value'-change, 7
Authenticity, 214, 215
Authority(ies), 11, 14, 15, 17–20,
22, 26–28, 31, 32, 38, 42, 43,
45–49, 54, 67, 70, 74n, 78, 81n,
82n, 85–87, 94, 99, 100, 108n,
113, 116, 117, 120, 124, 129,
131–133, 136, 137, 141, 144n,
149, 159–163, 163n, 164–166,
176, 179, 180n, 183, 197, 199,
199n, 200–205, 207, 208, 208n,
212; absence of, 214; aesthetic,
67; American, 200; attacks on,
49, 165; auto-destruction of,
105n; character of, 20; of
Christ, 27; in classroom, 97;
collapse of, 166, 195; contempt
for, 151; crisis of, 47; criticism of, 28; of death, 42; default of, 12, 201; dissolution of,
179; end of, 50; English, 200,
204; figures of, 103, 120, 158;
hang-up, 62, 62n; higher, 106;
highest, 17; idea of, 97; inhibiting, 197; institution of, 18; of
intellect, 197; intellectual, 15,
67, 124; interdictory, 137; interdictory nature of, 42; judgment
of, 27; lawful, 161; of mind,
199n; moralizing, 25; of Moses,
99; murderers of, 99; and obedience, 31, 32; old, 123, 200; of
the old, 186; opponents of, 94;
orders of, 136; of the past, 15,
23, 74n, 185, 192n; pedagogic,

18; personal, 11, 131; political,
165; recognition of, 179; relations, 54, 121; of resistance,
88; resolution of, 20; revival
of, 165; right, 17; of sabbath,
136; scheme of, 137; social,
199n; submission to, 25, 47;
teaching, 97; theory of, 149,
186; transferable, 67; true disestablishment of, 18; of truth,
20; untaught, 12; would-be,
105n
Authorship, 28, 30, 32, 34, 189,
197; religious, 27
Autonomous inner man, 53

Babel, Isaac, 81n;
    Collected Stories, 81n
Bad, 202, 211n
Balzac, 90n
Barbarians, 39, 40, 49, 159, 195n,
205; contemporary, 122
Barbarism, 35, 39, 46, 97, 143n,
144n
Barth, John, 55, 58n, 61n, 77, 103,
116, 121, 146; *The End of the
Road*, 55, 59, 72, 103, 128
Barth, Karl, 58
Bayle, 60
Beethoven, 10, 46, 93n, 173; *Ham-
merklavier*, 173
Behavior, 108, 133, 193; expressive,
144n, 174; perverse, 48; pub-
lic, 216; sexual, 147; sympto-
matic, 69; transgressive, 35, 44,
46, 69, 102, 112n, 127, 147,
150, 152, 155, 168, 182, 183,
184
Belief(s), 3, 126, 142, 142n, 145,
177; authoritative, 145; problems, 126; in unbelief, 172
Bell, Daniel, 129n
Benda, Julien, 83n
Bergman, 137; *The Seventh Seal*,
137
Bergson, 114
Black(s), 35, 43n, 81n, 91n, 92n,
93n, 102, 103, 112, 147, 187,
214; American, 94n; 'Black is
Beautiful,' 43n; 'Black is Brilliant,' 43n, 93n; caste, 92n; mil-

itant, 93n; moral, 164; physicist, 103; problem, 104n; young, 43n
Bonaventura, 185
Bottomore, T. B., 78n, 80n
Bourgeois, 40n, 66, 89, 90, 95n, 128n, 137, 201; black, 103n; class supremacy, 92; projector, 120
Boyers, Robert, prefatory note
Brando, Marlon, 204n
Braque, 52n
Breakthrough, 20, 24, 26, 36, 64, 76n, 151, 162n, 173, 181n, 191; in science, 106; tradition of, 185; transgressive, 152
Brewster, Kingman, 82n, 159n
Broch, Herman, 11, 42n, 187, 188n; *The Death of Virgil*, 187, 188, 188n; *The Unknown Quantity*, 42, 42n
Brown, Norman O., 197
Brown, Rap, 93n
Buber, Martin, 54n, 20, 121; *I and Thou*, 54n
Buddhism, 25
Buñel, Luis, 74n, 75n
Burke, Edmund, 63n, 64n, 65n, 66n, 140, 149; *Reflections on the Revolution in France*, 140; *The Works of Edmund Burke*, 63n
Bushnell, Horace, 36n, 37n, 38n, 82n; *God in Christ*; 37n
Bussy, Simon, 119n

Cadre(s): aesthetic, 112; defensive, 18; guiding, 76, 99, 126, 126n, 134n, 144n, 150, 150n; intellectual, 112; interdictory, 21; non-responsible, 99; scientific, 112
Cain, 118, 143; figure, 112n
Carnality, 142n, 144n
Carson, Johnny, 198
Case history(ies), 85n, 86n, 134
Catholic(s), 58n, 131, 182n; Roman, 31, 71n
Cause(s), 22, 37, 105n, 142n, 156, 168, 177n

Censorship(s), 108, 158n, 182, 182n
Cézanne, 52n
Chain: of feeling intellect, 173; images, 173; of intellect, 172; of interpretation(s), 38, 105, 217
Change(s), 6, 19, 25, 32, 34, 35, 114n, 135, 155, 157, 157n, 172, 189, 193, 215; interior, 21; mystiques of, 25, 35; technicians of, 107; theory of, 18
Chaplin, Charlie, 152
Character(s), 14, 20, 33, 34, 49, 53, 62, 70, 73, 73n, 87, 96, 98, 104, 105n, 114, 114n, 120, 130, 133, 160, 215; credal, 209; graven, 127; historical, 47; interdictory, 207; law-abiding, 151n; totalitarian, 113; weighted, 130
Chardin, 52n
Charisma, 105, 106, 108, 117, 162n, 163, 163n, 178, 213n; technique of, 209; theory of, 161
Charismatic(s), 24, 60, 92n, 94n, 106, 115, 123, 162n, 163, 192n, 209, 213n; contemporary, 123; modern, 106; of everyday life, 123; true, 106
Charmides, 105
Christ, 3, 9, 27, 31, 115, 130, 171, 213; *see also* Jesus
Christian(s), 61, 75n, 77, 91n, 170, 184, 213, 214n; animus, 171; churches, 71; criticism, 32; cultists, 120; cults, 209; culture, 187; cultus, 171; era, 60, 75n; godhead, 214n–215n; Jew-hatred, 171; mystery cult, 170; sentimentalism, 172; sentimentality, 211n; symbolic, 171; tradition, 30; transgressions, 51
Christianity, 137; new, 33, 75
Church(es), 2, 22, 34, 51, 51n, 61, 71, 74n, 75n, 78n, 93, 112n, 214n; death of, 51; self-glorification of, 49; militancy, 111; of one, 191; teaching, 34
Civility(ies), 50, 154, 159n, 184; antitype of, 92n; educated, 134; inhibiting, 168

Civilization, 47, 51, 83n, 103n, 106, 134n, 142n, 152, 167, 169, 188, 215; church, 51, 71; end of, 153, 154; repressive, 156; white, 112n

Class(es), 92n, 95n, 144n; conflict, 174; cultivated, 110, 112; culture, 144n; educated, 89, 134, 194n; leisured, 147; middle, 93; non-working, 107; presiding, 39; propertied, 57n, 172; re-educated, 20, 46, 50, 55, 67, 79, 98, 107n, 133, 147, 178, 210; true ruling, 166; upper, 101n; white working, 92n

Classroom, 2, 2n, 7, 15–17, 38, 58, 62, 73, 80n, 97, 98, 104, 132

Cleaver, Eldridge, 93n

Communist(s), 210, 215; Party, 156, 177n; state-party, 111n

Community(ies), 24, 60, 62, 66, 208; need-, 127; therapeutic, 124, 157

Comte, 32, 33, 45

Concealment(s), 10, 18, 38n, 48, 85, 191, 202; art of, 9; of (the) book, 189; intellectual, 210; self-, 44, 53, 55, 60, 72

Conduct, 2, 11, 133, 158n, 217n; codes of honorable, 116; of life, 17, 67, 144n; territories of, 106

Conrad, 189, 190; *Heart of Darkness*, 187–189

Conscience, 54, 82n, 88–90, 100, 181n, 207; American, 89; moral, 181n; negative, 180n, 181n; social, 90; transmoral, 181n

Conservatism, cultural, 37, 107

Conservative, 8, 57n, 149; purpose, 95n; movement, 126; vision, 66n; way of life, 152

Constitution (the), 158n, 159n

Constraint(s), 21, 70, 93, 216; of privileged knowledge, 35; social, 157

Contemplation, 186, 192; discipline of, 185

Contemporaneity, 92n; radical, 39, 96, 184, 185, 187, 194, 212; revolution of, 135

Contemporaries, 11, 95n, 116, 140, 163, 196; radical, 90n, 100, 213; true, 114n

Contempt, 55n, 65n, 151, 161, 166; democratization of, 150; dynamics of, 161; and rancor, 152; self-, 54n

Continuity(ies), 7, 12, 19, 193, 204n. 217; of interpretation, 15, 186; of presentation, 26; of resistance, 67; of theory, 132

Coser, Lewis, ed., 182n

'Counterculture,' 8, 37, 44, 90, 113, 169, 214

Cranch Report, 83n

'Creativity,' 26, 100, 151

Credal, 71; anti-, 69, 127, 151, 212; modalities, 144n; motifs, 127

Creed(s), 49, 50, 112n, 137, 151; anti-, 51, 127, 135

Crime(s), 35, 47, 55, 56, 65n, 99n, 163, 165, 166, 167, 168; and morals, 47; of passion, 206; primal, 99; of punishment, 162

Criminal(s), 43, 46, 55n, 64n, 93, 93n, 99, 112n, 113n, 116, 123, 163, 166, 168; cult of, 100; rehabilitation of, 167

Criminality, 46, 94, 100, 115–116, 166; political, 116; sphere of, 117

Critic(s) 19, 31, 32, 77, 90, 172; as artist, 74n; true, 88

Criticism(s), 4, 7, 8, 13–15, 18, 24, 27–33, 70, 77, 88, 90, 100, 109, 113n, 117, 130, 155, 163n, 168, 182, 183, 194n, 211; art of, 18; of authority, 28; Christian, 32; orgiasts of, 14; religion of, 8, 76n, 121, 163n; of repetition, 117; social, 42; true, 15, 18, 117; 'value,' 7

Cult(s), 20, 33, 54, 77, 98, 125, 134. 202, 209; Christian, 209; of the criminal, 100; of disobedience, 87; of educated civility, 134; of experience, 110; of genius, 65; of Jesus, 27; of the Jew, 79n; mystery-, 170; object, 99; of personality, 8, 54; victory, 171; of violence, 19; youth, 196

Cultural, 155n; achievement, 30; artifact, 85n; condition, 21; conservatism, 37, 107; development, 39, 55; disturbance, 89; document, 158n; egalitarianism, 52n, 101n, 146; history, 108; law, 167; orgiasts, 175; pietists, 22, 73, 73n; piety, 22; possibility, 115; problem, 76; psychopaths, 90; radicals, 37; revolution(s), 21, 103n, 147, 195, 205; revolutionaries, 44, 107; struggle, 96, 179, 179n

Culture(s), 4, 6, 8, 12, 14, 19–23, 25, 29–31, 33–36, 39, 41, 42, 44, 46, 48, 49, 51, 53, 54, 67, 67n, 69n, 70, 70n, 71, 73, 74n, 77, 83n, 85n, 88, 91n, 93, 94, 94n, 96, 99, 101n, 103, 106, 108, 113, 114n, 119n, 120, 123–126, 130, 130n, 136, 147, 150–152, 154, 155, 158n, 159, 159n, 161, 162, 163, 166, 170–172, 175, 178, 185, 194, 194n, 195, 202, 206–207, 215–217; American, 13n, 90, 90n, 93n, 102, 147, 196, 200; ancient, 174; anti-, 117, 128n, 178; anticredal, 137; architects of, 21; black, 91n, 101; bourgeois, 90; breakdown of, 19; Buddhist, 23; Christian, 187; class order, 164; commercial, 166; commercial technological, 8; conscious, 204; credal, 136, 137; defense of, 36, 57n, 76, 95, 202; destruction of, 15; dissolutions of, 197; end of, 152; English high, 200; fun, 109, high, 20, 20n, 68, 69, 69n, 70, 75n, 93n, 94n, 105, 106, 109, 156, 157, 168, 189, 193, 199, 216; impossible, 85n, 124, 135, 162n; inherited, 14, 103n, 148, 193; of Israel, 170; Jew(s) of, 46, 51, 83n, 95n, 112, 162, 198, 206; low, 106; objective, 70; pietists of, 20, 22; and politics, 14, 169; pop, 112n; rational, 70; received, 107; of the rich, 135, 135n; Roman, 110; scientists of, 69n; student, 53; theatrical, 111; theoretical, 193, 194n, 211n; theory of, 51, 66n, 68, 126, 132–133, 173, 200n; and therapy, 35; true, 46, 61n, 70n; of truth, 49, 61, 68, 110, 150, 160, 178, 197; universal, 46; unprogressive, 188; war of, 20, 106; wasp, 101; western, 66n, 92n, 127, 146, 180n; working class, 91n; youth, 103n, 106, 174, 196

Cunningham, Lawrence, ed., 186n; Brother Francis, 186n

Curiosity, 159n, 169; intellectual, 82n

Dada, 128n

Daube, David, 154n

Davis, Angela, 107, 137, 195n, 196n

Davis, Sammy, 82

Death, 14n, 42, 48, 56, 61, 63, 65n, 70, 71, 75n 112, 114, 116, 129, 131, 135, 136, 139, 163, 179n, 182n, 204n, 207; of the church, 51; dealers, 71, 189; figures of, 106; of God, 58; of teaching, 6

Deceits, 31, 63; of escape, 34; of mind, 42; of resistance, 31

Decriminalization, 116, 165

Defilement, 143n, 159n; carnal self-, 142n

Definitions, 144n

Demands, 175; instinctual, 102; interdictory, 175; Jewish moral, 53n; moral, 70, 104n, 133, 141, 152, 195

Democracy, 39, 104n, 126, 162n; authentic, 135; of emotions, 172; of love, 172; political, 6

Denial(s), 16, 28, 69; language of, 75n; of reality, 80n; self-, 98

Deprivation, 114n, 150; self-, 207

De Sade, 129

Descartes, 57

Desire(s), 32, 84, 85, 143n, 188, 207; limits of, 207; and power, 207

Destruction, 11, 103, 128n, 151, 198, 206; of aristocracies, 125; of culture, 15; of the family, 107; of historical memory, 78;

Destruction (cont'd)
  of ideal existences, 78; of reverence, 124; self-, 198; of truth, 14
Desublimation, 184, 185; theory of, 182
Deviancy, 90; moral, 107
Deviant(s), 90, 115, 123, 182; and straights, 46; black, 103n
Dewey, John, 115
Disciple(s), 10, 59, 162, 173, 174, 176, 176n, 179, 216; of Moses, 161n; rich, 176n; true, 172
Discipline(s), 2, 3, 3n, 11, 15-16, 23, 33, 34, 38, 47 48, 61, 71, 98, 114n, 125, 127, 152, 159n, 172, 175, 179, 190, 192, 192n, 196, 201n, 208n; of containment, 190; of contemplation, 185; credal, 111n, 112n; hermeneutic, 200n; historical, 106, 107; interdictory, 195; of judgment, 144n; of limit, 61; of modesty, 191; objective, 174; organizational, 111n; pedagogic, 217; of pictures, 3n; repressive, 144n; self-, 178; technological, 144n; of theory, 2; visionary, 2
Disestablishment(s), 20; rhapsodies of, 195; superiority of, 172
Disobedience, cult of, 87
Disorder(s), 16, 50, 182, 197, 207
Disrespect, 164n, 177, 203n; for self, 100
Dissolution(s), 97, 179; of authority, 179; of cultures, 197; of historical memory, 97; of interdictory, 208; of respect, 100; therapeutic, 98
Distance(s), 5, 19, 22, 27, 111, 132, 139, 172, 212, 214; historical, 199n; humane, 172, 175; inner, 5, 100, 111, 134; proper, 134, 178
Dostoyevsky, 34, 100; The Devils, 100
Dress, 183, 183n; modern, 77
Dru, Alexander, ed., 159n
Duchamp, 52n

Du Bois, W. E. B., 43n, 93n, 94n, 103n
Durkheim, 44, 44-45, 100, 116, 123, 144n
Duty(ies), 4, 6, 17, 52, 143n, 159n, 166, 216; pedagogic, 14

Educated: classes, 89, 134, 149n; man, 39; re-, 39, 89, 107, 126, 160, 164, 165n, 167, 172, 180n, 183, 184; transgressively, 100
Education, 32, 93, 144n, 194n, 195n; higher, 196; of intellects, 3; mass, 42, 94-97; moral, 192; object of, 61; re-, 46, 49, 83, 107, 176n, 191; totalitarian, 210; of the young, 145n; universal higher, 13
Egalitarianism, 94, 203; cultural, 52n, 101n, 146
Ego(s), 5, 53, 110, 163, 191, 203; identity, 145n
Elias, Norbert, 134n; Über den Prozess der Zivilization, 134n
Eliot, T. S., 13n, 69n, 216; Notes Toward A Definition of Culture, 216
Elite(s), 42, 69n, 96, 127, 140, 146; anti-credal, 126, 157; credal, 126; ex-religious, 146; new, 12
Emptiness, 21, 49, 62, 64n, 114, 115, 120, 130, 131, 132, 188; therapeutic, 164
Enfantin, 75
Engels, Frederick, 20, 84n
Enlightenment(s), 43, 88, 100, 112, 146; of therapy, 55
Equality, 102, 122, 130; of results, 172; universal, 171
Erasmus, 133, 180n
Erikson, Erik H., 49, 180n, 181n, 207; Young Man Luther, 180n
Eros, 9, 24, 67n, 180, 206; symbolic, 214; and Thanatos, 67n
Erotic(s), 110, 131, 134; arenas, 168; caprice, 214; circles, 85, 130; combat, 130; health, 197; manicons, 138; sphere, 127, 179-180, 179n, 180n, 212; strategy, 135
Eroticism, 133, 138, 146, 172, 207

Ethic(s), 39, 60, 120, 157; bio-, 89; of conscience, 207; of honesty, 60, 63; of self-deprivation, 207; true, 207
Eve, 143, 152
'Everything new' syndrome, 21
Evil, 7, 23, 112n, 123, 150n, 165, 187, 188n
Existentialists, 111, 182n, 212, 214
Existenz, 213, 214
Experience(s), 8, 14, 20, 24, 34, 38, 64, 73, 77, 86, 98, 102, 122, 138, 139, 140, 154n, 181n, 198n; assaults of, 63, 73, 85, 86, 110; cult of, 110; cultic, 196; essential, 154n; intellectual, 139; literary, 97; national, 89; original, 196; polytheist of, 132; quest for, 8; quest of, 122
Expression, 67, 112n, 215; self-, 37n, 50, 77, 174
Expressional quest, 36, 64, 65, 65–66, 165, 179, 205; questioning, 174; self-, 93
Ezekiel, 7

Facts, 5, 7, 24, 85, 88, 157, 158, 163, 164; neurotic, 87; and reasons, 117–120; social, 157; superiority of, 159
Faith(s), 22, 23, 25, 27–32, 35, 44–46, 50, 75n, 77, 80n, 83, 118, 171, 181n, 213, 214n; in Christ, 171; as criticism, 29; in criticism, 29, 31, 77, 88; cultivated, 29; and culture, 30; in 'faith,' 51; of Israel, 75n; Jewish, 171; leaps of, 214; militant, 111n; pasts of, 75n; steadfast, 35, 114n; and truth, 117; virtuoso of, 29, 31, 34; vision of, 34
Family(ies), 97, 106, 204n, 208n, contemporary, 97; destruction of, 107; modern, 203; order, 208n; romance, 28, 203; working-class, 107
Fanon, Frantz, 15, 43n, 50, 93n, 145, 146, 216
Fascism, 50, 151
Fear, 109n, 163, 166, 175; lawful, 164; thresholds of, 165

Fields, W. C., 205
Flesh, 183, 184, 188; rehabilitation of, 189, 197
Follower(s), 24, 28, 32, 59, 77, 110, 111, 210; cult-, 171; student, 10
Fonda, Jane, 156
Footnote(s), 2n, 31
Force, 161, 191; physical, 148, 159
Forgetfulness, 75n, 133, 185
Form(s), 38n, 44, 46, 51, 51n, 64n, 65, 67, 70, 106, 205, 207; art, 154n; authoritative, 197; catholic, 44; contempt for, 151; of culture, 93n; of disciplines, 179; of existence, 111; of fighting, 130; of government, 93n; interdictory, 35, 117, 118, 152, 162, 189, 197, 207; interdictory-remissive, 70; moral, 63, 64, 72, 147; moralizing, 20, 151; political, 149; public, 157n, 163; of rationalization, 69; of resistance, 110; of respect, 146; of revolution, 101; social, 3n
Forman, Maurice Buxton, ed., 117n; *The Letters of John Keats*, 117n
Freedom(s), 12, 20, 30, 35, 39, 42, 45, 46, 50, 60, 94n, 124, 129, 136, 158n, 159n, 168, 174, 206, 214; academic, 18; existential, 136; fighters, 106, 186; inner, 39; of inquiry, 101; new, 12; of press, 158n; of speech, 158n, 159n; of the therapeutic, 130
Freud, 2, 10, 14, 16, 33, 35, 36, 45, 46, 47, 58n, 66n, 69, 69n, 84, 84n, 85n, 86, 89, 93n, 99, 100, 104n, 107, 115, 133, 142, 146, 152n, 153n, 185, 186, 210, 212, 215, 216, 216n; *Character and Culture*, 153n; *Dora: An Analysis of a Case of Hysteria*, 84n; *General Psychological Theory*, 69n; *The Interpretation of Dreams*, 36, 85n; *Moses and Monotheism*, 99; *The Psychopathology of Everyday Life*, 142; *Totem and Taboo*, 86, 86n, 99n

Freudian, 80, 108, 164n, 203; bio-ethic, 89; dichotomy, 108n; doctrine, 88; therapeutic model, 14–15
Fromm, Erich, 78n
Fry, Roger, 52n
Functionalism, 51n, 209

Gandhi, 123n
Geertz, Clifford, 25, 34n, 114n; Terry Lectures, 25; *Islam Observed*, 25, 34n
Geis, Bernard, 195n, 196n
Genesis, 109n, 202n
Genius(es), 13, 24, 26, 27, 29, 31, 32, 45, 46, 50, 65, 77, 87, 99, 103n, 137, 151, 151n, 170, 172, 186, 212; apostle-, 7; and apostle, 27; commercial, 71; critical, 109; of criticism, 27; cult of, 65; heterodoxies of, 87; moral, 45; neurotic, 109; order of, 100; theatrical, 137; true, 151n; work of, 151n
Godard, 157n
Godhead(s), 9, 20, 21, 22, 58, 100, 166; Christian, 214n–215n
God-term(s), 3, 9, 18, 21, 39, 48, 49, 53, 55, 58, 62, 67, 68, 70, 100, 104, 112 116, 127, 129, 131, 150, 209, 214n, 215n; anti-, 184, 185; dead, 112; female, 74; true, 197
Gods: dead, 48; risen, 135; rush-hour of (the), 76–77; true, 72; western, 76
Goethe, 121, 133, 133n; *Elective Affinities*, 133, 133n
Good, 118, 136, 207, 211n; and bad, 202; critical, 90; and evil, 112n, 165
Goodman, Paul, 149
Gouldner, Alvin W., 76n; *The Coming Crisis of Western Sociology*, 76n
Government(s), 22, 93n; worker's, 177n
Grace, 17, 121, 163, 164
Grading, 154n
Gramsci, 51n
Griffiths, D. W., 92n

Growth, 178
Guides, 17, 22, 24, 50, 150; museum, 195n
Guilt, 7, 47, 61n, 93n, 109n, 121, 155, 156, 160, 164, 169; false, 48, 50, 75n, 109, 113n, 156, 167, 183n; knowledge of, 61n; provokers, 160; sense of, 99, 100, 155, 215; true, 94n, 100, 155, 156, 157, 167, 185; virtuoso of, 186n
Guiltlessness, 139, 181n
Guru(s), 6, 8, 9, 12, 13, 24, 53, 162n, 172, 178, 193, 197n, 205, 208; of experimental Life, 97; humanist, 108n; revolutionary, 90, 112n

Habit, 115, 195
Harnack, Adolph, 22, 23n; *Outlines of the History of Dogma*, 23n
Hatred: Jew-, 1, 40n 170; self-, 1, 112n, 188n; transgressive, 35
Haydn, 2, 3, 10, 93n, 173
Health, 32, 197; quest for, 48; as religion, 77
Heath, 149n
Heisenberg, Werner, 40, 41
Hermeneutic circles, 14, 19, 76n, 94
Hippies, 169, 170
History, 10, 68n, 108, 136, 142, 171, 174, 201; contemporary intellectual, 105n; primal, 86, 99, 120, 123, 202, 216
Hitler, 46, 64, 137, 138, 152, 158
Holy men, 197, 198, 204, 205
Honesty, 55, 61, 130, 202; ethic of, 60, 63
Hopkins, 3
Horror(s), 57, 98, 129, 156, 170, 181n, 189, 204, 216
Hostility(ies), 14, 20, 105n, 107, 125, 140, 151, 200; to culture, 8, 20, 42, 150, 216; sexualized, 163n; of suppliants, 163
Huizinga, 83n; *Geschichte und Kultur*, 83n
'Humanization,' 48
Hume, 145, 145n, 146, 198n
Humiliation, 32, 138, 139, 142, 171

228

Id, 112n, 115, 116
Idea(s), 2, 5–8, 13, 13n, 14, 19, 24, 33, 39, 60, 65–67, 69, 82n, 131, 142, 145n, 183, 183n, 190, 191, 208; organization of, 33; Freudian, 35; Socratic, 8; theatre of, 6, 131
Ideal(s), 103, 116, 121, 152, 207, 211; repressive, 112n
Idealization(s), 107, 108n
Identity: crisis, 78, 79, 203n; ego, 145n; institutional, 190; problem of, 78; quester, 207; seekers, 179; of self, 165; shrinkage, 200; suicide, 80n
Ideology(ies), 13n, 44, 71, 202
Illich, Ivan, 91, 92
Imagination, 100, 143n; historical, 194n; liberal, 198n; Protestant, 35
Immediacy(ies), 22, 23, 31, 43, 144n, 145, 188
Immobility, 84, 136, 147, 152, 178
Impulse(s), 43, 44, 53, 109, 115, 143n, 144n, 152, 182, 195, 199n
Indirections, 6, 9, 10, 52, 72, 184
Infinite, 37n, 214n; plasticity, 127; torment of the, 211, 214
Inhibition(s), 21, 43, 52, 53, 73, 108, 115, 133, 152, 156, 179; of civilization, 103n; neurotic, 136; racist, 102; white, 102
Innocence, 6, 160, 179n
Instinct(s), 98, 112, 115, 150; theory, 115
Institution(s), 5, 18, 22, 52, 65n, 70, 92, 100, 102, 108, 112n, 127, 144n, 154n, 189, 191; academic, 88, 96; democratic, 162n; political, 125; powerless, 18, 205; repressive, 93; sacred, 6, 8, 199n, 217; teaching, 209; theatrical, 125; therapeutic, 9, 51
Intellect(s), 12, 13n, 25, 43n, 59n, 70, 96, 111, 125, 140, 172, 197; cat house of (the), 88, 139, 172; chain of, 172; critical, 98; education of, 3; enforcement of, 6; feeling, 5, 8, 29, 32, 38, 53, 97, 109, 125, 156, 173,

174, 191, 198; force of, 101; temple of the, 6, 9, 12, 17, 198; virtuoso of, 207
Intellectual(s), 24, 29, 40, 48, 100, 106, 118, 127n, 147, 148n, 162n, 190, 200, 209, 213, 215n; aristocracy, 6; aspiration, 101; authority, 15, 67, 124; cadres, 112; capacity, 205; concealment, 210; curiosity, 82n; experience, 139; failed, 15; freelance, 190; gossip, 192; history, 105n; integrity, 53; interest, 48; as interpreter, 215n; justice, 3; modern, 31, 209; nullities, 3, 97; presence, 14; questions, 118; revolutionary, 43n; supremacy, 32; teaching, 4n, 5
Intellectualization, 73, 191; of self, 191
Intelligence, 14, 16, 88, 105n, 140, 142n; superior, 13
Intelligentsia, 51, 215n
Intemperance, honest, 29; refined, 29, 30
Interdict(s), 25, 35, 36, 38, 41, 42, 44, 45, 47, 49–51, 54n, 56, 68, 69, 70–74, 87, 93, 97, 99, 100, 101, 108, 110–112, 120–123, 126, 131, 138, 139, 141, 142, 147, 156, 160, 162, 163, 165–168, 174, 177, 183, 185, 186, 189, 196, 197, 202, 203, 207, 216, 217; authoritative, 104n; defense of, 71; inherited, 35, 142n; meaningful, 93, 99; order of, 167; recognizers of, 121; supreme, 119
Interdictory, 17, 23, 25, 49, 54, 73, 92n, 97, 106, 142, 158n, 166, 179; achievements, 185; analysis, 183; authority, 137; cadres, 21; character, 207; contents, 56n, 69; demands, 175; discipline, 195; dissolution of, 208; energies, 123; father-god, 99; figures, 101, 114, 117, 162, 176, 213; form, 35, 117, 118, 152, 162, 189, 197, 207; instruction, 42; intensity, 71, 72; life, 185; meaning, 103; mode, 184;

Interdictory (cont'd)
mood, 30; motifs, 22, 34, 51, 69, 81n, 116, 150, 169; nature of authority, 42; order 41; particularities, 160; primacy, 150; re-cognition, 121; rule, 165n; style, 71; symbolics, 127; thrust, 92n, 120; violence, 59
Interdictory-remissive, 42, 51n, 53, 53n, 141, 147, 148, 168, 171; forms, 70
Interdictory-transgressive, 195
Interior: change, 21; controls, 41; flexibility, 54; space, 1, 3, 10, 18, 21
Interpretation, 4, 10, 15, 17, 18, 36, 39, 47, 77, 84, 85, 130, 139, 159, 160, 160n, 162n, 173, 186, 202, 216; chain of, 38, 105, 217; continuity of, 15, 186; critical, 18, 130; therapeutic, 179
Interpreter(s), 10, 11, 24, 36, 39, 61n, 203, 215n; authoritative, 150; chain of, 14, 19; intellectual as, 215n; scientific, 39; teaching, 36; therapeutic, 77; true, 11
The Interpreter's Bible, 59n
Inwardness, 53, 117, 212; absence of, 113; contempt for, 55n; residual, 55, 57
Irresponsibility, 197
Israel, 4n, 21, 68, 75n, 92n, 99, 155, 170, 172, 202, 203; future of, 75n; tradition of, 109n
I-Thou, 53n

Jacob, 109n, 201, 202, 209
James, 2, 13n, 52n
James, Henry, 13, 58n, 67, 72, 204; The American Scene, 204; What Maisie Knew, 67
James, William, 58n, 95n; Psychology, 95n
Jesus, 9, 10, 16, 27, 116, 120, 121, 171, 180, 185, 213, 213n; see also Christ
Jew(s), 25, 40n, 47, 51, 53n, 77, 78, 79n, 80n, 81, 83, 84, 86, 89, 109n, 112, 135, 170, 171, 177n, 213; American, 81n, 198; contemporary, 75n, 80n;

cult of (the), 79n; of culture, 46, 51, 83n, 95n, 112, 162, 198, 206; definition of, 78; emancipation of (the), 79n; essence of (the), 79n; ex-, 77n, 78, 78n, 81n, 86, 171, 176n; non-Jewish, 112n, 170, 171; particularity of, 171; psychological, 216n; real, 78n, 79n; sabbath, 78n, 80n, 82; true, 202
Jew-hatred, 1, 40n, 170; Christian, 171
Jewish, 92, 138, 182n; anti-, 171, 177n
Jewry, 176n; ex-, 170
Job, 65n, 109n, 131
John XXII, 114n
Jones, Ernest, 85n; The Formative Years and the Great; Discoveries, 85n
Joodeyism, new, 75n
Judaism, 75n, 79n, 80n
Judgment(s), 27, 56, 135, 141, 181n, 203; of authority, 27; danger of, 202; discipline of, 144n
Justice, 17, 56, 112, 116, 124, 125, 152, 161, 162, 170, 172, 177n, 202; compensatory, 102, 104n; destruction of, 124; intellectual, 3
Justification(s), 19, 23, 24, 28, 41, 49, 70, 71, 125, 148, 162n; through faith, 181n; inner, 17, 148; language of, 209; order of, 24; personal, 136; self-, 165, 174

Kafka, 61, 65, 109, 164n; The Penal Colony, 164n
Kairos, 190n
Kant, 55, 142n, 143n, 144n, 151n, 159n, 198n; Kant's Critique of Aesthetic Judgment, 151n; The Doctrine of Virtue, 143n
Kennedy, John F., 149n, 204
Kenney, Father Gregory, 71n; Sex and the Young Catholic, 71n
Kierkegaard, 25, 26, 28, 29, 31–34, 53, 87, 90, 128n, 158, 159n, 169, 180n, 182n, 212, 212n, 213, 214n; Attack Upon Chris-

tendom, 28n; *Concluding Unscientific Postscript,* 212n; *Either/Or,* 128n; *Journals,* 158, 159n, 182n
King, Martin Luther, 92
Kluckhohn, Clyde, 68n; *Culture,* 68n
Knowledge, 3, 5, 8, 10, 19, 23, 61n, 66n, 74n, 117, 125, 130, 131, 133, 161n, 162n, 163, 165n, 167, 174, 177, 191, 198n, 199n; cultureless, 126; dead, 3, 5; factories, 124; false, 62; of guilt, 61n; hermeneutic, 11; industry, 7, 9, 12, 76, 96, 97, 108n, 193; of inescapability, 22; inherited, 21; managers, 193; personal, 9, 29, 97; privileged, 9, 10, 15, 23, 24, 30, 35, 61n, 72, 97, 117, 118, 124, 125, 169, 175, 193; renascence of, 175; self-defensive, 72
Köster, Kurt, ed., 83n
Kroeber, A, L., 68n; *Culture,* 68n
Kropotkin, 149
Kyodan, P. L., 77

Laing, R D., 197, 197n
Language, 192; of denial, 75n; of justifications, 209; locker room, 184; of morals, 141; of romance, 207; of spontaneity, 151; of trust, 113
Law(s), 17, 25, 40n, 56, 56n, 67, 70, 111n, 112, 116, 121, 158n, 159n, 163, 165–167, 197; codes of, 162; cultural, 167; doctrine of, 143n; of duty, 143n; Jewish, 120; of mediocrities, 96n; and morality, 57n; and oracles, 161n; and order, 84, 98, 112, 120, 151; order of, 56; sociological, 111n; submission to, 144n
Lawrence, D. H., 158n
Leach, Edmund, 106; Reith Lectures, 106
Leader(s), 108, 108n, 110, 111, 142; empty, 131; ideal, 111; rebel, 152n
Learning(s), 13, 14, 16, 25, 62, 87, 198n; book-, 126, 207; higher, 87, 95, 125; re-, 136

Lenin, 16, 20, 148
Levi-Strauss, Claude, 134n; *Mythologiques,* 134n
Liberation, 13n, 44, 48, 61, 184
Life, 60, 62, 70, 100, 106, 110, 112, 115, 131, 132, 144n, 152, 174, 183, 189, 190, 205, 211; academic, 130; aestheticizing of, 135; apostles of, 71; artistries, 110; color, 112n; experimental, 49, 97; interdictory, 185; love of, 142n, 143n; meaningful, 160; moral, 208; political, 198n; public, 46, 111, 112; styles, 12, 90, 152, 164; therapeutic, 208; work of, 64
Limit(s), 16, 21, 30, 36n, 40, 41–43, 46, 59, 123, 129, 148, 159n, 203n; art of, 36, 165; of desire, 207; disciplines of, 61; of power, 207; of prudence, 217; reconstructed, 71; ritual, 168; science of, 41–43, 159, 163; self-, 167; systems of, 64
Limitlessness, 159n
Links, 15, 38, 173; in chain of interpretation, 105; in chain of interpreters, 19
Locke, 141
Love, 9, 33, 63, 64n, 65n, 84, 133, 138, 145, 146, 161n, 166, 170, 172, 175, 179, 181, 197, 208, 214; acosmic, 10, 208; affair, 145; democracy of, 172; of humanity, 170; of life, 142n, 143n; object, 145; sexual, 142n
Loyola, 186n
Luther, Martin, 26–28, 31, 49, 179n, 180n, 181n, 182n, 215n; *Table Talk,* 27
Lutheran: jurisprudence, 162n; psychologizing, 214n; symbolic, 181n

Machiavelli, 19, 209
Mailer, Norman, 103n, 104n, 154n; *Advertisements For Myself,* 104n; *An American Dream,* 154n; *Deer Park,* 154n
Man, 21, 32, 33, 39, 51, 54n, 79, 84, 88, 120, 160, 196; civilizing, 186n; contemporary, 45,

231

Man (*cont'd*)
79, 103; educated, 39; European, 188; of leisure, 129; moral, 163; natural, 152–154, 154n, 188; one-dimensional, 144n; plastic, 210; psychological, pref. note, 143n, 144n, 178, 205; re-educated, 153; species-, 84, 130, 131; superior, 30; theorist of, 214; transgressive, 120; universal, 120
Mann, Thomas, 92; *The Magic Mountain*, 92
Manner(s), 24, 64, 153, 184, 200; mild, 134
Mannerliness, 8
Mao, 83n
Marcuse, Herbert, 103n, 108n, 144n, 205–207
Marx, Karl, 1, 16, 33, 40n, 44, 58n, 78, 78n, 79, 82, 83, 84n, 89, 90, 112n, 116, 117, 160, 172, 173, 200, 201, 210, 216; *Capital*, 83; *Early Writings*, 78n; *The Process of Capitalist Production*, 84n
Marx, Groucho, 58n
Marxism, 18, 126, 127
Marxist, 4, 16, 18, 40n, 80, 120, 144n, 170, 176n, 211; example, 89; movement, 126, 127; optimism, 112n; party, 18; symbolic, 40n; synthesis, 40n; theory, 78, 79, 201
Master(s), 3, 9, 11, 61n, 176n, 179, 179n, 201n; of culture, 172; and disciple, 59, 173, 174, 176; of moral theology, 71n; non-, 124; of privacy, 173; true, 58n
Mazzola, John W., 5
Mead, Margaret, 91
Meaning(s), 41, 43, 54n, 86, 87, 88, 108, 115, 129, 131, 147, 158n, 160, 160n, 162n, 176, 185, 211, 214; inner, 112n; interdictory, 103; order of, 47; of pain, 65n; sociological, 150; of speed, 135n; totemic, 175
Meaninglessness, 136
Mediocrities, 96; law of, 96n
Memory, 174, 183, 186, 187, 195n;

historical, 4n, 39, 78, 79, 97, 128n, 135, 174, 184; destruction of, 78, dissolutions of, 97
Messiah, 120, 121, 170, 196, 204, 209, 214n
Metamorphosis(es), 25–27, 31, 32, 34, 43, 78, 79, 81–84, 92n, 102, 104, 106, 113n, 120, 122, 136, 138, 149, 155, 157n, 161n, 184, 187, 189, 213; Jacob, 203n; political, 148; of rejection, 150; sociological, 29; of therapy, 80; *Abrahamic/rabbinic*, 203; *ancient/modern*, 159; *anti-political/dissolution of power*, 149; *artists/apostles*, 73; *artists/paratherapists*, 151; *Aunt Angela/ Stalin*, 107; *authority/obedience*, 27, 32; *'charismatic'/ technological*, 117; *Christian/ unchurched*, 162; *commercial/ political*, 92n; *credal/political*, 104n; *culture/politics*, 213; *danger/money*, 196; *dis-ease/ ease*, 88; *economic/political*, 138; *Either/Or*, 25, 26, 34, 128n; *fame/money*, 130, 201; *Family/Society*, 168; *famous/ money*, 155; *friend/disciple*, 179n; *genital/oral*, 102; *God/ Man*, 84; *good/evil*, 82, 120; *healer/killer*, 154; *hidden (or abstract) criminality/normality*, 113n; *historical/political*, 216; *horse/god*, 213; *input/output*, 136; *intellectual/charismatic*, 106; *interesting/boring*, 141; *Jacob/Jake*, 78; *Jake/Gala*, 211; *Jake/Man*, 84; *Jew/ bourgeois*, 79; *Jew/Science*, 81; *Judeo/Christian*, 79; *Judeo-Christian/Mother Nature destroyer*, 81; *leader/teacher*, 176; *Lenin/Stalin*, 44, 108, 173; *love/death*, 74, 138; *Masses/ one*, 112n, 187; *master/crippled pet*, 122; *media/message*, 158n; *Messiah/man*, 213; *money/energy*, 90; *money/Jew*, 83; *Naphta/Illich*, 92, 93, 94; *neither/nor*, 29; *normal/ab-*

normal, 120; *obedience/authority*, 27, 28, 32; *obvious enemies/ objective friends*, 97; *open-mouthed/power driving*, 187; *organization/charismatic*, 28; *permanent revolution/boundless greed*, 84; *personal/theoretical*, 29, 217; *Protestant sentimentalism/modern sociology*, 161n; *race war/cultural revolution*, 92n; *rationalizing/irrationalizing*, 150; *reconciliatory/dichotomizing*, 213; *rehabilitator/waster*, 189; *retold/ -tailed*, 213; *sado/machochistic*, 183; *Saul/Paul*, 31, 34, 170, 171, 213; *sex/violence*, 157n, 158n; *sexual/political*, 138; *sexuality/violence*, 184; *Socrates/Plato*, 25; *solitude/ loneliness*, 192; *success/failure*, 216; *successor/functional equivalent*, 192; *superb student/master punter*, 82n; *technological/ 'charismatic,'* 177; *think/enact*, 193; *truth/faith*, 117; *Uncle Tom/Mooney*, 107; *victim/ hero*, 113n; *x/y*, 25

Michelangelo, 46

Mill, John Stuart, 46, 47, 47n, 89n, 90, 140, 141; *Dissertation and Discussions*, 89n; *The Spirit of the Age*, 141

Milton, 217

Mind(s), 3, 4, 4n, 6, 10, 11–13, 13n, 18, 19, 23, 33, 35, 46, 49, 60, 61, 64, 66n, 67, 70n, 71, 88, 91n, 106, 141, 145n, 173, 179n, 185, 190, 191, 198n, 199n, 205, 206, 211, 214, 216; anti-, 42, 216; changes in, 35; changes of, 21; confidence in, 198n; deceits of, 42; life of (the), 12, 24, 42, 48, 197; music of (the), 189; smallness of, 216; state of, 78; training of, 199n; violation of, 24

Mindfulness, 3, 4, 73n, 130, 198n

Mindlessness, 46, 189

Mishima, Yukio, 155; *Sun and Steel*, 155

Misunderstanding, 1, 10, 50, 179

Mobility, 147; upward, 178

Modern(s), 20, 39, 164, 173, 187; art, 52n, 67, 75n, 114, 151, 151n, 157; culture, 57n, 70, 216; masses, 110; politics, 210; revolutionary, 138; state, 148

Money, 7n, 8, 12, 33, 78, 79n, 83, 84, 96, 97, 101n, 102, 104n, 117, 124, 133, 157n, 201n

Monroe, Marilyn, 82

Moore, Bishop, 105n

Moral(s), 21, 27, 36, 47, 100, 141; Jewish, 86; language of, 141; questions, 131; sense, 72, 147

Morality, 30, 44, 57n, 127, 140, 143n, 152, 178; bourgeois, 157n; established, 140; genesis of, 99; new, 140; passionate, 147; Reformation, 52

More, 180n

Morrell, Lady Ottoline, 118n, 119n

Moses, 99, 162; disciple of, 161n

Movement(s), 4, 4n, 15, 33, 52, 55, 56n, 62, 63, 141, 176n, 177n, 200, 206, 209; antinomian, 89, 116; fascist, 50; gnostic, 147n, 150, 150n; historical, 210; Marxist, 126, 127; mass, 42; messianic, 171; of modernity, 20; national, 177n; Nazis, 138; political, 146; protest, 92n, 155; social, 13; therapeutic, 164, 165, 176n, 208, 209, 213; totalitarian, 131, 210; transgressive, 74; Trotskyist, 111n; youth, 145n

Mozart, 26

Multiversity, 125, 127, 154n, 191, 193

Murder, 56, 101, 119, 122, 127, 154n, 206; self-, 55, 63, 143n, 154

Music, 2, 4, 46, 165n, 174, 175, 196

Mussolini, 50

Mystiques, 183; of change, 25, 35; computer, 125; flesh, 184; of problem solving, 125; self-, 189; technological, 144n; transgressive, 172

Myth(s), 61n, 211; phallic, 43n

233

Naipaul, V. S., 176n
Name changes, 81n
Natural man, 152–154, 154n, 188
Nazis, 137, 138, 210
Need(s), 17, 145
Negro(es), 103n, 104n; white, 104n
Neuroses, 39, 157; historical, 55; of immobility, 84
New (the), 204; prophet of (the), 15; tradition of (the), 123, 185
Newton, 72n
Nietzsche, 7, 33, 54n, 55n, 56, 77, 79, 82, 153n, 164, 170, 172; *Beyond Good and Evil*, 55n
Nihilism, 150, 150n
Nixon, R. M., 149n, 204
No, 10, 122, 136, 181
Normality, 116, 153, 154

Obedience(s), 26–28, 31, 32, 38, 53, 59, 67, 73, 87, 103n, 123, 152, 156, 186; critical, 107
Object(s), 32, 143n; of education, 61; public, 5; sacred, 125; of therapy, 179; of transference, 186; truest, 11; of understanding, 1; of worship, 33
Objectivity, 1, 4, 5, 12, 17, 108, 126, 197
Old Testament, 109n, 195n
One (the), 176n, 187; unrecognized, 90
Oppositions, 5, 20, 21, 30, 169
Order(s), 9, 16, 20–22, 27, 39, 48, 49, 56, 70, 112, 120, 122, 136, 141, 151, 170, 186n, 197, 207, 208, 208n, 210, 215; academic, 18; anti-credal, 54n; of authoritative persons, 56; of authority, 136; civil, 22, 106; class, 164; constraining, 71; of creation, 1; credal, 53n; of decision, 26; of descent, 28, 106; established, 132; historical, 42; hoppers, 9, 21; hopping, 12, 117, 209; humane, 134; idea of, 199n; inherited, 139; institutional, 88; interdictory, 41; interdictory-remissive, 141, 142; of interdicts, 167; of justifica-

tions, 24; of law, 56; of meaning, 47; moral, 150, 159n, 169; perverse, 102; political, 18, 19, 55, 127, 166; primal, 28; principle of, 17, 18; prophetic, 116; public, 47; right, 91, 92, 101, 167, 182, 183; social, 12, 21, 36, 76, 77, 104n, 106, 147, 148, 153, 159, 166, 175, 195, 212, 215; teaching, 25, 88, 199n; totalitarian, 210; of truth, 144n
Organization(s), 25, 142, 209; charismatic, 22–23, 28, 34; credal, 51, 118, 163n–164n, 176n, 180n; scientific, 118; social, 9, 27, 31, 45
Orgiasts, 14, 19, 24; cultural, 175; democratic, 162; self-conscious, 98
Orgy, 98, 113, 144n, 162n, 196, 202
Originality(ies), 16, 24, 26, 44, 48, 151, 151n
Orrill, Robert, prefatory note, 104
Orthodox(ies), 28, 87

Paratherapists, 76, 77, 91, 112n, 124, 137, 142, 214
Paratherapy(ies), 141–143, 142n
Parent(s), 12, 14, 28, 75n, 90, 92, 128n, 169n, 185, 202, 203, 208n; rich, 204; supportive, 122; true, 38
Past(s), 7, 12, 15, 22, 39, 48, 78, 82, 99, 101, 105, 117, 129, 174, 186, 188, 193, 194n, 195n; authority of (the), 15, 23, 77n, 185, 192n; black, 101; immediate, 87
Patient(s), 36, 126, 137, 179; therapist-, 121
Peckenpah, 157n
People, the, 83, 112, 113, 149, 176n, 212; 'Power to the People,' 148, 170; unprofessional, 148, 149
Performance(s), 7, 10, 11, 12, 14, 33, 36, 98, 102, 133, 135, 191, 209, 217; critical 11; public, 147

Perón, 177n
Personal, 6, 11, 25, 32; authority, 11, 131; experience, 8; gift, 9; justification, 136; knowledge, 9, 29, 97; re-cognitions, 9; superiority, 82n, 94n, 125; teaching, 125; understandings, 12, 17, 197
Personality(ies), 8, 44, 73n, 74n, 115, 122, 153, 187; cult of, 8, 54
Perversion, 113n, 181, 182, 182n, 183
Philo, 159n, 161n; *Works of Philo,* 159n
Pietist(s), 21; cultural, 22, 73, 73n; of culture, 20, 22; moderns, 182
Piety, 61 161n; cultural, 22; of silences, 27
Pinal, Silvia, 74n
Pinter, 73; 'Old Times,' 73
Pirandello, 103, 104, 113n, 122, 127n, 128, 130, 133; *Il giuoco delle parti,* 127n; *The Rules of the Game,* 103, 113n, 128
Plato, 10, 14, 16, 21, 25, 26, 56n, 93n, 132, 173, 202; *The Republic,* 132
Pleasure(s), 9, 20, 28, 66n, 100, 110, 143n, 156, 191; literary, 63; pursuits of, 7, 20, 52n, 88, 89, 103, 129, 156
"The Plowman," 174
Point of view, 211, 211n
Political, 152, 174; authority, 165; criminality, 116; decline, 101n; democracy, 6; dramaturgy, 137; enemies, 44; form, 149; game, 166; history, 63; institutions, 125; kunstler, 137; life, 198n; medicine, 122, 216; men, 110; metamorphoses, 148; movement, 146; order(s), 18, 19, 55, 127, 166; power, 18; psychiatrist, 50; religion(s), 51n, 210; representatives, 106; resolution, 104n; science, 10; selves, 111; sense, 202; sides, 4n; theatre, 9, 12, 92n, 123
Politics, 14, 17, 27, 31, 33, 41, 44, 46, 52, 66n, 93n, 97, 101n, 110, 123, 127, 131, 138, 148, 149, 151, 153n, 156, 157, 169, 170, 173, 174, 199, 200, 209, 210, 213, 216; anti-, 151; art of, 156; fun of, 156; mass, 131; modern, 210; practical, 209; revolutionary, 146; and therapy, 53; total, 52, 157n; totalitarian, 157n; transgressive, 173
Position(s) 12, 16, 29, 52–53, 59, 88, 112n, 116, 152, 153n, 157n, 179, 216; critical, 76n; institutional, 95n; marketing of, 6
Possession, 11, 12, 114; state of, 49
Possibility(ies), 77, 139, 141, 146, 150, 189, 213, 215; closing of, 119; opening of, 70, 215, 216; repression of, 108n
Power, 17–20, 22, 33, 41n, 42, 46, 47, 54n, 64n, 65n, 66n, 87, 94, 141, 143n, 144, 148, 148n, 153n, 161, 165, 166, 174, 176, 188, 199, 200, 207; American, 200; and authority, 20, 22, 165, 166; criminal, 161; game, 148; healing, 141; holders, 148, 204; idea of, 65n; limits of, 207; 'Power to the people,' 148, 170; price of, 166; quest for, 207; seekers, 16, 134; sexual, 143n; state, 148; of the state, 56; strategist of, 20; struggle, 144n, 149; struggle for, 4, 18, 19, 31, 39, 40n, 46, 77, 91, 104n, 112n, 123, 143, 145, 149, 175, 188n, 209; technicians, 178; technicians of, 123, 175; technique of, 5; transference of, 148; wheel of, 19; world, 101n
Praxis, 16, 44, 148; critical, 116
Preaching, 2, 35, 97, 214
Predecessors, 1, 6 11, 45, 48, 61n, 95n, 120, 151; primitive, 165n; and successors, 124
Presence(s), 54n, 56, 100, 155; inhibiting, 214; intellectual, 14; presiding, 16, 22, 25, 46, 47, 49, 52, 57, 59, 62, 78, 88, 104n, 121, 146, 163, 166, 207; teaching, 110
Primitive(s), 103n, 140, 153n, 168, 189; art of (the), 104n; col-

Primitive(s) (*cont'd*)
lege-trained, 8; historical, 152; iniquity, 166; men, 143n; predecessors, 165n; rudeness, 8; society, 106; spiritualizers, 120; state, 153n; true, 162
Principle(s), 8, 12, 19, 43, 44, 53, 62, 123, 139; of order, 17, 18; pedagogic, 201; Protestant, 215n
Prison(s), 105n, 166, 168
Privacy, 60, 173
Productivity, 95n, 155n, 192
Professor(s), 6, 7, 12, 48, 51n, 95n, 124, 129
Professoriat, 97
Progress, 24, 70, 130, 151
Property, 41n, 161n, 205
Prophecy, 8, 15, 17, 24, 33, 40, 76, 214n; tradition of, 7–8
Prophet(s), 7, 10, 76, 116, 118, 161n, 186, 214n; false, 205n, 208; of the new, 15; of transgressiveness, 205; true, 76; war, 111
Protagoras, 17
Protagoras, 56n
Protest(s), 7, 92n, 133, 137, 156, 169, 170, 173; critical, 28
Protestant(s), 54n, 75n, 77, 182n, 214n, 216; agonizings, 32; distinction, 34; era, 215n; ex-, 209; 213; imagination, 35; liberal, 209; pathos, 22, 23, 34, 100; principle, 215n; psychologizing, 215n; reformers, 134; tradition, 34, 114n, 181n; virtuoso, 31
Proudhon, 149
Proust, 52n
Prudence, 10, 19, 217
Psychiatry, 36, 163n
Psychoanalysis, 46
Psychological: Jew, 216n; man, pref. note, 143n, 144n, 178, 205; self-portraits, 114; warfare, 91n
Psychologizers, 47, 48, 120
Public, 17, 19, 26, 32, 133, 142, 146, 168, 191; actings out, 138; affairs, 38, 198n; appearances, 154n; behavior, 216; darkness,

158n; enactment, 206; entertainers, 110; form, 157n, 163; image, 105; instabilities, 36; life, 46, 111, 112; men, 17; networks, 17; objects, 5; order, 47; oversexualization, 184; performances, 147; policy, 95n; relations, 191; school, 93, 101n; self, 60; Soviet, 19; sphere, 127; wisdom, 56
Publicity, 5, 8, 17, 48, 50, 60, 103, 151, 161, 168, 191; universal, 48
Punishment(s), 22, 50, 56, 61, 65n, 116, 149, 150, 163, 165, 166, 168, 202; capital, 112n, 168; compensatory, 164; crime of, 162; lawful, 164; physical, 166; theory of, 167

Quotation marks, 39, 43, 74n, 135, 201n

Radical(s), 113, 126n, 138, 195n; chic, 67; cultural, 37; technological, 37
Ramsay, 145n
Raphael, 52n
Rationalization(s), 69, 118, 146, 177; criminological, 167; mass, 47; of the symbolic, 70
Rationalizers, 19, 72n
Reality, 2, 25, 55, 63n, 77, 78, 111, 132, 136, 144n, 150, 201n, 206; aestheticizing of, 206; contemporary, 132; denial of, 80n; established, 206; historical, 111; social, 182
Reason(s), 4, 10, 14, 30, 37n, 57, 70, 108, 117–120, 123, 132, 146, 157n, 198n, 206; enlightened, 206; for hope, 155; infinite therapeutic, 108; of state, 4; technological, 19
Recognition(s), 7, 9, 106, 111, 121; defensive, 72; personal, 9
Recognizers, 7; of interdicts, 121; self-, 172
Re-educated, 39, 49, 126, 160, 164, 165n, 167, 172, 180n, 183, 184; classes, 20, 46, 50, 55, 67, 79,

236

98, 107n, 133, 147, 178, 210; man, 53; self-interpretations, 80n; young, 201

Refinement, 29, 30, 185

Reform(s), 83n; college, 154n; social, 7

Reformers, 31, 186n; Protestant, 134

Rehabilitation, 55, 116, 162, 167; of criminals, 167; of flesh, 189, 197; idea of, 162; theories of, 167

Reich, Charles, 197

Rejection(s), 70; metamorphosis of, 150; therapeutic, 216; world, 23

Release(s), 21, 23, 185, 217; id, 115; therapist of, 50n; of aggression, 35; from old penalties, 169; of transgressive behavior, 150

Religion(s), 27, 34, 35, 73n, 75n, 79n, 117, 146, 151, 171, 173, 194n, 210; civic, 89, 90, 102; of criticism, 8, 76n, 121, 163n; functional, 32; political, 51n, 210; pretend, 173; and science, 209

Remembrance, 188, 193, 217n

Remission(s), 22, 25, 34–36, 49, 54, 70, 71n, 73, 120, 126, 136, 140, 159n, 189, 203

Remissive, 49, 73, 142, 170; action, 73; energies, 118; fantasy, 158n; figures, 147; interdictory-, 42, 51n, 53, 53n, 70, 141, 147, 148, 168, 171; modalities, 25; motifs, 35, 81n, 150, 168, 210, 216; openings of possibility, 215; roles, 93n, 104n, 133; space, 72n, 170; spiritualizers, 120

Remissiveness, 73; cultic, 196

Renunciation(s), 46, 206, 208

Repetition, 62, 117, 179

Repression, 3, 7, 42, 68, 69, 71, 108n, 112n, 144n, 197, 214; humanist, 134

Repressive, 13n; civilization, 156; discipline, 144n; guiding cadre, 134n; ideals, 112n; implication,

103n; institution, 93; modalities, 144n; preparation, 196; symbolics, 153, 184; teachings, 134

Research, 8, 11, 12, 124, 125, 192; and development, 9, 124; entrepreneurs of, 124; gimmicks, 14; grant industry, 7; and human development, 124; paymasters, 53; personality, 124; scientific, 101; workers, 33, 174

Resistance(s), 34, 44, 55, 59n, 67, 75n, 84, 85, 110, 131, 136, 138, 139, 171, 188, 189; absence of, 146; concealed, 130; continuity of, 67; deceits of, 31; non-, 130; strategy of, 110; student, 205; of truth, 22

Resolution(s), 186; credal, 104n; political, 104n

Respect, 26, 103, 109n, 124, 126, 143n, 146, 163, 164n, 174; absence of, 138, 139; civil, 175; dissolutions of, 100; reciprocities of, 138; self-, 100, 138; for truth, 215; for unequals, 172

Responsibility(ies), 16, 41n, 97, 124, 142, 167, 191, 197, 207; pedagogic, 5; of world power, 101n

Restraint(s), absence of, 38; of inherited culture, 103n

Retribution, 167

Revelation(s), 10, 38n, 48, 52n, 53n, 58, 59, 60, 152, 191, 202; Mosaic, 86; self-, 60

Reverence, 17, 56, 112, 116, 124, 161, 172; destruction of, 124; and justice, 124, 125, 152, 162, 170, 172

Reversal(s), 27, 28, 32, 35; character of, 27; of roles, 121

Revolt, 46, 47; pathology of, 163n

Revolution(s), 8, 20, 23, 24, 44, 47, 80n, 81n, 82, 101, 103n, 144n, 152, 166, 174, 183, 193, 200, 201, 214; absolute, 211; of contemporaneity, 135; counter-, 81n; cultural, 21, 103n, 147, 195, 205; managerial, 193; Mosaic, 86; permanent, 144n, 157n; scientific, 193

Revolutionary(ies), 19, 24, 36, 43, 44, 66n, 82n, 83n, 94n, 97, 107, 116, 127n, 129, 152, 174, 195, 201; action, 205; acts, 44, 168; answer, 144n; Argentinean, 176n; art, 84; chain-breakers, 173; character type, 151; child, 66; cultural, 44, 107; culture, 23; gurus, 90, 112n; intellectuals, 43n; jargon, 177n; model, 107; modern, 138; place, 88; politicians, 148n; politics, 146; prophecy, 214n; rhetoric, 112n; rich, 46, 66n, 129, 155, 157; role, 151–152; scientific, 44; sensuality, 19; starletdom, 137n; students, 170; theory, 200
Rey, Fernando, 74n
Rich, 135, 135n, 147, 185, 205; European, 88; revolutionary, 46, 66n, 129, 155, 157
Rieff, Philip, 39, 40, 41, 84n, 111, 111n, 153n, 190n; *Fellow Teachers,* pref. note, 200n; *The Mind of the Moralist,* pref. note, 2n, 115n, 135, 215, 216n; *The Triumph of the Therapeutic,* pref. note, 45, 89, 135
Riesman, David, 82n
Rights(s), 6, 17, 18, 22, 77, 105n, 149, 150, 155n, 161, 166; authority, 17; civil, 92n, 176n; new, 137; order, 91, 92, 101, 167, 182, 183; radical, 149; student, 6, 155n
Roehm, Captain, 113
Role, 133, 134, 201n; changers, 179; institutional, 132; of leader, 108; limit, codes of, 162; player, 137, 214; playing, 111, 214, 215; prophetic, 7; remissive, 93n, 104n, 133; reversal of, 121; revolutionary, 151–152; of teacher, 108
Romans, 59n
Romanticism, 13, 30, 146n, 198n, 207
Roosevelt, Franklin Delano, 149n
Rousseau, 145n, 146, 152, 163, 173, 198n

Rules, 129, 130, 165n, 167, 211; to art, 151n
Russell, Bertrand, 118n, 119n, 194n, 195n; *Autobiography 1872– 1914,* 118n; *Mysticism and Logic,* 118n, 194n
Ryan, Alan, 40n

Sabbath, 80n, 136
Sacred, 88, 114, 161n; city, 192; document, 158n, 159n; institution(s), 6, 8, 199n, 217; object, 125; world, 2
Saint Francis, 185, 186, 186n
Saint-Simon, 32, 33, 45, 75
Saint Theresa, 185
Sanchez, Thomas, 60
Sartre, J.-P., 80n, 214, 214n; *Anti-Semite and Jew,* 80n
Scheler, Max, 182, 182n; *Ressentiment,* 182n
Schleirmacher, 214n
Scholar(s), 2n, 6, 12, 74, 82n, 83n, 95n, 118, 128n, 133, 148, 148n, 157n, 158n, 162, 190; of meanings, 162n
Scholar-teacher, 1, 4, 9, 13, 191
Science(s), 3, 7, 18, 32, 33, 36n, 40–46, 52, 63, 65–68, 70, 89, 106, 110, 123, 124, 129, 159, 159n, 165, 169, 173, 186, 189, 193, 194n, 197, 201n, 209, 210; and art, 36; behavioral, 63, 125, 157; catholic, 44; and culture, 119n; and democracy, 39; dynamics of, 45; humanistic, 42; of limits, 41–43, 159, 163, 165; moral, 68, 70, 133; natural, 158, 158–159, 159, 159n; political, 10; positive, 32, 33; rationalizing, 20; social, 32, 68, 98, 120, 158; of society, 32; of symptoms, 69; and technology, 45
Scientist(s), 24, 41, 73, 100, 147, 165n, 169, 192n, 193, 194, 194n, 200n; of culture, 69n; non-, 193; social, 68, 76, 106, 168, 208
Scofield, Paul, 113n
Secular, 51n

Self, 21, 36, 38, 49, 60, 100, 113, 124, 127n, 152, 191; apostles of, 66; apostleships of, 65; concealed, 60; control, 160n; deceitful, 202; deceitfulness, 109n; deification, 188; display, 218; disrespect for, 100; estrangement, 79n; fulfilling permissions, 108–109; identity of, 165; idolatries of, 32; performing, 36; portraits, 114; private, 59; promotion, 60; protection, 61; public, 60

Sensibility(ies), 45; failed, 155; pseudo-, 44, 45, 63; true, 155

Sentimentality(ism), 145, 146, 146n, 180n, 206; Christian, 172, 211n

Sex, 44, 145; gospel, 61; manuals, 98

Sexual: acrobatics, 152; act, 145; action, 143, 146; behavior, 147; display, 101; encounters, 123; energy, 207; exhibitionism, 157n; images, 184; love, 142n; power, 143n; struggle, 144n

Sexuality, 63, 101n, 127, 143, 144, 144n, 145, 146, 165n, 179, 180, 184; liberated, 144n; symbolics of, 181

Shattuck, Roger, 128n

Silberman, Charles, 66n

Silence(s), 27, 37, 72, 154n, 181n, 187, 189, 193; art of, 208; of listening, 30; piety of, 27

Sin(s): mortal, 71n; original, 128n, 167; originality of, 128n; penalty of, 17; remedies for, 22; terminal, 178

Smith, Preserved, 180n; *The Life and Letters of Martin Luther*, 180n

Social: designers, 80; direction, 20; fact, 157; formation, 155; order(s), 12, 21, 36, 76, 77, 104n, 106, 147, 148, 153, 159, 166, 175, 195, 212, 215; organization, 9, 27, 31, 45; problems, 17; procedure, 23, 25; response, 115; science(s), 32, 68, 98, 120, 158; scientists, 68, 76, 106, 168, 208; stability, 88; strata, 88;

structure, 56; system, 162; teachers, 192; theorists, 145n; theory, 116, 145

Socialism, 101n, 172, 177n

Society(ies), 5, 9, 16, 17, 22, 32, 33, 44–47, 51, 79n, 106, 110, 132, 151, 152, 165, 195, 207, 217; American, 35, 108, 193, 200; civil, 79n; cultured, 50; cultureless, 38, 49, 50, 56, 71, 108n, 123, 125, 127, 158, 159, 178–180, 216; emancipation of, 80n; fatherless, 106; good, 136; new, 47, 50, 55; primitive, 106; science of, 32; unprogressive, 152; western, 51, 66n, 210

Society for the Propagation of the Gospel, 72

Society of Jesus, 88

Sociological: analysis, 21, 35, 182; contradiction, 14; law, 111n; meaning, 150; metamorphosis, 29; problem, 76; question, 138; rubric, 8; sense, 116; theory, 1, 75, 76n, 126

Sociology, 3n, 22, 32, 33, 36, 48, 79, 113, 116, 192, 192n 201n; American, 96n; reflexive, 76n; of religion, 34

Socrates, 25, 26, 105, 105n, 106, 110, 115

Solzhenitsyn, 211; *The First Circle*, 211n

Sorel, Georges, 67n, 145, 146, 211, 211n, 214n; *Reflections on Violence*, 211n

Soul(s), 16, 21, 55, 59, 60, 103, 120, 132, 160n, 161n, 165, 194n

Space(s), 1, 3n, 21; inner, 181n; interior, 1, 3, 10, 18, 21; remissive, 72n, 170; social, 147

Species-Man, 84, 130, 131

Spencer, Herbert, 38n

Sphere(s), 44, 46, 144; of action, 45; of activity, 42; aesthetic, 212; of criminality, 117; erotic, 127, 179–180, 179n, 180n, 212; private, 127; public, 127

Spirituality, 91n, 170, 215; inherited, 91n; revivals of, 215

Stalin, 16, 41n, 66n, 112, 210
Stanislavsky, 137; method, 162
State(s), 4, 12, 18, 22, 54, 56, 91n,
  95n, 105n, 125, 131, 148, 149,
  153n, 156, 166; apparatus of,
  166; functionaries, 198n; hospital, 125; primitive, 153n; warring, 153n, 155, 199; welfare,
  54, 56, 76, 94n, 152
Steiner, George, 199n, 200n; Eliot
  Lectures, 199n; *In Bluebeard's
  Castle,* 199n
Stevenson, Adlai, 149n
Struggle(s), 27, 61, 67n, 80n, 86,
  112n, 149n, 153n, 205, 212;
  class, 96; cultural, 96, 179,
  179n; economic, 144n; for
  power, 4, 18, 19, 31, 39, 40n,
  46, 77, 91, 104n, 112n, 123,
  143, 145, 149, 175, 188n, 209;
  sexual, 144n; social, 5; for survival, 191
Student(s), 1–3, 2n, 3n, 5–7, 9–16,
  10n, 24, 38, 47, 52–54, 54n,
  59, 60, 87, 92, 95–98, 107, 117,
  122, 124, 130, 132, 140, 141,
  153n, 154, 154n, 155n, 158,
  169, 169n, 170, 172–174, 178,
  179, 183, 190–192, 197, 203,
  205, 205n; communities, 62;
  criminology, 196; Jewish, 1;
  radical, 75n, 124; revolutionary,
  170; true, 38; virtuoso, 13
Study, 2, 6, 9, 96, 97, 192, 194n,
  201n; life of, 13, 19
Style(s), 151n, 196, 197; bourgeois,
  201; critical, 14, 19; life, 12,
  90, 152, 164; original, 130;
  paranoid, 14; protest, 170;
  transgressive, 138
Sublimation, 108n, 185, 186, 215
Sublime, 64n, 66n
Submission, 203; to authority, 25,
  47; to law, 144n; of the powerful, 166
Successors, 117, 120, 124, 155n,
  190; true, 200n
Suicide, 12, 55, 56, 58, 63, 80n,
  136, 138, 139, 155; identity,
  80n
Super-ego, 43, 52, 90; symbolism,
  115

Superiority, 11, 197; of disestablishments, 172; of facts, 159;
  moral, 19; personal, 82n, 94n,
  125
Survival, 72n, 103n, 139, 157, 188,
  202; struggle for, 191; therapy
  of, 139
Swift, 146, 198n
Symbol(s), 53n, 142, 160n; literary,
  61; of symbols, 33
Symbolic(s), 19, 21, 39, 40n, 42,
  70, 148, 149, 150n, 153, 157,
  164, 171, 181n, 183, 184, 214;
  authoritative, 164; Christian,
  171; compliance, 85n; of contradiction, 150; desublimating,
  181; distancing, 171; emancipative, 111; Eros, 214; failing,
  148, 183; interdictory, 127;
  justifying, 164; lawful, 144n;
  Lutheran, 181n; Marxist, 40n;
  Nietzschean, 171; rationalization of (the), 70; repressive,
  153, 184; of sexuality, 181
Symptom(s), 14, 54n, 69, 79, 201n
System (The), 90, 113n, 142, 158,
  164, 167; social, 162

Taboo(s), 86, 123; ancient, 211
Talented tenth, 43n
Talmud, 79n, 81n, 116, 117
Task, 10, 36; pedagogic, 15
Teacher(s), 1, 2, 4, 6, 9–13, 15–17,
  19, 24, 36n, 37, 38, 41–43, 59,
  66n, 73, 82n, 83n, 91n, 92, 94,
  105–112, 105n, 108n, 117, 122,
  124, 130, 130n, 132, 145n, 150,
  153n, 154n, 156, 161, 163n,
  166, 167, 173, 179, 190, 191,
  196, 198, 207, 208, 217, 218;
  duties as, 216; duty of, 4; good,
  98, 111; great, 106, 109n, 117;
  greatest, 19; social, 192; social
  welfare, 54n; true, 38; work of,
  10
Teaching(s) 2, 10n, 11–13, 17, 18,
  28, 35, 38, 88, 98, 104n, 123,
  125, 130, 131, 134, 154n, 155n,
  183, 205, 215; Abrahamic, 211n;
  baptismal, 205; death of, 6; exegetical, 16; generations, 186;
  great, 106; and learning, 13;

negative, 187; non-, 14; peace cry, 141; presence, 110; privilege, 9; repressive, 134; rhythms of, 13; of self-limit, 167; therapeutic, 46; as therapy, 212; true, 88; unprogressive, 13

Temptation, 3, 114n, 130, 185, 190; ultimate, 188

Tension(s), 4n, 24, 110, 112n, 165

Terror(s), 44, 63, 64, 64n, 65n, 66n, 166, 186, 209, 210, 211n; aesthetic of, 66n; black, 102; racist, 94n; true, 131, 186

Theatre(s), 64n, 109, 120, 131, 168; hospital-, 51, 123, 157; political, 9, 92n, 123; state-sponsored, 110

Theorist(s), 1, 3, 6, 23, 24, 36n, 48, 64, 76n, 86, 128, 134, 144n, 145n, 146, 150n, 168, 175, 198n, 200; critcial, 183, 193; good, 145n; of man, 214; priestly, 7, 76, 100; social, 108n, 145n; of therapy, 35, 216

Theory(ies), 5, 16, 47, 59, 76n, 99, 100, 103n, 105n, 115n, 121, 132, 133, 137, 144n, 146, 161n, 164n, 183, 189, 193, 203, 217; aestheticizing, 144n; anarchist, 148, 149; of art, 132; of authority, 149, 186; of censorship, 182n; of change, 18; of charisma, 161; class, 129n; continuity of, 132; critical, 33, 183, 195, 196, 207; of culture, 51, 66n, 68, 126, 130n, 132 133, 173, 200n; of desublimation, 182; disciplines of, 2; instinct, 115; justifiable victim, 211; Marxist, 78, 79, 201; of punishment, 167; revolutionary, 200; of rehabilitation, 167; social, 116, 145; sociological, 1, 75, 76n, 115n, 126; transference of, 16; Trotskyist, 112n

Therapeutae, 159n, 161n

Therapeutic(s), 1, 9, 45, 47–51, 53, 55, 56, 63, 67, 76, 77, 78n, 86n, 87, 88, 90, 104, 108, 112n, 113–116, 120–123, 127n, 128, 130–132, 135, 137, 139, 147, 151–154, 159, 159n, 174, 178,

208–212, 214–216; affect, 184; anticulture, 117; behavior of, 174; device, 179; doctrine, 59n; enactment, 117; model, 14–15; prose, 43n; pre-, 113n, 164; procedure, 86, 216; purposes, 126; relation, 36; true, 196

Therapist(s), 9, 46, 48, 54, 59, 76, 86, 91, 99, 108, 110, 117, 120–126, 128, 129, 132, 135, 145n, 179, 208, 209; good, 145n; movement, 178; of need communities, 127; and patients, 126; race, 94n; of release, 50n

Therapy(ies), 9, 23, 25, 34, 35, 49, 50, 53–55, 59, 61, 73n, 85n, 88, 96, 104n, 105, 108, 116, 120–122, 131, 136–138, 170, 186, 209, 210, 212, 213; business, 108; demo-, 174; enlightenment of, 55; indignation, 147; mass murder, 170; metamorphoses of, 80; of militancy, 111n; object of, 179; permanent, 53, 63, 107, 131; racist, 81; self-destruct, 150; shakedown, 104n; of survival, 139; teaching as, 212; theorist of, 35, 216; of therapies, 50

Thomas (Aquinas), 58, 58n; *Summa Theologica*, 57–58

Thought, 8, 13n, 14, 102, 141, 160n, 161; scientific, 42

Tillich, Paul, 181n, 190n; *The Interpretation of History,* 190n; *The Protestant Era,* 181n, 190n

Tocqueville, 90

Tolstoy, 20, 27

Torah, 25

Totalitarianism, 114, 124

Tradition(s), 14n, 15, 26, 34, 40, 80, 95n, 121, 126, 146, 175, 203, 203n, 204n, 205n; academic, 15; apophatic, 28; of breakthroughs, 185; Christian, 30; of Israel, 109n; Judeo-Christian, 94n; of the new, 123, 185; oral, 15, 26, 187, 192; of prophecy, 7–8; prophetic, 116; Protestant, 34, 114n, 181n; teaching, 14

Traditioning, 185–187

Transference, 9; negative, 43n, 91; object of, 186; positive, 43n, 94; of power, 148; of theory, 16; true, 186
Transgression(s), 25, 39, 44, 46, 51, 108, 111, 117, 121, 147, 155, 162, 163, 164, 166, 168; Cain's, 119; Christian, 51; rhapsodes of, 197; theatre of, 111
Transgressive(s), 44, 60, 70–71, 72, 100, 106, 114, 117, 129, 138, 144n, 163, 170, 171, 179, 187, 188; action, 115, 148, 183, 188; activity, 43, 156; acts, 102, 163, 215; behavior, 35, 44, 46, 69, 102, 112n, 127, 147, 150, 152, 155, 168, 182–184; behaviorist, 121; black, 94n; capacity, 100; component, 208; energy, 51; figure, 127; functioning, 123; heroics, 43n; imaginings, 163; intellectualizing, 62; interdictory-, 195; leadership, 126; lifestyles, 164; mode(s), 17, 102; motifs, 169, 170; protest movements, 155; public meaning, 92n; quest, 207; sense, 47, 127, 162, 164, 179, 179n, 197; thrusts, 163; top, 164
Transgressiveness, 44, 101, 115–116, 123, 129, 139, 166, 170, 188; prophet of, 205; rationalizing of, 170
Transgressors, 56, 121, 162
Trilling, Lionel, 81n, 198, 198n, 199n; Thomas Jefferson Lecture, 198n
Trollope, 13n; 'The Belton Estate,' 13n
Trotsky, 16, 111n, 112n, 148n
Truth(s), 7, 16, 18, 20, 23, 37n, 49, 53, 61, 68, 71, 83, 85, 108n, 109n, 110, 111, 141, 144n, 145n, 147, 150, 160, 161n, 163, 174, 178, 189, 197, 206, 212; critical, 19; destruction of, 14; eternal, 213; and faith, 117, 118; force of, 199n; inner, 164; order of, 144n; organization of, 108; resistance of, 22; of resistance, 44, 55, 59n, 67, 84, 131; respect for, 215; self-perpetuating, 85; and superiority, 196–197; theoretical, 85n; and untruth, 60
Type(s): anti-ideal, 211; character, 53, 151, 159; characterless, 77; corporate managerial, 149n; counter-ideal, 88; ideal, 1, 21, 45, 55, 87, 93n, 114, 131; teaching, 191; transgressive, 170

Unbelief, 66n, 121, 145, 145n, 172
Understanding(s), 1, 4, 10, 21, 76, 88, 92n, 175, 178, 190–192, 210; apostles of, 77; personal, 12, 17, 197; self-, 89, 90
University(ies), 4, 6, 8, 9, 11, 12, 37, 52, 55n, 82n, 83n, 91n, 96, 97, 125, 126, 169, 175, 190, 191, 193, 205; American, 15; true, 124
Untruth, 54, 60, 80n, 212
Urban, G. R., 40n; *Can We Survive Our Future?*, 40n
Utopia, 33, 138, 139, 162n

Vadim, 157n
Value(s), 7n, 24, 68n, 69n, 70n, 80, 83, 98, 109, 130, 184, 201n; actor-managers, 7; criticism, 7; infinite, 136; meaningful, 98; new, 40; relation, 78, relational, 137n; ultimate, 98
Vermeer, 52n
Victim(s), 12, 50, 61, 118, 127, 128n, 130, 154n, 157, 166, 167, 211
Violence, 14, 49, 50, 59, 66n, 71, 130, 149, 152, 154n, 155, 187, 197, 205; cult of, 19; defensive, 131; interdictory, 59; legitimate, 148; rhapsodes of, 101; shows of, 157n; therapeutic, 59; visionary of, 154n
Virtuoso(i), 28, 72n, 185, 192; of faith, 29, 31, 34; of guilt, 186n; of intellect, 207; of prophetic views, 13; Protestant, 31
Von Bora, Katherine, 179n
Von Ranke, L., 96n

Waldo, Peter, 185
Wallace, 168n
War, 130, 135, 138, 170, 188n; for
    advantage, 53; class, 150; of
    culture, 20, 106; private, 138;
    Vietnam, 155, 156
Weber, Max, 2, 10, 13, 22, 23, 58n,
    93n, 108, 108n, 116, 121, 153n,
    161, 214n
Weil, Simone, 188n, 193, 193n;
    Iliad or the Poem of Force,
    188n; *Oppression and Liberty,*
    188n, 193n
Welles, Orson, 74
We-They, 53n
Whitehead, 169
Whitman, Walt, 78n

Wiesel, Elie, 66n; *Souls on Fire,*
    66n
Wilde, Oscar, 135n; *The Soul of
    Man Under Socialism,* 135n
Wisdom, 24, 90, 160n, 161n, 198n
Wrong, 17, 18, 149, 153n, 156, 159,
    160, 170

Xanthippe, 110
Xenophon, 105

Yank Brown at Yale, 82n
Yeats, 39, 194n
Yes, 122
Youth, 12, 92, 144, 156, 174, 196,
    201; black, 104n; student, 12

Zen Buddhism, 23

73 74 75 76 77 10 9 8 7 6 5 4 3 2 1

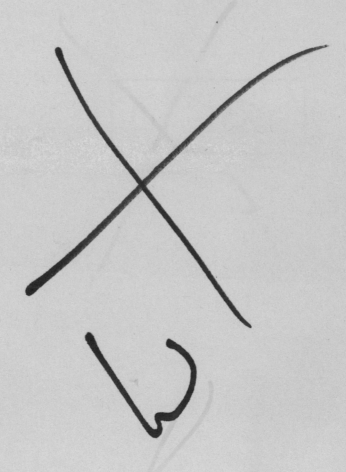